Seventh-day Adventist Higher Education in North America

Theological Perspectives and Current Issues

Seventh-day Adventist Higher Education in North America

Theological Perspectives and Current Issues

STEVE PAWLUK & GORDON BIETZ, coeditors

Pacific Press® Publishing Association
Nampa, Idaho
Oshawa, Ontario, Canada
www.pacificpress.com

Cover design by Gerald Lee Monks
Cover design resources from iStockphoto.com
Inside design by Nicola Johnson

Copyright © 2012 by Pacific Press® Publishing Association
Printed in the United States of America
All rights reserved

The authors assume full responsibility for the accuracy of all facts and quotations as cited in this book.

You can obtain additional copies of this book by calling toll-free 1-800-765-6955 or by visiting http://www.adventistbookcenter.com.

Scripture quotations marked ESV are from The Holy Bible, English Standard Version® (ESV®), copyright © 2001 by Crossway, a publishing ministry of Good News Publishers. Used by permission. All rights reserved.
Scripture quotations marked HCSB are taken from the Holman Christian Standard Bible ©, copyright © 1999, 2000, 2002, 2003 by Holman Bible Publishers. Used by permission. Holman Christian Standard Bible ©, Holman CSB©, and HCSB© are federally registered trademarks of Holman Bible Publishers.
Scripture quoted from NASB are from *The New American Standard Bible*®, copyright © 1960, 1962, 1963, 1968, 1971, 1972, 1973, 1975, 1977, 1995 by The Lockman Foundation. Used by permission.
Scripture quotations marked NIV are from the HOLY BIBLE, NEW INTERNATIONAL VERSION®. Copyright © 1984 by International Bible Society. Used by permission of Zondervan Publishing House. All rights reserved.
Scriptures quoted from NKJV are from The New King James Version, copyright © 1979, 1980, 1982, Thomas Nelson, Inc., Publishers.
Scripture texts credited to NRSV are from the New Revised Standard Version of the Bible, copyright © 1989 by the Division of Christian Education of the National Council of the Churches of Christ in the USA. Used by permission. All rights reserved.
Scripture taken from the HOLY BIBLE, TODAY'S NEW INTERNATIONAL VERSION®. Copyright © 2001, 2005 by International Bible Society®. Used by permission of International Bible Society®. All rights reserved worldwide.

ISBN 13: 978-0-8163-2613-6
ISBN 10: 0-8163-2613-4

12 13 14 15 16   •   5 4 3 2 1

Table of Contents

Foreword   7
ELLA SIMMONS

Introduction   13
STEVE PAWLUK AND GORDON BIETZ

Praise the Source of Faith and Learning   17
THOMAS H. TROEGER

Section 1: Theology of Seventh-day Adventist Higher Education

The Theology of Adventist Education: Its Heart and Soul   21
NIELS-ERIK ANDREASEN

Toward a Theology of Seventh-day Adventist Higher Education: What Makes Adventist Higher Education Adventist?   39
STEVE PAWLUK

Christian Higher Education: Passing the Mantle of Faith in a Secular Society   57
GORDON BIETZ

Understanding Christian Education   71
DAVID THOMAS

Section 2: The Value-Added Aspect of Seventh-day Adventist Higher Education

Nurturing the Adventist Mind: What Seventh-day Adventist Education Can Do for the Church   95
RANDAL WISBEY

The Adventist Advantage   105
HEATHER J. KNIGHT

A New Mission School Model: How Adventist Colleges and Universities Can Thrive and Fulfill Their Mission in the Twenty-First Century   111
DON WILLIAMS

Faith, Young Adults, and the Campus Experience   127
V. BAILEY GILLESPIE

The Mission of Seventh-day Adventist Higher Education: Redundant or Complementary?   147
STEVE PAWLUK

The Caring Questioner: A Model for Educators   167
DOUGLAS HERRMANN

Table of Contents

Section 3: External Perspectives

A Place for "Dreamers of Day": The Heritage Distinctions of Higher Education in America   *181*
E. GRADY BOGUE

We Are Higher Education, and We Change Not   *197*
JAMES A. TUCKER AND PRISCILLA TUCKER

Faith-Based Higher Education: Reflections by an Accreditor   *213*
GERALD D. LORD

Truth and Tenure   *223*
TED W. BENEDICT

Section 4: The Future of Seventh-day Adventist Higher Education

Awareness and Perceptions Among Adventist College-Bound Youth Regarding Adventist Higher Education   *233*
VINITA SAUDER, LORETTA B. JOHNS, AND JIMMY KAJAI

Broadening the Context of Challenges Facing Adventist Higher Education   *259*
RICHARD OSBORN

Responsible Partisans: Ethics and Intellectual Accountability in Adventist Higher Education   *279*
CHARLES SCRIVEN

Where Might We Go From Here?   *293*
STEVE PAWLUK AND GORDON BIETZ

Appendix

Author Information   *295*

ELLA SIMMONS

Foreword

There is an ongoing conversation in the church surrounding the fundamental nature, required content, and expected outcomes for Seventh-day Adventist education. The dialogue began in the nineteenth century with the initiation of Adventist education and has continued through the twentieth century to the present. Indeed, it appears that the conversation has intensified during the past several decades in various forms ranging from casual observations to serious theological and academic debates. Today church members—leaders, education professionals, pastors, parents, students, and others—are asking the question: What is Adventist education?

Some would have the response to the question of definition be an educational model that is the antithesis of so-called secular education. Others would have the declaratives support a mirror image of secular education with spiritual value added. Still others would assert that it is simply education for Adventists by Adventists, that no more is required. Although this is an oversimplification, purpose is integral to its identity. Indeed, there is some element of truth in all of these positions.

The church's perspectives, expectations, and principles are expressed in the distinctive characteristics of Seventh-day Adventist education derived from the Bible and writings of Ellen G. White that point to the redemptive aim of true education: to restore human beings into the image of their Maker. Its resultant unique educational philosophy determines its values and the emphases placed on these values along with methods by which the values are taught for shaping the worldview of its students and the future of the church. While, in some instances, the intellectual climate of today's Seventh-day Adventist colleges and universities and their attendant opinions regarding academic freedom offer a challenge for the church, generally Seventh-day Adventist tertiary institutions play a vitally effective role in preparing students for service to the church and the world.

Students come to college and university today with overwhelming expectations that range far beyond coursework and degrees. They expect and need guidance for understanding and applying the knowledge and skills they acquire. They are hungry for direction and models for life and purpose. They rely on higher education for the meaning and purpose of life, the cultivation of character, and insight to the challenges, problems, and issues of their local contexts and the global community.

These young people expect their college or university to aid in their emotional and spiritual development. They yearn for enhanced self-understanding, preparation for responsible citizenship, and the development of personal values. These also, they expect as outcomes from their higher education experiences. Toward these ends, today's students expect their institutions to encourage and support their personal expression of spirituality and practice of religion (see Reports From the Higher Education Research Institute [HERI] Graduate School of Education & Information Studies, UCLA, 2000–2009). Staggering as they are, these expectations are congruent with experience and outcome targets—the goals and objectives—of Seventh-day Adventist education. Adventist education was created, and exists, for these purposes.

At its inception Seventh-day Adventist education was conceived to be true education, rather than mere schooling. It was to be holistic in nature involving the harmonious development of the physical, mental, and spiritual characteristics of the learner. Its outcomes were to be the preparation of the student for joyous service in this life and joy in wider service throughout eternity in the life to come. From the beginning, the aim of Adventist education has been to aid the learner in the formation of Christlike character, the establishment of a uniquely Seventh-day Adventist pattern of Christian living, and a commitment to service. Just what does this entail and by what means are these ends achieved? What are the required in-puts, structures, and methods? What are its impediments? What must be excluded? Are there absolutes? Is there any flexibility?

Foreword

Throughout its existence, the Seventh-day Adventist Church has maintained its allegiance to the guidance of foundational principles and methodological elements it was given for creating and achieving the outcomes of true education. In this guidance lie answers to the questions of identity and definition for Adventist education.

Since, in the greatest sense, the work of education and the work of redemption are the same, one must consider first the theology of Adventism that determines the theology of Seventh-day Adventist education. This understanding then provides direction for the content and focus Adventist education—what is included and how it is presented. If Adventist education is to be truly Adventist, there first must be a complete explication of the essential elements of Adventism. The church must answer the question, What does it mean to be Seventh-day Adventist? It must articulate the absolutes of Adventism in a more explicit way, and it must operationalize its definition for education.

The system of education instituted at creation was to be a model throughout human existence. God was both the Knowledge Base and the Teacher. In Him are "all the treasures of wisdom and knowledge" (Colossians 2:3, NKJV). "To God belong wisdom and power; counsel and understanding are his" (Job 12:13, NKJV). Originally, humankind communed directly with God in their education and learned of Him through His works. However, the effects of sin cut earthly students off from learning of God in this face-to-face contact, and to a significant degree, it distorted the messages of His works.

Therefore, the learner must go to God's Word for an accurate revelation of God. Scripture must be the gold standard of truth, and as such given the highest place in the educational process. What education can be higher than this? What can equal it in value? "The true 'higher education' is that imparted by Him with whom is 'wisdom and strength' (Job 12:13), '[For the LORD gives wisdom, and from his mouth] cometh knowledge and understanding.' Proverbs 2:6" (White, *Education*, 14).

Current church policy for education acknowledges that God is the Source of all true knowledge in all its forms. It implies a unity of all truth as it emanates from and reflects God's character as Creator and Sustainer of this world and the Redeemer of the human race. Thus, the primary object of Seventh-day Adventist education in all its content and process forms is to direct the mind of the learner to God's revelation of Himself and His works in and through the person, ministry, sacrifice, and mediatorial acts of His Son for humankind.

The world has had its great educators, people of impressive intellect and extensive research who have stimulated thought and uncovered vast bodies of knowledge. Yet, as far back as they go in the history of discovery and education, the Light of the world was before them. Where truth has been found in their research and teaching, they are only reflections of the True Light.

For example, "Rightly understood, both the revelations of science and the experiences of life are in harmony with the testimony of Scripture to the constant working of God in nature" (White, *Education,* 130). Revelation is not antithetical to reason. Undeniably, the work of true education is to train learners to be critical thinkers, not simply reflectors of the thoughts of others. In this process students must be directed to the sources of truth—God's truth, and to the unlimited domains of research and discovery in nature and revelation. These must be pursued in tandem as God intended.

God's principles of education remain unchanged. The principles of education that He has given are the only safe guide. "They are steadfast for ever and ever" (Psalm 111:8, NKJV). Ellen White observes that, "The discipline and training that God appointed for Israel would cause them, in all their ways of life, to differ from the people of other nations. This peculiarity, which should have been regarded as a special privilege and blessing, was to them unwelcome.... To be 'like all the nations' (1 Samuel 8:5) was their ambition. God's plan of education was set aside, His authority disowned" (*Education,* 49, 50).

The recent history of higher education reflects this same rejection. After shedding the dogma of the Dark Ages, many academics have overcorrected and assumed a hostile stance against religious influences and scriptural guidance in research and education. It has become academic chic to disdain all things of faith. Many scholars measure themselves by themselves only, and define rigor and reason by the absence of faith and godly authority.

Nevertheless, the same Spirit sent by Christ to instruct His first cohort of teachers has been commissioned to instruct educators and scholars today. This same instructor will lead to the results God originally intended from education. "This is the end to which true education tends; this is the work that God designs it to accomplish" (White, *Education,* 96).

The experiences of the ancients are examples and warnings for educators today. "These things happened to them as examples and were written down as warnings for us, on whom the fulfillment of the ages has come. So, if you think you are standing firm, be careful that you don't fall!" (1 Corinthians 10:11, 12, NKJV). "With us, as with Israel of old, success in education depends on fidelity in carrying out the Creator's plan. Adherence to the principles of God's word will bring [success]" (White, *Education,* 50). "God's work in all time is the same. The Teacher is the same. God's character and His plan are the same. With Him 'is no variableness, neither shadow of turning.' James 1:17" (White, *Education,* 50).

To violate this truth is to deny the heart of Seventh-day Adventist education. The pursuit of education apart from God is at best reckless, at its worst foolishness. Ellen White says it is "to seek to be wise apart from Wisdom; to be true while rejecting Truth; to seek illumination apart from the Light, and existence without the Life; to turn from the Fountain of living waters, and hew out broken cisterns, that can hold no water" (*Education,* 83).

Regardless of perspectival differences, most who treasure Adventist education agree that conceptually it is characterized by a tenacious pursuit and presentation of truth, truth which is in and of God. Most agree also that its processes and purposes are those Jesus modeled in His life on earth and articulated through His Word.

While this book does not attempt to answer the essential questions regarding Adventist education, it provides food for thought and urges responses in the pursuit of a definitive model of Seventh-day Adventist higher education for the twentieth-first century and beyond. It is a collection of perspectives and more questions on a range of topics pertaining to the nature and expectations of Seventh-day Adventist education. The writers engage the reader in analyses of issues, opportunities, and challenges of higher education. They explore perspectives and possibilities from the inside on the theology, value-added aspects, and future of Adventist education with a few offerings of external perspective.

Some readers will undoubtedly disagree with some of the ideas and perspectives proclaimed or implied here, as is expected in response to any ideological offering. However, the reader is encouraged to think beyond the current presentation. Ideally, the reader will accept the challenge of engaging divergent thoughts as a stimulus in the continuous pursuit of the nature of true Adventist education. Perhaps, then, these pages will lead to more conclusive deliberations that will yield the definitive outcomes necessary to sustain Adventist education through these end times in a victorious return to direct communion with God in the courts of heaven where real learning will commence.

STEVE PAWLUK AND GORDON BIETZ

Introduction

This book has been over three years in the making. The joined-at-the-hip proximate causes for its writing are pragmatism and stewardship.

Pragmatism has prompted much thoughtful deliberation about the mission and future of Seventh-day Adventist education, and not just higher education, because of enrollment of a declining proportion of Seventh-day Adventist young people relative to the growing membership of the church. Although a few of our colleges and universities are maintaining, or even growing, others are declining from their peak enrollments of a few decades ago. This, of course, affects the resources which our denomination's educational institutions have at their disposal, resulting in the need to make some critical choices related to how to best execute our mission and to make responsible strategic decisions.

Stewardship, in this case, is not used in the sense of financial responsibility, although that is certainly an important part of the concept, but we use it in the broader sense of fiduciary responsibility to God's kids, to the church, and to society. (We purposely chose to refer to our students as "God's kids" for several reasons. It is common to think of our students as customers, as clients, or as "our products." While each of these metaphors may be, in some regard, instructive, they make it easy to overlook the reality of how important each of our students, regardless of denominational or faith background, are to God.

And we wish to signify that closeness to God's heart by using the more informal and endearing term "kids" rather than "children." This also reminds us that, as educators, we are, not only engaged in a profession or a service, but we have been given a sacred trust as we participate in God's creation of productive human beings.)

Peter Drucker asserted that management is "doing things right, and leadership is doing the right things."[1] He also reminded us that "Management by objectives works—if you know the objectives. Ninety percent of the time you don't."[2] As administrators and professors in Seventh-day Adventist higher education, we want to manage and lead well. We want to ensure that we are leading our institutions in the right direction and not just making effective tactical decisions. We recognize the personal sacrifice that is represented by each student who attends our institutions. We realize that family, the church, and society share the costs to support each student's education. And we consider that a sacred trust. A sacred trust that requires conscientious stewardship.

This book follows in the footsteps of James Tunstead Burtchaell, Richard T. Hughes, Arthur Holmes, Robert Benne, and others who have inquired about the mission of Christian education. To our knowledge, although the Seventh-day Adventist denomination has a history of being involved in education almost from its beginning; and although we represent one of the largest denominational school systems in North America with 837 elementary schools, 109 secondary schools,[3] and 13 colleges and universities,[4] there has been no prior attempt to collect, in one source, philosophical and theological foundations for our policies and practices. It appears that our system has evolved in a pragmatic manner and that decisions have been made mostly with an eye to practical results and finances. It is our hope that this conversation-in-writing will foster prayerful evaluation of both our direction and trajectory.

We invited contributions to this book from those thoughtful and courageous voices which have expressed important ideas and perspectives in journal articles, at meetings of the Association of Adventist Colleges and Universities, on task forces on the mission and essentials of Seventh-day Adventist higher education, and around the proverbial water cooler; not because they necessarily agree with each other, but because they need to be heard and seriously considered. We've probably inadvertently overlooked some, who we invited to provide a chapter, and we regret that others, who we invited to provide a chapter, were unable to participate due to their already heavy responsibilities.

All of our chapter contributors are, or have been, employed in higher education. We intended this book to serve as a printed conversation, a virtual focus group, of those who have dedicated their careers to the mission of Seventh-day Adventist education. This does not mean that other voices are unimportant. The conversation about mission needs to include all stakeholders and constituents. And we hope that this book will prompt many more conversations, in person, in groups around the water cooler, in periodicals, in committee meetings, and at board meetings.

This book attempts to reflect conversations and ideas that have been percolating in, and about, Seventh-day Adventist higher education for years. We've made no attempt to present "The One Correct Idea" in these chapters. Instead, we present the considered views of people who have served Seventh-day Adventist education consistently and well, and who have thought long and carefully about the purposes of Seventh-day Adventist education.

Although the authors will present different opinions, they offer important commonalities as well.

- They care about education.
- They care about Christian education.
- They care about Seventh-day Adventist education.
- They have personally contributed time, influence, and money, to Seventh-day Adventist higher education.
- Although there is no single, published, mission statement for Seventh-day Adventist higher education, they are writing as genuine supporters of its tacit mission.

Even though the language of the North American Division Web site suggests a focus on students engaged in K–12 education, the principles identified in the mission are noteworthy for higher education as well.

> We believe that the Creator's design is for "whole person" development—mental, physical, and spiritual—and that, no matter what your religion or philosophy of life, an Adventist school education can help your child make better moral decisions and grow up to become a trustworthy community leader.[5]

We did not edit the chapters so that they would agree in every detail or so that they would sound alike. We wanted each voice and personality to come through as you read their perspectives on how we can best serve God's kids. So each chapter will present one or more important ideas regarding the purpose, mission, and future of Seventh-day Adventist higher education.

We hope that in these pages, you will find strong inspiration, helpful answers, and new questions.

We hope that this book will prompt

new directions in your conversations and planning sessions.

We hope that this book will create a little cognitive dissonance that leads to new insights and innovations.

We hope that this book will result in deeper understanding of, and appreciation for, the essential unity and the healthy diversity that are found among and between the various Seventh-day Adventist institutions of higher education.

References

[1] Peter F. Drucker, cited in http://www.albertarose.org/articles/quotes/peter_drucker_quotes.htm.

[2] Ibid.

[3] E-mail to Steve Pawluk from Elaine Furrow, NAD Office of Education, February 23, 2010.

[4] http://www.adventistcolleges.org/.

[5] http://www.nadeducation.org/v, accessed June 7, 2010.

PRAISE THE SOURCE OF FAITH AND LEARNING

Thomas H. Troeger (born 1945)

Praise the source of faith and learning
Who has sparked and stoked the mind
With a passion for discerning
How the world has been designed.
Let the sense of wonder flowing
From the wonders we survey
Keep our faith forever growing
And renew our need to pray:

God of wisdom, we acknowledge
That our science and our art
And the breadth of human knowledge
Only partial truth impart.
Far beyond our calculation
Lies a depth we cannot sound
Where your purpose for creation
And the pulse of life are found.

May our faith redeem the blunder
Of believing that our thought
Has displaced the grounds for wonder
Which the ancient prophets taught.
May our learning curb the error
Which unthinking faith can breed
Lest we justify some terror
With an antiquated creed.

As two currents in a river
Fight each others' undertow
'Til converging they deliver
One coherent steady flow.
Blend, O God, our faith and learning
'Til they carve a single course
While they join as one returning
Praise and thanks to you their source.

Praise for minds to probe the heavens,
Praise for strength to breathe the air,
Praise for all that beauty leavens,
Praise for silence, music, prayer.
Praise for justice and compassion
And for strangers, neighbors, friends,
Praise for hearts and lips to fashion,
Praise for love that never ends.

This hymn is traditionally sung, to the tune of "Ode to Joy," by the assembled students, faculty, and staff at La Sierra University's Academic Assembly at the beginning of each academic year.

Section 1

Theology of Seventh-day Adventist Higher Education

NIELS-ERIK ANDREASEN

Chapter 1

The Theology of Adventist Education: Its Heart and Soul

Seventh-day Adventists have written and spoken voluminously about education, and so they should for this reason alone. The church began its strong commitment to education a mere eleven years after the organization of the denomination (1863), with the establishment of Battle Creek College, in the same year the first official denominational missionary was sent abroad (1874). At the present time, over seventy-four hundred schools, colleges, and universities enroll a student population of 1.5 million, a number equal to approximately 10 percent of the official church membership worldwide. This represents an enormous commitment of church resources, both people and finances, to education.

From the outset, the purpose of education in the Adventist Church was to prepare its young adults for effective witness to the gospel and active participation in the mission outreach of the church. This signifies that from its feeble beginnings following the "Great Disappointment" in 1844 the community of believers, which became known as the Seventh-day Adventist Church nineteen years later, was committed to affirming faith through understanding, especially of Scripture and of current events as well. Thus the emotional trauma of the Disappointment and the subsequent confusion was overcome by prayerful, but rational, thoughtful reflection and study. A correspondence between the church leaders and particularly James White at the Battle Creek, Michigan, headquarters and John N. Andrews, who lived in Rochester, New York, in 1864, reveals the importance of education in the earliest years of the Seventh-day Adventist Church.[1] The leaders extended a call for Andrews to join the staff at headquarters which Andrews declined, explaining that the present urgent work of the young church required him to live near a good library (Rochester Seminary) so he could carry on with the theological and apologetic work he was doing. This commitment to overcome disappointment and confusion with new understanding soon led to formal educational activities in an Adventist college, with a faculty, students, and regular curricula of study. Since that time, education, both formal and informal, has played a consistent and central role in Seventh-day Adventist life and faith.

At first Adventist education adopted the standard or common curricula of the time for studies in humanities, classics, and science, with added subjects in Bible.[2] It was assumed by the denomination's educational leaders that if the Adventist schools enrolled Adventist students, engaged Adventist teachers, and pursued Adventist educational goals, on an Adventist campus, they would deliver a type of education appropriate for the church and its mission. That turned out to be an inaccurate assumption, as is demonstrated by the tensions in the first Adventist college during the early years, leading even to its temporary closure. At issue was the nature of the education provided in the Adventist college.[3]

By the end of the nineteenth century, certain educational reformers began to reshape Adventist education in a new mold. The urban Battle Creek College was moved to rural Berrien Springs and renamed Emmanuel Missionary College as a way of refocusing the education it offered around a curriculum of work and study, designed to prepare students for ministries and services of importance to the growing church. E. A. Sutherland, first president of Emmanuel Missionary College who led out in this change, also helped establish Walla Walla College in College Place, Washington,[4] and Madison College in Tennessee.[5] Other early Adventist colleges in Massachusetts, Tennessee, California, and Alabama were similarly located in rural settings and incorporated agriculture and work study opportunities in the curriculum and in their operations. Indeed, as the North American church grew and expanded toward the west and south in the thirty-year period between 1874 and 1905, eleven colleges were established—one every three years on average, beginning with Battle Creek College in Michigan (1874) and concluding with the College of Medical Evangelists in California (1905). They all shared the search for a type of education suitable to the young and growing church with its ambitious worldwide mission.

Each of these new educational institutions was coeducational and developed business enterprises enabling students to work their way through college. Meanwhile the new curriculum emphasized practical preparation for life and professional preparation for denominational work, both nationally and especially in overseas mission fields. This development was followed early in the new century by the first comprehensive guide to the idea of a unique Adventist education by E. G. White herself.[6] While this book does not deal with the technical aspects of education, such as admission standards, curriculum design, faculty development, and graduation requirements, it does set out a philosophy, or better a theology of education that is unmistakable in its direction and goal. Interestingly, it does not refer to the education as Adventist, or Christian, or denominational, preferring instead the term "true education,"[7] meaning that the early Adventist educators conceived of these educational ideals as possessing general value for all of education, and not just for the denomination. They thought of themselves and in some cases were clearly recognized as educational reformers.

It is also worth noting that none of these early "reformed" Adventist colleges carried the word *Adventist* in their name, a common practice, and even expectation in more recent times. Evidently, the educational leaders who shaped these Adventist schools concluded that the new directions in the curriculum they instituted and a strong commitment to ministry and mission service would adequately define their Adventist character. Perhaps in naming these colleges they may have wished to downplay the denominational definition of their educational program, recalling that the sponsoring church began essentially as a reform and revival movement among the established Christian churches. Whatever the reason, unlike Lutheran, Reformed, and Catholic institutions that were given "religious" names, the Adventist institutions were named after their location (Walla Walla, Loma Linda), or after the organizational unit in the denomination to which they were attached, in some cases with the term "missionary" attached. As a sole exception, Battle Creek College became Emmanuel Missionary College after its move.

The professions of particular importance to the Adventist mission included ministry, teaching, medicine, and nursing. The preparation of healthcare professionals led to the establishment of a health sciences institution, the College of Medical Evangelists, now Loma Linda University (1905), for the preparation of doctors and nurses. That in turn required upgrading of the preparatory science programs in the undergraduate colleges, eventually forcing them to seek institutional accreditation, and with that some standardization of their curricula of study, bringing them once again closer in line with common curriculum designs and learning objectives. The potential impact of that development on the unique understanding of education in the Adventist Church continues to be felt even to the present, and has led to the rediscovery that Adventist students taught by Adventist teachers perhaps in a rural church-owned college with work study campuses, along with a strong focus on church mission, alone will not assure the special character of Adventist education. Attention must also be given to the way in which the curriculum designs, teaching methods, materials and objectives, learning experiences, and educational outcomes are developed and implemented. For as these became ever more standardized, as a result of conforming with normal educational expectations in all accredited institutions, the distinctly Christian and Adventist character of the entire intellectual life in an Adventist college had to be articulated anew. The question is this, In addition to Adventist teachers and students meeting on an Adventist-owned campus, committed to the Adventist mission, what else does it take to make education uniquely Christian and Adventist? What is the "heart and soul" of an Adventist education that remains after all the familiar or normal characteristics of the Christian educational institution have been accounted for? This question deserves careful attention among Adventist educators. Attempts to answer it have proved both complex and promising. They have drawn Adventist educators into an examination of the history, philosophy, and practices of education within Christendom. And in general, they have forced educational administrators and teachers to examine the unique character of the shared intellectual life in an Adventist educational institution. It is at this point that the question of the philosophy (or theology) of Adventist education becomes central, and for its elucidation a backward glance at the long history of Christian education in general may be instructive.

In his helpful primer, *Building the Christian Academy*,[8] Arthur Holmes traces that history and development of Christian education from the early Christian centuries, through the scholastic period, into the Renaissance and Reformation, and on to modern times, first in Europe, then the United States, and the rest of the Christian world. The premise of the book is that Christian education from its beginning adopted the framework of teaching and learning already in existence within the classical world and fitted it to its Christian educational objectives. That is to say the curriculum of study itself chosen by Christian educators was not particularly unique. However, explains Holmes, Christian education added a "heart and soul" that made it unique. If this principle were to be considered for our time, it would mean that from a historical perspective at least,

Christian educators should not expect to make their education uniquely Christian merely by modifying the curriculum, dropping some courses of study, adding new ones, changing some textbooks and syllabi, setting different exams, or selecting a different learning environment. Historically speaking at least, the outer framework of Christian education is not as determinative for its uniqueness as may have been thought. Rather, its Christian character will emerge from its distinctive Christian "heart and soul." This is not too surprising, since Christian students and teachers still have to master the disciplines of science, social science, literature, languages, law, and the applied sciences of engineering and medicine, and so on, along with their study of religion and Scripture, as do all other students. And upon graduation, they will ply their trade in the secular world using common knowledge and skills along with all other graduates. Christian education is not special education, and Christian knowledge is not unique, known only to Christians. The church long ago rejected Gnosticism, the idea that Christians devote themselves to esoteric knowledge, only accessible to Christians for their unique use. Instead, it embraced common knowledge communicated in common and familiar ways, but with a unique Christian "heart and soul." Diversions from that historic approach have generally proved disappointing or even disastrous, and led both teachers and students astray and, where attempted, have turned historic and biblical Christianity into a sectarian religion. In the process, students became disappointed or marginalized in the world where Christians live, serve, and witness.

Fortunately, Adventist educators have nearly always steered away from promoting a special esoteric education and instead have committed their educational resources to seeking common education and disseminating common or shared knowledge that has stood the test of time. But that urgently raises the quest for the "heart and soul" of its education to new levels of importance: What exactly makes Christian education Christian and Adventist education Adventist in a world requiring the acquisition of common or shared knowledge, and how do the ideals of Christian education emerge, both historically speaking and in our educational institutions today? In seeking an answer to this question, it is interesting to consider the relationship between education and the formation of Christian faith as understood by Adventists.

The foundation of Christian faith was laid by Jesus Himself and He did it through a process of education. Some have observed that Jesus began His adult life as a carpenter, and it is certainly true that He grew up in a carpenter's home, and presumably learned that trade as a young adult. But the moment He left home, He changed profession and became a teacher, not attached to a school, to be sure, but an itinerant teacher, of the kind well known in antiquity. People who knew Him called Him Teacher, Rabbi, and even established teachers of the day acknowledged Him as a fellow teacher with a national following (John 3).

Working as an educator then, Jesus taught by parables, sayings, "sermons," and symbolic acts. His methods of instruction were not remarkably different from those used by other teachers of His time, but He used them effectively and according to the gospel record, He earned a reputation with common people as a very good teacher. It is also generally acknowledged that Jesus taught about the kingdom of heaven. That is to say, He taught life practices and faith commitments for people who expected a better world from the hand of God. But from our perspective, the most remarkable thing about His teaching is the subject matters He used to convey His thoughts—they were generally quite secular in nature (that is drawn from the affairs of the world around Him), interspersed with concepts found in the Scriptures to be sure, but mostly drawn from the daily life of His students. The experience of farmers, tradesmen, fishermen, soldiers, builders, tax collectors, priests, and rulers all appear frequently in His teachings. And the subjects that formed the case studies of His instruction include economics, government relations, labor relations, family life, illness and health, arrogance and prejudice, generosity and greed, international relations and local issues, pride and humility. I have often thought that had Jesus visited an academy or college in our time, and attended classes, He would have felt quite at home with the subjects taught. I also think that He would allow no lesson to close without a life-changing conclusion—a take-home educational moment, as it is fashionably called today, but that merely represents good pedagogical practice at all times. Therefore, the first take-home lesson regarding the foundation of Christian faith is that it takes its beginning from Jesus Himself, that He used education to convey it, that His teaching material is quite secular in form and context, and that it always points the students to some life-changing concept, often at odds with established practices and thinking. In this process, He identified the "heart and soul" of His educational work, namely the call for us to serve others better and to love God more, in response to His urgent invitation to enter God's kingdom now. In short, the foundation of the Christian faith was established by Jesus Himself. He used a process of common education for its elucidation, but gave it a "heart and soul" that made it uniquely Christian. In so doing, Jesus Himself established a pattern for Christian education in all time.

This "heart and soul" of Christian education, its essence, draws the teacher and learner, as it did Jesus and His followers, to the realization that all truth is God's truth. That principle concerning the way Christians approach the learning process was accepted by many thought leaders throughout Christian history. It implies that the outer form of Christian education (the curriculum of study) shared with common education does not make it "secular," or anti-Christian, since all truth belongs to God in the first place. Jesus established that fact with His teaching material and the lessons He drew from it. Though at times forgotten over the Christian centuries, this principle was articulated anew in the Protestant Reformation and is celebrated in the reformed tradition, for example, by Dutch theologian Abraham Kuyper, one-time prime minister of the Netherlands and founder of the Free University in Amsterdam, who brought great clarity to its meaning: "In the total expanse of human life there is not a single square inch of which the Christ, who alone is sovereign, does not declare, 'That is mine!' "[9] While not using this expression, E. G. White, in her treatment of true education, also affirms the unity of all truth under the aegis of God's creation. From a simple blade of grass (biology) to the vast galaxies (physics), there exists a unity impressed upon it all by the Creator. And from the beginning of time to its end, a connecting link is provided by God's provident care for His creation.[10] Such unity of knowledge impressed upon it by the Creator, and the connecting links between it, may not be obvious at first, and may appear elusive even after years of contemplation, but Christian educators proceed from the conviction that in the final analysis, all truth is God's truth. Therefore, though it deals with secular subjects, the work of Christian education is sacred.

This characteristic of Christian education may well be its most profoundly important feature for our time, for it touches both the teacher and students and the matters being studied. For the teacher, the unity of all truth under God's providence leads to an awareness of the enormity of the educational task along with a sense of humility before it. It is therefore not uncommon for the most brilliant, educated minds to become aware in a deeply felt way of the presence of God in the subject under study. For the students, it means that education becomes holistic. In its simplest form, holistic education implies that all aspects of learning contribute to shaping the students into whole beings, with physical, intellectual, and spiritual qualities, and further that such education seeks the maturing development of all these aspects of human life. That does not occur merely by having the students engage in rigorous intellectual pursuit while performing physical labor or athletic activities and participating in religious services. Rather, it requires the student to discover that all truth does belong to God, and that the whole human being must engage in the learning process and become enriched by it in order to fully and genuinely appropriate that knowledge as intended by the Creator. Approached this way, education makes teachers and students believers in God and leads them to worship Him.

E. G. White pondered this principle of true education in some of her most often quoted statements. "Higher than the highest human thought can reach is God's ideal for His children. Godliness—Godlikeness—is the goal to be reached."[11] How can this happen? Adventist theology of education has not really addressed how these lofty goals of education can be reached at the practical level where teaching and learning occur. Too often Adventist educators have simply surmised that E. G. White is here equating education with redemption[12] and describes what the redeemed human being will experience in the presence of God, when redemption has done its work, which is "To restore in man the image of his Maker, to bring him back to the perfection in which he was created, to promote the development of body, mind, and soul, that the divine purpose in his creation might be realized—this was to be the work of redemption. This is the object of education, the great object of life."[13] Therefore, religious activities, such as Bible study, prayer, and devotion are generally considered the proper ways to achieve this level of personal growth. Rarely do Christian educators imagine that these lofty goals are actually achieved by an ordinary educational process dealing with the very ordinary subjects of education, and taking place in a school, a lecture hall, a library, a laboratory, and happening in front of teachers. But in fact, when these ordinary educational activities are imbued with "heart and soul," education becomes Christian. As a result, the broken image of God is restored in man, godliness and godlikeness do emerge in humanity, so that the extraordinary experience often associated with what typically happens in the church pew will actually occur on the school bench as well. That, in fact, is what Christian education promises and what Jesus modeled in His teaching work. In short, it is not just added elements of a religious nature, such as Bible classes, school prayer, or the elimination of certain secular subjects from the curriculum that enables education to reach its noble goals. Rather, it is the "heart and soul" of Christian education, meaning those transforming qualities that when infused into common education, enable it to reach its most noble goals, and make it Christian. That is what we mean by Christian education or "true" education.

As a consequence, the difference between ordinary education and Christian education may not be visible on the surface or even in the educational institution's catalogue of subjects and courses of study. History, math, biology, literature, and so on, may look very much the same in Christian and secular education. For example, the Christian chemistry teacher does not inject some religion into the periodic table or chemical reactions, but rather attributes the ordinary truth of chemistry to God, as His truth. The readings and laboratory activities may be identical to or like those of all other chemistry classes. The topic of chemistry itself does not display any unique features of a distinctly Christian character. Here is no Christian chemistry different from secular chemistry. Alchemy is not Christian chemistry—it is bogus science! However, when chemistry is taught by a Christian educator, the "heart and soul" of Christian education are on display. They hold that all truth is God's truth, such that when teachers approach their subjects of study, they approach God in humility and marvel, and students come to the subjects with mind, body, and spirit as whole beings in search of the Divine image in which they were made. Such a transformation of common education to Christian education is an inner transformation, like a conversion, and that is what makes it Christian. But how does it work itself out in a classroom, a lecture hall, the libraries, and laboratories in our time? How does it modify the teacher's and student's mind-set? And how does it manifest itself following graduation in the life of an educated Christian? What precisely is that "heart and soul" of Christian education?

When speaking of the heart of Christian education, we most readily think of the idea that we learn in order to serve. All education provides the student with a huge amount of human capital and Christian education adds to that a heartfelt desire to spend this capital on others to help meet needs and fulfill promises. The Campus Compact organization, with its emphasis on service learning and civic engagement, represents current initiatives to put a heart back into education that otherwise might remain selfish and self-serving. These worthy initiatives in no way diminish or obviate the central place of the heart in Christian education, but only underscore its importance. This heart is not a natural part of education, for in fact education left to itself draws attention to the learners' preoccupation with themselves, and easily leads to pride and selfishness. By itself, education provides knowledge, and knowledge leads to power, and power brings with it opportunities to benefit oneself in many different ways. Many parents desire to have their children graduate from the most prestigious universities on the grounds that it will give them unprecedented opportunities in life, to seek positions, gain influence, and become wealthy, even at the risk of becoming proud and self-serving. This alone illustrates the enormous opportunities and risks which are made possible with the acquisition of knowledge. It is no wonder that the first human temptation recorded in the Bible is the temptation to become wise, and the tempter was the most cunningly clever of all God's creatures, the serpent. This classic temptation was not a temptation to disobey, but to become wise, and hence powerful, and the attractiveness of this offer was great enough to produce the worst case of disobedience in all of human history. Therein lies an important insight: Education with a heart, simple as it sounds, does not come naturally or easily, even in a so-called Christian school or college; it must be sought deliberately and intentionally. The difference between common education and Christian education is enormous. The work of the Christian educator is hugely important, and life changing, namely to turn students away from the goal of seeking self-serving opportunities toward a life goal of selfless care for others. For Seventh-day Adventist educators, the service objective always will give priority to the activities with a history of special importance to our church, such as healthcare, relief and development among the disadvantaged, protection of children and the elderly, and so on. Meeting these urgent needs with competent, unselfish, and generous service expresses the heart of Adventist education.

Some Christian theologians have proposed that human nature possesses within it noble and unselfish thoughts that can turn any education with its concomitant abilities and powers into something good. The goodness deposited in the life of humans by the Creator Himself, it is thought, is not all lost to selfish aggrandizement. That may well be, as illustrated in the "noble savage," or the natural goodness of a person. Nevertheless, left without direction, this natural goodness, such as it is, embellished by education can and often does turn into something demonic and selfish, without proper protection. Christian education, that is education with a heart, provides the best protection possible against falling into selfishness, by relentlessly impressing upon the students the truth that one learns to serve. All educational achievements, all of them essential for growing into "godliness," "godlikeness," are intended for the benefit of others, and for the common good of all. In the hands of Christian educators, knowing becomes caring. Understanding becomes compassion. Achieving becomes sharing. That is the heart of Christian education and uniquely of Adventist education.

At times Christians have noted how some well-educated people, even believers, have become selfish and hateful toward others, despite the best efforts by their teachers to point them to the heart of education. And so they have proposed that the most effective way to address this risk is to limit education in some way or other so as to protect students from being led astray by certain areas of learning or simply by learning too much. For example, some have proposed to eliminate some subjects, such as literature, philosophy, or art, and so on, from the curriculum, particularly subjects that are theoretical with no apparent practical application that could possibly be of benefit to others. Others have proposed to limit useful education to high school or undergraduate college, in the hope that the heart of education will occupy a larger place in the life of the student and not be diluted by endless preoccupation with learning more and more, some of it considered mostly useless! I have generally found that this does not provide lasting positive results for Christian education and that its heart is not protected by such constraints. Rather, effective Christian educators nurture the heart of their students by demonstrating how all areas of education serve others. Therefore, all courses of study that prepare for service in some way belong in Christian education, and additional study that enhances and expands service is desirable and valuable. That is the standard for determining what to include and exclude, and how much education to pursue. It is the ability to be of use for the good of others that makes any subject suitable for Christian education. That is the heart test of Christian education, its final exam. It asks, Can I benefit the common good with what I learn? Will someone be helped to live better as authentic human beings created in the image of God because of what I teach or learn?

In this connection someone may well ask, for example, how reading literature can be of service to anyone! It can help with effective communication, in speech, and in writing; it can help understand human nature, its fears, uncertainties, its hopes and dreams; it may help understand and obey the ethical demand that guides our moral obligation toward others in everyday living. Even very complex subjects of study may be helpful for a life of service if only by protecting the student from reaching simplistic conclusions and easy answers to what are arguably complex questions in many areas of life. Simplistic and all too easy answers can be damaging by depriving the student of wholesome humility before the whole world along with respect for all of life within it. For example, learning from ecology, geology, or astronomy that much of the early history of the earth and the universe still remains shrouded in mysteries, can protect students from arrogance and from accepting untested solutions to today's problems in the environment and climate. Similarly, unraveling the human mysteries in the study of psychology can lead to empathy on the part of the student toward others and can make the student more understanding of the situation others are facing and help find realistic and workable solutions to their problems. There is hardly a field of study but that its heart can be uncovered and laid bare by a good Christian educator and turned into an opportunity to serve others. That is the first characteristic of the theology of Christian or "true" education—it has a big heart. Its goal is to serve, to help, to comfort, to seek the welfare of others in an understanding, constructive, and empathetic way. Christian education is never undertaken for its own sake. Christian education evokes the ethical demand—teaching us how to seek the good of others and indeed to seek the good of all God's creation in a way that is never self-serving. The goal of education, explains E. G. White, brings joy of service in this life and expectation of higher joy of wider service in the life to come. That goal of education is its heart.

The soul of Christian education, on the other hand, points to the essential character of all Christian intellectual life and it also identifies some of the deeply personal benefits of a Christian education. Therefore, it is a bit more difficult to explain and put into practice. It is closely related to the well-known statement by E. G. White, that the object of education is for students and teachers together to reach "higher than the highest human thought can reach—that is God's ideal for his children."[14] This ideal is remarkable for its extraordinary, even imaginative quality, namely to reach beyond ordinary human abilities, but also because it differs so radically from the familiar but unsustainable and ineffective way by which educators so often seek to capture the soul of their educational work, by making it more "human," so to speak. For a Christian educator, on the other hand, seeking the soul of education means making it more godlike. It is that part of education that restores the image of God in both the teacher and student. Christian education sanctifies. For Seventh-day Adventist educators, this sanctification of necessity gives special attention to those spiritual convictions that have special importance for our church, the Sabbath, the Second Advent, the message of salvation, and so on. These convictions define the soul of Adventist educators.

Some have suggested that the best way to nurture the soul of Christian education—to make it decidedly more Christian in character—involves modifying or altogether eliminating subjects that could be threatening to the divine presence, and limiting the height to which the human mind is actually allowed to reach. Such eliminations and limitations might include, for example, certain kinds of music from the music department, certain types of literature from the English department, theories about origins from the biology and physics departments, Freudian psychology from the behavioral sciences departments, communist ideology and socialist economics from the political sciences department, and philosophy, especially existentialist philosophies, from all departments, and so on. Indeed, Christian education is right in setting aside certain subjects and placing limits on others that do not contribute positively to the formation of its heart and distracts the search for its soul. Christian education does set priorities. Not every subject is suitable for Christian education and some subjects may actually become distractive or be detrimental to its soul. And yet any such eliminations and limitations by themselves do not assure that Christian education recovers its soul in what is being taught, and may indeed give educators a false sense of security that all is well. Indeed, in some cases, leaving certain subjects out of discussion may actually make them into something like a forbidden fruit that both teachers and students are tempted to taste outside the Christian classroom. And in other cases, eliminating or limiting certain areas of study may in the final analysis simply reflect the prejudices or fears of educators and that would be counterproductive. The soul of Christian education does not emerge by skirting difficult subjects, but by probing for all God's truth where it may be found. In other words, the soul of Christian education does not emerge simply by removing presumed obstacles to its emerging, but by deliberately seeking its actual presence. Therefore, in addition to the occasional eliminating from the curriculum of study things that are neither profitable nor helpful, specific efforts must be made to seek and nurture the soul of Christian education wherever it can be brought to expression within all subjects being taught. But how?

The answer to this question takes us close to what is meant by true piety, which is a faith that transforms the inner being of every believer. True piety is not a naive faith that believes uncritically, or leads to an unexamined life. It is a self-understanding more than a worldview. A pious person is someone, whether student or teacher, who knows himself or herself to be a child of God, created and nurtured by God's life-giving power, and affirms the One God, the Father of us all, Creator and Sustainer of the whole world. Those affirmations, not preconceived ideas about the world and life within it, are the starting point from which education with a soul begins, as Scripture also teaches with its profound statement that the fear of God is the beginning of wisdom (Proverbs 1:8). That conviction, and not cultural, ideological, and philosophical preferences, determines the subjects to be studied, and guides their exploration and investigation. If such piety is the starting point at which the soul of Christian education first appears, its ending point is doxology—praise of God, for those higher than ordinary human thoughts that emerge throughout the teaching and learning process. Indeed, one sure indication that teachers and students have experienced the soul of Christian education is that they feel moved to praise God for what they have learned.

Christian schools and universities generally include chapel services, vesper, and worships in their curriculum or co-curriculum in order not to leave God out of the educational process. In some cases, chapels and worships, or prayers before lectures, are seen as the permanent, non-negotiable residue of Christianity in a Christian college or university, to keep it from becoming secular, as it were. In other words, religious exercises may be retained as a visible indicator that the education remains Christian. Such thinking would be backward, and generally leads to endless criticism by students who quickly detect if chapels are designed for religious pretense rather than for real worship. In true Christian education, it is not chapel that makes it Christian, by providing it with its Christian soul once a week. Rather, that soul belongs in all teaching and learning activities—in the lecture room, the laboratories, and libraries, while chapel and all religious exercises provide an opportunity for doxology, a moment to praise God for the soul of education that makes it truly Christian. How can that become real?

Education opens the mind to extraordinary explorations and unequaled discoveries. Discovering new mysteries of the world and life within it, extending our understanding of them in new directions through research, artistic and applied learning—all of that and more leaves the truly educated person speechless before the privilege of limitless learning opportunities, and inspires moments of praise and joy. It is an extraordinary idea—higher than the highest human thoughts ever imagined! While proud educators may feel self-aggrandizement and pride at such moments, the truly pious Christian educators experience a sense of gratitude for the gift of learning new truth, all of which ultimately belongs to God. That is the soul of Christian education at work in the teacher and student. Therefore, if the heart of Christian education motivates the educated person to seek the common good for all, the soul of Christian education leads to assurance of faith and thus doxology, namely the praise of God for enabling students and teachers to reach goals higher than the highest human thought can grasp.

Some Christian educators may respond that if the soul of Christian education leads to spontaneous praise of God, religion has been introduced unnaturally in subjects where it does not belong placing the integrity and objectivity of learning at risk. God, they will say, is not part of the argument or database or discovery in an ordinary curriculum of study that Christian education shares with other types of education. For example, history, they say, is the study of human events, not speculation about the side which God took in a war or in an election. Biology is the scientific study of life using well-established methods of investigation, and should not be overshadowed by expressions of marvel over its ever unfolding mystery, no matter how impressive. And math is pure logic, not a defense in support of the existence of God. Nevertheless, despite these reservations, the soul of Christian education comes to expression in the teaching of these subjects. How can that happen without the risk of it being used for trivial or extraneous purposes?

Rather than attempting to write God into the social sciences, biology, and even math textbooks to make certain of a Christian soul being present in these subjects, it would be far better to begin with the premise that all truth is in fact God's truth, including the truth of social sciences, natural sciences, and even logic. Accordingly, the interactions between individuals and people groups over the centuries, the emergence of social and political systems, and the events that make up our heritage—all this is of God. God does not have to be added to these subjects in some unnatural, artificial, or extraneous way. He is there already, that is, He is in the discoverable and emerging truth of these subjects. Similarly, the life sciences with their mysteries of life and death, reproduction and regeneration, the cycles of growth, from the largest forms of life to its smallest building blocks along with their chemical reactions—all belong to the truth of God. We do not have to inject God in unnatural ways into our laboratories, so long as we know that we are studying His world. And even logic, pure math, is God's truth and we do not have to add Him to it, as it were. If it were not so, our God would be too small, and not to be taken seriously. Because Christian educators know this, they revel in God's presence while teaching their subjects, for they know they are humans invited to seek God's truth and help dispense it. They have understood the meaning of piety for educators and they are giving Christian education its soul back. Therefore, the soul of the educated Christian grows in step with the acquisition of new learning and understanding. Each new discovery enlarges the awareness of God's presence in the life of a Christian educator. And that compels the Christian teacher and student to sing the doxology and to worship as a natural response to such an extraordinary invitation to learn.

Taken together, the heart and soul of Christian education are its most fundamental and compelling character traits. One of these, the heart, enlarges the educated Christian's desire to serve others and meet their needs. It enables the students to hear the ethical demand and to pursue the common good for all God's children, including their redemption from sin and destruction. The other, the soul, enlarges the educated Christian's personal understanding of God in step with a growing understanding of the subject being taught and learned. As the heart of Christian education blesses others, its soul blesses those who teach and learn by sanctifying them. Taken together, they are transforming education, and that transformation happens not just in the cocurricular activities of service learning and worship services, but in the very educational process when Christian educators lead their students to think more of others the more they learn in their chosen fields of study, and to think better of God the better they themselves understand the subjects under investigation.

In conclusion: The heart and soul of Christian education and the Adventist college and university

Taxonomy means classification, and when applied to Adventist educational institutions, it asks about their unique classification in relation to other types of educational institutions. Most Adventist colleges and universities share a common classification with other similar institutions. For example, Andrews is one of over two hundred national, comprehensive doctoral degree granting universities. Most other North American Adventist institutions are classified as regional bachelor's or master's degree institutions. Loma Linda is classified as a health sciences university. All are considered four-year institutions, meaning that they grant at a minimum the bachelor's degree. All are regionally accredited, and they provide students with standardized curricula for like institutions, even to the point of listing in their catalogues mostly similar or even identical sounding course descriptions. All are independent, meaning private, as opposed to public, religious, and church-related institutions. Adventist colleges and universities share this kind of taxonomy with other North American institutions of higher learning.

This identification of what is shared with other institutions adds importance and even urgency to the question of the unique and limited taxonomy of Adventist colleges and universities. What is special about them? In response to this question, we at times refer to the unique aspects of our Adventist campus life and faith. For example, our campuses are smoke and alcohol free, offer vegetarian food along with other dietary practices, operate single gender residence halls, regulate social activities, require chapel and worship attendance, close on the seventh day Sabbath, commit to the fundamental teachings of the Seventh-day Adventist Church, and so on. While many other colleges and universities uphold a vibrant Christian life and faith on their campuses, few if any other religious colleges and universities practice such a very specific, denominational commitment to Christian life and faith as understood by Seventh-day Adventists. Thus the life and faith exhibited on an Adventist campus clearly contribute to, and some will say absolutely determine, the unique taxonomy of Adventist education in visible and tangible ways.

Both levels of classification of Adventist institutions of higher learning, the common one, shared by many other similar institutions, and the specific one, dealing with Adventist life and faith, are important and give special character and definition to every Adventist college and university. But there is more. In order for the education we offer to reach the full measure of a theology (some will say a philosophy) of Adventist education, as we have discovered from our own history and as outlined by Ellen G. White in her book *Education,* we must also capture the innermost heart and soul of the education we offer. Only then will all our very best and most promising thoughts about education come to expression in our institutions of higher learning. The heart of Adventist education is an unwavering commitment to a life of service, especially the areas of service enjoying a high priority in our church. Its soul comes to expression through a pervasive and deep commitment to faith in God and to the knowledge of His truth. While these two special characteristics may be barely visible to the casual observer, their potential impact on the students in Adventist education is profound and lasting. Without them, Adventist education may *look* Christian, but with them it will *be* Christian.

References

[1] Special Collection no. 250, J. N. Andrews/W. A. Spicer Collection, Center for Adventist Research, Andrews University.

[2] Cf. Meredith Jones-Gray, *As We Set Forth* (Dexter, MI: Thomsen-Shore, 2002), 80, 81.

[3] In 1881, President Sidney Brownsberger left Battle Creek College and Professor C. W. Stone took over his position for the rest of the school year. In 1882, Brownsberger was asked to return but had already accepted a position at a school in Healdsburg, CA. The school closed down but soon reopened under the administration of the blind minister, Wolcott H. Littlejohn. *As We Set Forth,* 4, 5.

[4] Walla Walla University was founded as Walla Walla College in 1892.

[5] Madison College was founded in 1904 as the Nashville Agricultural and Normal Institute (NANI), but was renamed Madison College in 1937.

[6] Ellen G. White, *Education* (Mountain View, CA: Pacific Press® Publishing Association), 1903.

[7] *Education,* 13, *passim.*

[8] Arthur Holme, *Building the Christian Academy* (Grand Rapids, MI: Wm. B. Eerdmans Publishing Co., 2001).

[9] James D. Bratt, ed., *Abraham Kuyper: A Centennial Reader* (Grand Rapids, MI: Eerdmans, 1998), 488.

[10] Cf. *Education,* 20–22, 99–101.

[11] *Education,* 18.

[12] Cf. *Education,* 15, 16, 28–30.

[13] *Education,* 15, 16.

[14] *Education,* 18.

STEVE PAWLUK

Chapter 2

Toward a Theology of Seventh-day Adventist Higher Education: What Makes Adventist Higher Education Adventist?

Introduction

Roman Catholics propose the importance of the sacramental principle, the belief that humans encounter the divine through the ordinary. Lutherans contribute their theology of paradox—*simul Justus et peccator*—to enrich Christian tradition. Mennonites strive to live lives of radical discipleship and embrace pacifism. The Reformed tradition reminds us that all the world belongs to God and so Christians should engage culture accordingly. Baptist groups emphasize restoration of this world to a state of "primitive godliness." Each of these unique perspectives of what it means to live the Christian life influences the content and the educational approaches of the institutions of higher learning associated with those denominations (Hughes, 2001).

Although Seventh-day Adventists publish a *Philosophy of Adventist Education* (http://www.nadeducation.org/dynamic.html?wspID=477, accessed September 26, 2007), it is not clear that we have fully developed how our particular understanding of the gospel should influence our curriculum, our policies, our educational approaches, and our educational expectations. The central question of this chapter is: How does (or should) the Seventh-day Adventist worldview affect our system of higher education? It is my premise that:

1. Seventh-day Adventism presents its belief system in documents such as its statement of twenty-eight "fundamental beliefs" (http://www.adventist.org/beliefs/fundamental/fundamental-beliefs.pdf, accessed September 30, 2009), explicating what is important to the believer's Christian life, but it has taken a mostly pragmatic, and somewhat evolutionary, approach to higher (and K–12) education. In doing so, we have inadvertently reflected society's spirit of anti-intellectualism described by John Stott, who points out that "The modern world breeds pragmatists, whose first question about any idea is not 'Is it true?' but 'Does it work?'" (1972, 14). It does not appear that we have honestly debated and clearly determined what it is that makes higher education distinctively *Seventh-day Adventist,* other than discussing lifestyle issues as they may impact the preferences and perceptions of parents, employers, and donors toward the institution.

2. Our denomination, while it certainly benefits from being a part of the larger Christian tradition (1 Corinthians 15:3), has also developed some important perspectives that can, and should, provide significant direction to our educational approaches. While this may seem idealistic to many, it is one of the premises of this chapter that compartmentalized Christianity is an oxymoron, and that Christian, and more specifically, Seventh-day Adventist belief, should affect our choices, policies, and curriculum, perhaps much more than any other factor—although, admittedly, other factors are important too.

3. One of the perspectives important to historical (and present Adventism) is the value given to "present truth." It is not the intention of this chapter to use the term in the same way that some prefer to use it, that is, pertaining to the an understanding of Scripture that is focused on some nostalgic golden age in denominational history. But it is one of the purposes of this chapter to examine the meaning of the term, to demonstrate its centrality to the Seventh-day Adventist movement, and to reclaim it as a vital working principle when applied to Seventh-day Adventist belief

and practices, including those pertaining to higher education. However, we may need to coin a new term that does not evoke the negative connotations that have been overlaid onto this term—*present truth*.

4. Another, possibly even more important and distinctive, of our denomination's perspectives is the organizing model of the great controversy. Much has been written about the meaning of the great controversy and what it says about the character of God, the nature of man, the meaning of salvation, and end-time events. Less has been written about what our understanding of the character and values of God mean when considered in connection with the curriculum (both formal and hidden), the policies, and the practices of Seventh-day Adventist higher education. We may be surprised to find out that at least some of our practices and policies inadvertently inculcate values that do not comport with what we deduce about the character of God.

I will not purport to present here a comprehensive theology of Seventh-day Adventist higher education, but to propose a modest impetus for serious, but respectful, conversation among higher education administrators, denominational leaders, and constituents, regarding what is distinctively Seventh-day Adventist about Seventh-day Adventist higher education, and how those essentials should guide our work in higher education. Indeed, if our faith tradition is to impact our everyday lives, and it should, what is better than to allow our understandings of scriptural principles to shape our curriculum, policies, procedures, and expectations of our students? This influence must go beyond merely proscribing certain forms of entertainment or foods or beverages offered in our dining halls or on-campus vending machines, and it must go far beyond dress codes or the "Rah! Rah!" method of teaching creationism in our science courses. Some of these things may, in fact, be important *when included in a comprehensive theology of Seventh-day Adventist higher education,* but they may also become mere proxies for what is important at best, or, at worst, distracters from what we intend to accomplish.

This chapter begins its approach to a theology of Seventh-day Adventist higher education by proposing that Adventism was incubated in the concept of present truth, that it is part of Adventism's DNA (a concept explicated by Tucker and Tucker elsewhere in this book); and that the single most important contribution that the Seventh-day Adventist denomination has made to Christianity is to provide the perspective offered by the great controversy paradigm. These two theological stances define and differentiate, to a large extent, who we are as Seventh-day Adventist Christians. If embraced, as they were by our Adventist forebears, these two doctrines will significantly impact, and likely change, who we are institutionally. I will attempt to illustrate how this might work out after considering these two theological perspectives themselves in some detail first. I will conclude the chapter by urging broad-based and honest denominational conversation so that we might, over time, develop a comprehensive theology of Seventh-day Adventist higher education. This subject has, in fact, been investigated somewhat by members of the Association of Adventist Colleges and Universities (AACU), which have spent several years reexamining the question, via at least one task force and a series of mission conferences, of what the mission and the "essentials" of Seventh-day Adventist higher education might be.

Present truth

Present truth is a term that is not widely used by contemporary Seventh-day Adventists. Oddly enough, just as the culture in which we live becomes more postmodern and pluralistic, the implications of present truth result in significant discomfort for many Seventh-day Adventists. Perhaps it is because the term has been usurped by various subgroups and offshoots of the Seventh-day Adventist Church and is used to describe teachings that purport to clearly, and without any shadow of doubt, identify what faithful Seventh-day Adventist should think and do. The tone of the publications and sermons asserting present truth is often frantic, judgmental, and generally devoid of nuance, leaving little room for individual opinion, critical thinking, or disagreement. We are called to rally 'round the speaker's or author's brand of sinless living or right belief, presumably traceable to early Adventist roots prior to some sort of contemporary compromising effects upon the pure doctrine. Many of the proponents of this type of present truth call for revival and reformation in our denomination pursuant to whatever particular insight they have developed, a call which often is accompanied by warnings of dire consequences for those who ignore them. Occasionally, these writings include threats of withdrawn support from, or even overt attacks upon, institutions or its employees that do not teach the particular viewpoint that is being promulgated as present truth. One may conclude that the term *present truth* is used, not to promote progressivism in our denomination, but rather to freeze our understanding of Scripture somewhere in the first half of the twentieth century. It is not clear why that time period is better or offers a more authentic Adventism than any other segment of our denomination's history, nor has a compelling case been made to explain why freezing our theological understanding in any one historical period is somehow better than seeking to make continual progress. As Richard Hughes reminds us,

> both the Bible and human experience make very clear, namely, that we are not gods, but finite human beings with very human limitations. This notion has enormous implications for those of us who serve as scholars. . . . If we take seriously this fundamental aspect of human experience, then we have no other choice but to search for truth (2001, 2).

It may be time for our denomination to reclaim the term *present truth* for what it actually did mean among early, pre-1920s, pre-fundamentalism, Adventists. George Knight clearly established the progressive nature of present truth in his book, *A Search for Identity* (Knight, 2000). He opens chapter 1 by asserting, "Most of the founders of Seventh-day Adventism would not be able to join the church today if they had to agree to the denomination's '27 Fundamental Beliefs'" (Knight, 2000, 17). His statement is probably no less true now that there are twenty-eight. Through the use of multiple examples from Seventh-day Adventist history, he clearly establishes that present truth is "fluid rather than static." He reminds us that Ellen White, a founder of our denomination who spoke under the influence of divine inspiration, stated in 1850 that "we have the truth, we know it, praise the Lord." Yet, fifty-three years later, in 1903, she wrote that "there will be a development of the understanding, for the truth is capable of constant expansion. . . . Our exploration of truth is yet incomplete. We have gathered up only a few rays of light" (Knight, 2000, 20). Perhaps it is not only the case that truth is progressive, but even that those widely believed to have the prophetic gift mature in their understanding as well (Thompson, 2005 and 1991).

Rather than circumscribing diversity and discussion, the doctrine of present truth originally celebrated the priesthood of all believers, the active work of the Spirit in each believer's life, and the need to protect open inquiry so that our denomination could continue to be led of God. This is illustrated in J. N. Loughborough's statement, which he prepared for the *Review and Herald,* and to which he referred when discussing the organization of the Adventist denomination,

> "The first step of apostasy is to get up a creed, telling us what we shall believe. The second is to make that creed a test of fellowship. The third is to try members by that

creed. The fourth to denounce as heretics those who do not believe that creed. And fifth, to commence persecution against such" (White, 1985, 453).

James White agreed, stating, "now I take the ground that creeds stand in a direct opposition to the gifts [of the Spirit]." He continued, "Making a creed is setting the stakes, and barring up the way to all future advancement" (White, 1985, 454). This assertion was made in the context of discussion about whether or not to organize as a denomination. Evidently, in time, the allure of certainty prevailed, and our denomination now has both a book that describes our fundamental beliefs in exquisite detail, as well as a church manual that defines proper belief and practice for Seventh-day Adventists and their congregations (http://www.adventist.org/beliefs/church_manual/Seventh-day-Adventist-Church-Manual-17thedition.pdf, accessed September 26, 2007).

Ellen White, one of the founders of the Seventh-day Adventist education system, whose works are sometimes misused to stifle discussion and viewpoint diversity, consistently upheld the doctrine of present truth in both word and example.

During a school board meeting in St. Helena, California, an elderly Mrs. White voiced her strong concern over what seemed, to her, to be an unreasonable application of the *Testimonies* when a board member referred to her earlier letter to contradict her opinion in favor of granting admission to two children who were younger than the standard of ten years old, which was based, in part at least, on Mrs. White's earlier letter.

"My mind has been greatly stirred in regard to the idea, 'Why, Sister White has said so and so, and Sister White has said so and so; and therefore we are going right up to it.' God wants us all to have common sense, and He wants us to reason from common sense. Circumstances alter conditions. Circumstances change the relation of things" (White, 1981, 315).

Elsewhere, Ellen White championed present truth and an attitude of open-minded searching by suggesting that God might be compelled to use the desperately dangerous approach of sending, or at least permitting, heresies to arise among believers who rest too confidently in the established views of truth. She encouraged "a most critical examination of the positions which we hold," asserting, in what sounds very much like the critical thinking goals expressed in many universities today, that "God would have all the bearings and positions of truth thoroughly and perseveringly searched" (White, 1948, 707, 708). Such statements suggest that the concept of present truth held by this founder of our denomination was aimed, not only at seeking new truths, but at validating currently held truth as useful for the present time. This does not sound like counsel to stay safely in the middle of the box or to become a "shallow ground believer," but seems to recommend a fairly vigorous attitude of challenge, verification, and exploration. Indeed, her intemperate language challenges all believers, let alone university professors and students, to "Agitate, agitate, agitate" (White, 1948, 707). Her use of terms is further suggestive of the academic attitude of critical thinking similar to that delineated by Paul and Elder (2008). For example,

> It is important that in defending the doctrines which we *consider* fundamental articles of faith we should *never* allow ourselves to employ arguments that are not *wholly* sound. These may avail to silence an opposer, but *they do not honor the truth*. We should present sound arguments, that will not only silence our opponents, but will bear the *closest and most searching scrutiny* (White, 1948, 708; emphasis supplied).

Ellen White herself, over a period of years, evolved from holding the belief that eternal hellfire was a necessary motivational tool to the assertion that eternal damnation was "repugnant" and a misrepresentation of the character of God (Thompson, 2005, 75).

It is this vigorous Ellen White that has led Seventh-day Adventist schools of every level and type to cite, even if not consistently practicing, one of her most famous statements against the function of education to create mere conformists.

> Every human being, created in the image of God, is endowed with a power akin to that of the Creator—individuality, power to think and to do. The men in whom this power is developed are the men who bear responsibilities, who are leaders in enterprise, and who influence character. It is the work of true education to develop this power (White, 1952, 17).

The Seventh-day Adventist denomination was founded on and built by the courageous and vigorous doctrine of present truth. It is time that we affirm and reclaim it. It is a doctrine of significant importance to us and to our educational system, for it functions in our denomination in a manner much like the First Amendment does in our nation or like the policy of academic freedom does in research universities across the land. Affirmation of the historic doctrine of present truth protects freedom of speech, freedom of press, and freedom of association in the

Seventh-day Adventist Church. It allows for the vigorous clash of ideas and the comparison of insights without automatically calling into question one's loyalty to God or to the church. Affirmation of the doctrine of present truth is requisite for Seventh-day Adventism's return to the humility enjoined upon us by Scripture, motivated by an appreciation of the fact that God is infinite and we are not. Such an openness of mind would do much to once again enable interested observers to describe Seventh-day Adventists as "people of the Book."

Pre-fundamentalist Adventists, from the mid-1800s through the founding of the Adventist denomination and up to the 1940s or so, understood that God is God and we are not. As Hughes puts it, "The sovereignty of God, therefore, means that I am not God, . . . and that my knowledge is always fragmentary and incomplete" (2001, 86.) Early Adventists understood that infinite God could not be explained by finite humans, but that each of us is capable of approaching an understanding of God, like the diversity of Bible writers (Thompson, 2005, 52), based on our background, our interests, our personalities, and our culture, and that "comparing notes" between ourselves would allow us, us a group, to develop a progressively clearer understanding of God's self-revelation in His words and in His works. As knowledge increases, as science advances, and as we are more able to grasp the meaning of our world and its place in God's universe, we must remain open-minded, understanding that *present truth is truth for today,* it is different than truth was for yesterday, and it will most likely be insufficient tomorrow.

Understanding and practicing this historic Adventist doctrine would have huge implications for our tertiary educational system. But, before we do so, let's consider the model of the great controversy.

The great controversy paradigm

The great controversy paradigm has provided Seventh-day Adventists with a valuable model that allows us to answer, with convincing clarity, how evil originated and why a just God allowed, and continues to allow, it to exist; why bad things happen to good people; and why God doesn't answer every prayer request in the affirmative. It provides a cogent explanation for why Jesus was born, lived, died, and was resurrected. It provides us with an overarching perspective for understanding current and historical events, and a context for our personal lifestyle choices. It reminds us of the most important things.

First Corinthians 15:3 indicates that some beliefs are of "first importance." This implies a taxonomy of beliefs, suggesting that other doctrines or Fundamental Beliefs might be of secondary, or even, tertiary importance. But in Adventism, the great controversy theme and its implications could be considered as being of "first importance."

One aspect of the great controversy theme that remains insufficiently explored, at least in terms of its application to education, is the subtheme of the overarching value of liberty and individual freedom of choice. The book of Revelation portrays Satan as the coercive power that seeks behavioral compliance through financial, regulatory, and punitive means (Revelation 13:16, 17). In remarkable contrast, Jesus, God, respectfully "stands at the door and knocks," inviting, educating, and persuading (Revelation 3:20). It is Satan who is the enforcer. Jesus is the Educator, explaining potential outcomes and reminding us of the necessity of counting the cost (Luke 14:28–33). His respect for an individual's personal choice is not only awesome, but it comports well with postmodern sensibilities. Urban anthropologist Jennifer James, posits that the only way that one can induce another person to change is to "tell them a better story," which they may then seek to incorporate into their own story and experience (Jennifer James, "Thinking in the Future Tense," speech given at 2005 Annual Meeting of the Southern Association of Colleges and Schools Commission on Colleges in Atlanta, GA, December 3–6, 2005).

It is interesting to compare this position with current research regarding motivation for moral action. Tom Tyler reports that research indicates that "sanctions explain only a minor aspect of rule following: in one study, around 5 percent and incentives around 10 percent" (Rhode, 2006, 216). The central theme of the great controversy paradigm is that God is so completely pro-choice that He was even willing to accept the blame cast upon Him by Adam, Eve, and the serpent in Genesis 3, ultimately paying the penalty for their disastrous decisions with His own life on the cross.

Seventh-day Adventists have long understood that the great controversy theme provides elegant insight into the unseen cosmic battle between good and evil. We recognize that things are not what they seem on this earth, but that there is a deeper level of reality (Ephesians 3:10; 6:12; 2 Corinthians 4:18; 5:7). Along those same lines, Seventh-day Adventist education exists not just to help students learn a living and to do well and to do good in this present life, but it is a preparation for eternity. Thus, in Seventh-day Adventist thinking, according to the North American Division Office of Education mission statement, education and the work of redemption are intertwined (http://www.nadeducation.org/dynamic.html?wspID=477, accessed September 27, 2007). One might profitably consider, however, whether the term *redemption* refers only to obtaining eternal salvation, or whether it might also include the broader meaning of redeeming the dignity, understanding, and stature of the individual regardless of whether he or she is ultimately "saved."

There is a mission-related urgency in Seventh-day Adventist education that should cause us to vigorously examine how best to design and apply our system of education. If it is to be a vehicle of renewal for our own children, for other Christians, and for "pre-Christians" (McNeal, 2003, 59) who enroll in our schools, what then is the appropriate balance between stimulating students to engage in the risks (albeit within certain constraints) of open exploration and, on the other hand, the safety of certainties and truths that have withstood the test of time?

Is there a proper place in Seventh-day Adventist higher education for indoctrination? Can higher education be Seventh-day Adventist and still embrace academic freedom, which enjoys honest and rigorous inquiry into the complexities of our world and the diversities of human experience? The answers to the question often seem to be dependent on our own personalities, our experiences with our own children, or our memories of our own youth. Most of us believe that we turned out fine, so we conclude that the educational system that "worked" for us ought to be a good one for others, perhaps merely requiring minor tinkering in its replication.

But we need to reflect on the extreme risk taken by God in permitting the great controversy to unfold. It is difficult, especially for those of us who are parents, to fully realize how committed God is to freedom, if we do not stop to contemplate the level of personal risk that He assumed in order to offer His created children liberty and choice. It was a universal risk that ultimately demanded the life of His own Son.

But the heavenly Father chanced the danger, and engaged with humanity person-to-person. As Philip Yancey points out, referencing the Creation story of Genesis,

"In a remarkable scene, God parades the many animals before Adam 'to see what he would name them.' What a strange new sensation for omnipotence! The creator of the universe in all its vast array assumes the role of Spectator, waiting 'to see' what Adam would do" (Yancey, 2002, 34).

Yancey then confesses,

"I sometimes wonder how hard it has been for God not to act in history.... What is the cost of God's self-restraint?" The Scriptures answer that question plainly. It cost the Son's life.

Nevertheless, in a millennia-long process, God showed us that truth is stronger than untruth, that lepers become clean when touched by one who is whole, and not the other way around, and that when God and sinners eat together and talk together, the danger is worth it.

It is important to understand, however, that we know of no guarantees for safety in God's economy. In spite claiming "promises" such as those found in Proverbs 22:6 and 1 Corinthians 7:16, there are Biblical evidences and many personal testimonies that indicate other outcomes. We find that we must continue to hope, a concept that makes little sense in a risk-free environment, in God's grace (Romans 8:24).

Risk is, in fact, risky. Adam and Eve, living in the very presence of God, made a fatal choice. Cain, growing up in a godly environment not far removed from the blessings of Eden where his parents spoke with God face-to-face, became a murderer. One-third of the angels, who had been living in God's presence, nevertheless, rebelled. Life is not safe, but without risk, it is not really the life for which we were created. The great controversy story forcefully reminds us of that dangerous but vital truth. *Free will is not safe, but it is what makes us human in the image of God* and thus, in God's estimation at least, it is worth it. Administrators and faculty members are compelled, by this great controversy truth, to inquire if the corollary is true, that without academic freedom and spiritual risk, Seventh-day Adventist higher education is not really education, and perhaps, it is not even Seventh-day Adventist.

While choices have consequences, humans' freedom of choice is valued so much in the great controversy story, that God neither compels nor rushes decisions. To use Ronald Heifetz's phrase (1994), God allows the problem to "ripen." God knows that our characters and emerging values are the result of slow learning, occurring in fits and starts. Eroding prejudices and biases, emerging readiness to learn, unfolding realizations, recognizing and learning from mistakes, and learning to evaluate and take advice takes time, lots of it. Learning is not accomplished in a day, a few months, or even during the four years of higher education. However, four years of higher education can permit students and faculty to take a "time out" from regular life, to come aside to the sanctuary provided by the ivory tower, and to focus on the educational and moral development of each student in a client-advisor relationship (as opposed to a parent-child or, God forbid, a customer-merchant relationship).

The great controversy theme also teaches that history will culminate in a summative conflict between good and evil. Revelation 13 is interpreted by Seventh-day Adventists to mean that toward the end of time as we know it on this earth, the coercion of the beast will be so extreme that people who will not comply with the beast power will not be permitted to buy or sell or engage in the regular activities of life. Instead, they will, according to our present understanding of prophecy, be persecuted, arrested, and threatened with the loss of life in order to compel them to comply with the beast power. It will take a certain kind of courageously independent individual to remain sufficiently faithful to be willing to stand for his or her beliefs even though almost all of civilization will follow after the beast. It seems that with this belief firmly embedded in the consciousness of Seventh-day Adventists, our higher education system should seek to assist students to become more *individualistic* rather than increasingly compliant and conforming. Graduates of Seventh-day Adventist higher education ought to be better independent thinkers rather than better belongers.

People who can stand up to peer pressure, civil compulsion, and injustice must be given opportunity to practice critical thinking, make choices, evaluate the consequences, and adjust their course after experiencing the results of their choices, not some arbitrarily imposed external "consequences" as we euphemistically refer to them. They must learn to value liberty over compliance, risk over safety, and moral courage over conformity. The curriculum (formal and hidden), policies, and procedures of Seventh-day Adventist higher education should be consistent with these values.

Application

So what do these two great and historic themes of present truth and the great controversy mean, in practical terms, for Seventh-day Adventist higher education? Here is a handful of propositions:

1. Our educational task should be one of exploration and openness to God's leading as we seek new truths and refine applications of current truths. To borrow a phrase from Theodore Hesburgh, the Seventh-day Adventist university must be the place "where the church does its thinking" (Hughes and Adrian, 1997, 64). While it is certainly important for Seventh-day Adventist institutions of higher education to produce ministers, teachers, physicians, and nurses who will further the institutional mission of the Seventh-day Adventist Church, Seventh-day Adventist colleges and universities should be much more than religious vo-tech institutions. And while Seventh-day Adventist institutions of higher education have an important role in the preservation and transmission of knowledge and understanding that has stood the test of time, they must also be the organizations that prompt and enable the church to expand current understandings in view

of emerging data, consider new paradigms or seek new insights, and to allow the Spirit to move as new information becomes evident.

The Seventh-day Adventist university must be not only the servant of the church but also the probing conscience of the church. University professors have been given the gift of time to read, to think, and to research—to be the research and development engineers in our church. The church must allow them to utilize their gifts, in developmentally appropriate ways for their students, and in conversation with constituents such as students' parents, pastors, and church leaders, to further the denomination's refinement of its ability to apply the gospel to today's, and not only yesterday's, issues and needs.

2. Our academic task should consist of neither indoctrination nor coercion. Not unless we wish to foster beastlike powers. Not unless we want to produce short-term gains, which can easily be negated once our college graduates are faced with faith-shaking information at graduate school or in the workplace. Some parents do not like to hear this. Many parents of students and many denominational leaders believe that they are paying higher education to indoctrinate students in more sophisticated ways than we were able to in the K–12 setting, or to remediate deficiencies resulting from "insufficient" K–12 indoctrination or resulting from attendance at schools that are not Seventh-day Adventist. Parents pay tuition. The denomination subsidizes universities and colleges. These institutions of higher education exist, in the minds of many, to ensure that as many young people as possible, will think "correctly" and, perhaps more importantly, will become, or remain, loyal Seventh-day Adventists. However, the great controversy paradigm teaches us that even though we may have the authority and ability to indoctrinate, we should not.

It shows us that, contrary to what we sometimes feel as parents and guardians, persuasion and choice constitute the best way to encourage true faithfulness, as Ellen White asserted in her chapter on educational discipline (1952). And history has repeatedly made the compelling case that faithfulness is not the same as loyalty. Behavior can be coerced. Faithfulness cannot. The beast demands compliance. God invites faithfulness. So should our colleges and universities.

This attitude will require that we place less emphasis on compelling certain outward actions through dress codes, dining restrictions, entertainment choices, required attendance at religious functions, and orthodoxy of belief; and more emphasis on ensuring that our students are engaging the principles of the gospel and are evaluating Jesus Christ and His enhancement of their lives. Our emphasis should be on a religious experience that adds to our students' lives, rather than one that continually subtracts from their lives, even if, according to our own estimation and experience, the things that we are subtracting are harmful. We don't dispel darkness by evacuating it, but by admitting light and displacing it.

Ellen White (1952) warns us that this more open approach will not appear as efficient or successful to uninformed onlookers and donors as a more coercive approach, but it will, in the end, be more productive because our students will have made choices for themselves, will have tested their resilience when questioned by peers, and will have internalized the principles of the kingdom for themselves.

3. Our curriculum should inform and inspire wonder at God's ingenuity. As they learn to exegete God's Word and to exegete God's works, our students' minds will be stretched, and once stretched, they will not return to their original shape. Seventh-day Adventist higher education should cause our students to become aware that there is often more than one correct answer to questions and that good answers must often be derived on the basis of incomplete information in complex contexts. Rather than discouraging our attempts to find truth, that orientation should motivate students (and faculty members) to become intensely curious about the unknown. As new information becomes available, it allows us to consider

God in more nuanced terms, much in the same way as adult children slowly become increasingly aware of the much greater complexity of the lives of their parents than they recognized as young children or teenagers.

Present truth, and the risks taken by God in the great controversy to ensure free will, enable the gift of curiosity. A certain level of comfort with ambiguity and paradox may evidence a more resilient faith than a four-year package neatly tied and closed up. Vigorous investigation can only lead, in the long term, to deeper understanding. Overprotecting our university and college students stunts their development as thinking and resilient believers, and achieves the very opposite of the purpose of Seventh-day Adventist higher education.

Professors are specialists in their disciplines. This means that they have become proficient in using the tools developed by their discipline to seek truth. It is important to ask Seventh-day Adventist professors to be proficient in explaining to students how a Seventh-day Adventist belief system shapes their interpretation of findings that result from their discipline's investigations. In many cases, discipline-derived truths and a Seventh-day Adventist understanding of truth fit together well. In some cases, a Seventh-day Adventist understanding of truth corrects discipline-derived truths. In others, discipline-derived information will shed light on the meaning of Scripture. In other cases, a Seventh-day Adventist understanding of truth and discipline-derived truths conflict in ways that the professor has not yet solved. This is why we call our truth *present* truth, and academic honesty requires that the professor disclose that to university students as well. Faithfulness to God impels the professor to explain to students why, in view of an unsolved complexity, he or she remains a Seventh-day Adventist believer. This offers an important model for students in higher education, so that students can, after leaving the support of the Seventh-day Adventist college or university, understand how to honestly deal with the questions that they will inevitably encounter as they continue lifelong learning.

4. Our teaching style should be constructivist and learner-centered, not authoritarian and teacher-centered. I am not proposing the extreme constructivism which posits that there are no absolutes or objective truths. But we must be constructivist in the sense that we admit that reality is filtered through perception, that each of us lives in his or her own reality, and that no finite reality can access the Absolute in its entirety. Thus, we continually seek the Absolute, but recognize that it is a search that will continue through eternity with "new truths to comprehend" (White, 2000, 190). We are constructivists in our humility. Even Jesus, presumably a Master Teacher and Spirit-led, was unable to teach His disciples all that they needed in three years. He expressed frustration as well as an understanding of the importance of learning readiness (Matthew 17:17; John 4:21–23; John 16:13, 14).

5. Learning should be differentiated because present truth is in the eye of the beholder and because the great controversy paradigm values individual choice. This will require professors and students to enter into a client-advisor relationship where the more educated and experienced faculty member informs the client of options, advises why one option or another seems best to him or her under the current circumstances, and then allows the student to draw conclusions and make choices, thus leading to another round of discussions and learnings. Thus it is the student who thinks, explores, and occasionally runs into dead ends, that experiences the excitement of learning and the exhilaration of discovery. An aside: Most professors love discovery and have gone into higher education so that we could be paid for reading, thinking, speaking, and writing about things that interest us. We enjoy our profession because it affords us the opportunity to teach and write about what we are discovering. But then, in an act of high academic disrespect, we often deny our students the very same opportunity of discovery, insisting that they make *our* discoveries *theirs,* testing them on how well they did so, instead of fostering their love of discovery and the development of scholarly habits of mind.

Conclusion

It is important, and very possible, for Seventh-day Adventist higher education to be good higher education and to be Seventh-day Adventist. Reaffirming, exploring, and faithfully applying the historic Seventh-day Adventist themes of present truth and the great controversy will enable us to be true to the history and calling of Seventh-day Adventist Christianity as well as to effective higher education. Daring to look findings and evidences, even disquieting ones, in the eye will strengthen the intellectual backbone of believers. Upgrading our curriculum, our teaching and testing approaches, and our campus life policies in alignment with these time-honored Seventh-day Adventist perspectives, would enhance the many good things that we already offer our students. That openness could also leaven and invigorate our churches and our communities. It may frighten those who are unaccustomed to our churches being something more than "a club where religious people can hang out with other people whose politics, worldview, and lifestyle match theirs" (McNeal, 2003, 1). But, allowing present truth and the great controversy themes to shape our policies and practices will bring Seventh-day Adventist higher education in closer alignment with biblical principles as well as its historic denominational roots, while preparing it to take the next step in effectiveness and service to the kingdom.

Bibliography

Heifetz, Ronald A. *Leadership Without Easy Answers.* Cambridge, MA: Belknap Press of Harvard University Press, 1994.

Hughes, Richard T. *How Christian Faith Can Sustain the Life of the Mind.* Grand Rapids, MI: Wm. B. Eerdmans Publishing Co., 2001.

Hughes, Richard T. and William B. Adrian. *Models for Christian Higher Education.* Grand Rapids, MI: Wm. B. Eerdmans Publishing Co., 1997.

Knight, George R. *A Search for Identity: The Development of Seventh-day Adventist Beliefs.* Hagerstown, MD: Review and Herald® Publishing Association, 2000.

McNeal, Reggie. *The Present Future: Six Tough Questions for the Church.* San Francisco, CA: Jossey-Bass, 2003.

Paul, Richard and Linda Elder. *Critical Thinking: Concepts and Tools.* Dillon Beach, CA: The Foundation for Critical Thinking, 2008.

Rhode, Deborah L. ed. *Moral Leadership: The Theory and Practice of Power, Judgment, and Policy.* San Francisco, CA: Jossey-Bass, 2006.

Stott, John. *Your Mind Matters.* Downers Grove, IL: IVP Books, 1972.

Thompson, Alden L. *Inspiration: Facing Hard Questions, Finding Honest Answers.* Hagerstown, MD: Review and Herald®, 1991.

_____. *Escape From the Flames: How Ellen White Grew From Fear to Joy—And Helped Me Do It Too.* Nampa, ID: Pacific Press® Publishing Association, 2005.

White, Arthur L. *The Ellen G. White Biography,* vol. 5. Hagerstown, MD: Review and Herald®, 1982.

_____. *The Ellen G. White Biography,* vol. 1. Hagerstown, MD: Review and Herald®, 1985.

White, Ellen G. *Education.* Nampa, ID: Pacific Press®, 1952.

_____. *True Education.* Nampa, ID: Pacific Press®, 2000.

_____. *Testimonies for the Church,* vol. 5. Mountain View, CA: Pacific Press®, 1948.

Yancey, Philip. *Finding God in Unexpected Places.* London, England: Hodder & Stoughton, 2002.

GORDON BIETZ

Chapter 3

Christian Higher Education: Passing the Mantle of Faith in a Secular Society

"And the Word was made flesh, and dwelt among us."[1] Communicating God's character by the Ten Commandments was inadequate. It took the Incarnation, God's becoming flesh, for the fullness of His character to be revealed.

That is the sum total of why Adventists support faith-based higher education. We must do more than implant certain concepts and information in the minds of the young. The Word must become flesh every day, in every class, in every contact with every student through every employee. Here God's love may be manifested in the lives of mentors in a living, learning environment that welcomes a diverse milieu of students from functional and dysfunctional homes, from rich and poor homes, from backgrounds of cultural Adventism, legalistic Adventism, and grace-filled Adventism. Out of all that diversity, Christian education should create a community that empowers conversations between the older and younger generations on what is important.[2]

Building a Christian worldview based on God's Word is crucial. To obtain a clear idea of what these conversations should involve, we need to first determine what outcomes we seek.[3]

Without the clarifying effect of . . . comprehensive and foundational reflections on the assumptions underlying religious education practice, the enterprise becomes an activity for which there are methods but no purpose, direction but no destination.[4]

Without clear convictions and a focused commitment to Christian education's purpose, there is a danger of losing direction. Harvard University, founded in 1636, is such an example. The original "rules and precepts" published when the school began, were overtly Christian.

> Let every Student be plainly instructed, and earnestly pressed to consider well, the maine end of his life and studies is, to know God and Jesus Christ which is eternal life (John 17:3) and therefore to lay Christ in the bottom, as the only foundation of all sound knowledge and Learning. And seeing the Lord only giveth wisedome, Let every one seriously set himself by prayer in secret to seeke it of him (Prov. 2:3).[5]

The university motto adopted in 1692 was *Veritas Christo et Ecclesiae,* meaning "truth for Christ and the Church." This phrase was embedded on a shield. . . and can be found on many buildings around campus including the Widener library, Memorial Church, and various dorms in Harvard Yard. Interestingly, the top two books on the shield are face up while the bottom book is face down. This symbolizes the limits of reason, and the need for God's revelation.[6]

Today, a Harvard education may justifiably be prized, but certainly not for holding to the founding principles of the institution. To avoid the road that many faith-based schools have traveled as they are absorbed into the secular society, there needs to be clarity of mission, a willingness among administration to hold to the mission, and an unambiguous understanding of the educational outcomes sought.

The goal of higher education conversations is encapsulated by the research findings of Steven Garber, who studied Christian graduates. He observes three common traits identified in mature Christian graduates who integrate belief and behavior.[7]

First: Convictions—a worldview sufficient for life's questions and crises

For six hundred years after the founding of the first colleges and universities in the Western world, all institutions of education were church institutions. All education was religious education with the purpose of building a coherent, faith-based worldview that answered life's basic questions: Who am I? Where did I come from? Where am I going? But today our innate drive for meaning in life is not met by thoughtful religious education. Vaclav Havel said, "The tragedy of modern man is not that he knows less and less about the meaning of his own life, but that it bothers him less and less."[8] The response in this culture when confronted with meaningful questions about life is too often a thoughtless "Whatever works for you." Adventist higher education posits an opinion about life, truth, and the source of truth. We share convictions. Our response to the questions of life is not, "Whatever!"

Neither is the Christian university's response to secularism an unrelieved diet of religious propaganda. Uninformed conviction based on a false confidence that has not been tested by exposure to a diversity of ideas results in fanaticism. Such an approach to Christian education might rightly be called brainwashing and doesn't prepare students with a worldview that is sufficient for answering life's questions.

If we are to educate young people to be thinkers rather than mere reflectors of the thoughts of others,[9] students must be confronted with a world of ideas, including those that may conflict with their own long-held beliefs. During this process, student ideas may change, and that can be unsettling—especially for parents who may be investing in private education for the express purpose of forming them in their own mold. The danger of a closed system of thought is that it may replicate dysfunction similar to the way inbreeding produces malformations.

Arthur F. Holmes, author of the classic book *The Idea of a Christian College,* suggests that Christian higher education provides the most advantageous setting for exploring new ideas.

> A Christian college does not exist to combine good education with a protective atmosphere, for Christians believe that the source of evil is ultimately within the heart, not without. The Christian college does not exist only to offer biblical and theological studies, for these are available in other kinds of institutions, and could be offered through adjunct programs at state universities without the tremendous expense of offerings in the arts and sciences. The distinctive of the Christian college is not that it cultivates piety and religious commitment, for this could be done by church-sponsored residence houses on secular campuses. Rather the Christian college is distinctive in that the Christian faith can touch the entire range of life and learning

to which a liberal education exposes students.¹⁰

Proper convictions that are able to stand the buffeting of secular worldviews are not built in a cocoon of protection where the growing mind like mold in Petri dish is fed only one thought. Nor are appropriate convictions formed by providing a smorgasbord of ideas, giving equal weight to all of them, and suggesting that students merely choose the ones that suit their fancy. The challenge is to have an appropriate balance between providing an intellectually secure environment that teaches convictions about truth and an intellectually diverse environment that fosters questions and an expanded understanding of truth.

Oliver O'Donovan, scholar in the field of Christian ethics, has said, "A Christianity which will bear witness to God's Word in Jesus will be a speaking, thinking, arguing, debating Christianity, which will not be afraid to engage in intellectual and philosophical contest with the prevailing dogmas of its day."¹¹

How does Christian education develop such thoughtful principled character? Ellen White has some appropriate suggestions:

> Instead of confining their study to that which men have said or written, let students be directed to the sources of truth, to the vast fields opened for research in nature and revelation. Let them contemplate the great facts of duty and destiny, and the mind will expand and strengthen. Instead of educated weaklings, institutions of learning may send forth men [women] strong to think and to act, men [women] who are masters and not slaves of circumstances, men [women] who possess breadth of mind, clearness of thought, and the courage of their convictions.¹²

Second: Character—a mentor who incarnates the worldview

In *The Abolition of Man,* C. S. Lewis suggests that diminishing the attention paid to values in education produces "men without chests." It also produces students whose responses to the great moral issues of the day demonstrate no character.

Building character in young people requires the Bible as a foundation. Martin Luther, in his characteristically bold style, says, "I would advise no one to send his child where the Holy Scriptures are not supreme. Every institution that does not unceasingly pursue the study of God's word becomes corrupt. . . . I greatly fear that the universities, unless they teach the Holy Scriptures diligently and impress them on the young students, are wide gates to hell."¹³

Character is formed—the Word becomes flesh—when a young-adult student connects with a mentor who lives the reality of a biblically based Christian life. Faculty and staff members interfacing with students provides the model for living the Christian life. Christian education is an immersive experience. In residential university life, character is developed inside and outside of the classroom. The development of character during the transition between home and life in the secular world depends on contact with mature Christian mentors whose worldview has developed through their own intellectual pilgrimage.

Information takes on meaning and character is developed as students see the integration of faith in the life of a mentor. When faculty and staff live lives of integrity and relate to students with love, the educational living-learning community becomes a transformational community.

As the old saying goes, a gentleman is one who uses the butter knife when he is alone. Similarly, character is what you are when no one is watching. Integrity of character is not so much taught as caught from faculty and staff of integrity. "One can acquire everything in solitude—except character."[14]

Third: Community—living out that worldview in company with mutually committed and stimulating people

The biggest problem the world faces today isn't related to building fuel-efficient cars or even saving the planet. The biggest problem today is how we get along with each other—Palestinian and Jew, Protestant and Catholic, Muslin and Christian, black and white. Education should model the life of Jesus. Higher education should create utopian communities where the grace and love of God is manifested by faculty, staff, and students. As one little girl prayed, "O Lord, make the bad people good and the good people nice."[15] We need more nice Christians—not just truth-filled Christians.

Alexander Astin's book, *What Matters in College? Four Critical Years Revisited,* testifies to the value of the living-learning environment when he describes the focus of the campus as having,

> A primary commitment to educating the undergraduate, a residential setting that not only removes the student from the home but that also permits and encourages close student-student and student-faculty contact, smallness, and a sense of history and tradition that generates a strong sense of community. This study has shown, once again, that this traditional model of undergraduate education leads to favorable educational results across a broad spectrum of cognitive and affective outcomes and in most areas of student satisfaction.[16]

In Alexander Astin's book, he says, "The student's peer group is the single most potent source of influence on growth and development during the undergraduate years."[17] The mission of Adventist higher education is to build faithful communities of learners through its scholarships, its programs, and its campus lifestyle guidelines, all of which support the mission of the Seventh-day Adventist Church.[18] In the world of technology—where Facebook replaces human interaction and Wii games replace intramural sports—we need communities.[19]

If education were simply the transmission of information, then we could take star teachers and transmit their classes to everyone over the Internet. But you don't sing in a choir on the Internet, you don't play in the orchestra through fiber-optic connections, and you don't play intramural sports on the computer screen. Quality education, secular or faith based, grows from conversations with mentors and peers as significant issues of life are addressed in community.

Richard Newhaus said, "It is by identifying with some Christian community and making its story and values one's own that character is naturally formed. Its moral heritage, proverbial wisdom, and moral exemplars create levels of expectation and a sense of accountability."[20]

How does an institution accomplish the goals of nurturing mature Christian graduates with deep spiritual convictions, strong character, and experience in a community that supports a Christian worldview? Without specific, intentional focus on the faith of the founders, an institution is vulnerable to inundation by a secular culture tsunami. A secular laissez-faire attitude is the easier road. This is illustrated in the trends outlined in *The Dying of the Light: The Disengagement of Colleges and Universities From Their Christian Churches* by James Tunstead Burtchaell.

Avoiding the secularization of an institution requires strength of character on the part of leadership. Spiritual life and church traditions must be prioritized—not only through required courses and integration of faith and learning across the curriculum, but also with behavioral boundaries and required structured religious events.

The challenge

Living in a secular society that is increasingly multireligious, how should we maintain a faith-based identity? We don't want a sterile, rigid, Shaker-like cultural identity that holds to a nineteenth-century approach to life in the world. Nor do we want a postmodern identity that simply reflects twenty-first century societal changes without holding to the faith of the founders.

Some religious higher education communities seek to stand outside the culture, but in so doing, develop their own culture. Jesus is our Example, and He was intimately involved with His culture to the point of being called a drunkard and a glutton.[21] His own instructions were to not be isolated from society, for He said the light of the gospel should not be hidden.[22] We are social beings and are naturally inclined to engage society. The question for us is how higher education interfaces a Christian worldview with a secular society without, on the one hand, losing its faith base or, on the other hand, living an isolated existence.

All education is about shaping human lives, so the question is, What kind of community is best for shaping human lives in the way of Christ?

Polar opposites

As we look at the place of Christian higher education in a worldly, materialistic secular society, there are two polar opposite perspectives. One extreme position is that there is no such thing as Christian education, for by the mere use of the word *Christian* before the word *education,* you are presupposing an outcome and therefore do not have freedom of inquiry. This, it is suggested, is indoctrination, not education. This approach would propose that all learning must be approached with an open mind and with no *a priori* convictions.[23] It suggests that in an environment of absolute academic freedom where there is a no-holds-barred pursuit of truth, the darkness of ignorance will be displaced by the triumph of the light of truth.

The other extreme is that Christian education possesses all truth and the educator need only to pass it to the mind of the learner. This approach might justifiably be called propaganda. The assumption is that education is simply giving someone else what you have and then they will be educated. When an institution focuses on "having the truth," teaching is simply providing information.

Neither of the above polarities can really be considered education. In the first place, the educator yields to the culture providing students a potpourri of perspectives, withholding judgment on any of them for fear of appearing judgmental and, in the opposite case, the educator seeks to clone his or her perception onto the student.

The challenge is clearly outlined by Joel Tate of the College of St. Joseph.[24]

> On the one hand, we say that we have the truth—and I don't believe we should flinch from that conviction! That means that there are people who don't have the truth and whose ideologies are flawed—dangerously so. That idea isn't readily tolerated for a university that exists in a postmodern world. The academy is more comfortable in the presentation of a potpourri of ideas leaving the student to decide on his or her own. Anything else appears too much like indoctrination or worse brainwashing.

Christian university an oxymoron?

Is "Adventist University Christian Education" an oxymoron? Is it possible for an institution to be both Christian and a university?

As Arthur Holmes says in the classic work *The Idea of a Christian College:*

> The medieval university was governed by a unifying religious perspective but education today is rootless, or at best governed by pragmatism and the heterogeneity of viewpoints that makes ours both a secular and a pluralistic society. The result is a multiversity not a university, an institution without a unifying worldview and so without unifying educational goals. The Christian college refuses to compartmentalize religion. It retains a unifying Christian worldview and brings it to bear in understanding and participating in the various arts and sciences, as well as in nonacademic aspects of campus life.[25]

It is the higher education institution with a unifying worldview that truly is a university. The university faculties bring together a unifying idea as compared to the perspective of university that brings together the universe of ideas holding firmly to none of them. The university that loses confidence in the value of the truth loses its reason for existence. It is simply a hodgepodge of perspectives that one could find on the Internet, and rather than a university, it might be called a chaosity. We would not tolerate a physics department that gives equal weight to the various theories about the shape of the earth. "Some say it is round but others say it is flat." We would not tolerate a chemistry department that taught alchemy. Neither should the Christian university give equal weight to theories of origins or ideas about salvation and the truthfulness of the Bible. The university, like the person of character, should stand for something.

So how does the university stand for something without being oppressive and indoctrinating in its stand? Where is the balance found between forcing faculty opinions on students and pretending to have no opinion about anything?

Extrinsic motivation

It would be ideal if all students who come for a university education were mature, motivated adults. Because that is not the case, extrinsic motivation is necessary for a wide range of behaviors that the university encourages.

To regard the institution that seeks to reinforce religious commitment as simply primitive in its moral development takes a very linear and narrow view of morality and spirituality. No one would suggest that requiring a wellness class is developmentally primitive for teaching habits of healthful living, nor would requiring practice be problematic for learning the violin; but somehow when it comes to spiritual development, extrinsic constraints that place students in an environment of worship for spiritual growth is intrusive and inhibits spiritual growth. Similar to the way violin practice is unprofitable for the person with no interest in learning to play the violin, it could be argued that required worships provoke rebellion for the student who doesn't desire spiritual growth. But rather than eliminating the requirement, it might be well to reflect on the motivation of the student for attendance at a Christian university. For students desiring spiritual growth, and who know why they attend a Christian university, the requirement component is superfluous—like the minister requiring the groom to kiss the bride.

For quality spiritual growth, worships must be of high quality, even as for learning to take place in the classroom more is required than attendance. It isn't enough to say that attendance is required—there must be such quality that the students will appreciate the product—even as the groom appreciates the bride.

Required worships are not only for the purpose of inculcating biblical truths, but are also for building community. When the university community gathers together in corporate worship, it builds unity and identity. The mere assembly of a diverse group of people to worship and focus on God deepens the understanding of the nature of the Christian church community.

An environment of appropriate external restraint on behavior is necessary in building a safe context for exploring the student's relationship with society. The cultural constraints of the Mennonites are broken by the sudden process of "wilding," where young people go into the world to sample all its sins and appeals and then choose between the Mennonite way or the secular world. The Christian university design is not to immerse students into the world, but to prepare them to navigate in the world while not becoming of it. Ideally, external restraints are loosened as students develop personal convictions about their place in the church and the world.

Piaget, whose theories of moral development have set the general standard, has said, "All morality consists in a system of rules, and the essence of all morality is to be sought for in the respect which the individual acquires for those rules."[26]

Secular use of rules

Even the most secular of societies and institutions recognizes the need for external constraint. In 1992, Andrew Martinez, a student, organized a "nude-in" protest in the main plaza of the University of California, Berkeley. He said he was trying to make a point about free expression at the birthplace of the 1964 Free Speech Movement. "What I am getting out here is there's a lot of social control going on here," he told the crowd at the nude-in.

The message caught on and nude spottings spiked on campus. Martinez, whose naked notoriety landed him on national television talk shows, was expelled the following year after the university rewrote its dress code to ban nudity. Even in a culture as liberal as Berkley, they found it necessary to make adjustments to their dress code to support their culture.

Judicious use of rules

As Ellen White spoke of education, she said,

> In the school as well as in the home there should be wise discipline. The teacher must make rules to guide the conduct of his pupils. These rules should be few and well considered, and once made they should be enforced. Every principle involved in them should be so placed before the student that he will be convinced of its justice.[27]

The university should be an environment to aid young people in their transition to adulthood. It is the goal to use the teaching-learning relationships to build trust that allows for discreet and personal advising, remembering that "it is better to request than to command," using Jesus' approach as the example, and remembering that we are fellow learners in the Christian walk.[28]

Enzle's and Anderson's research indicates that when students experience surveillance for the purpose of control, their intrinsic motivation for the given behavior actually decreases.[29] Wilson's and Lassiter's research suggests that excessive or unnecessary external constraint impedes intrinsic control associated with mature moral development and often increases, rather than decreases, the desirability of a forbidden behavior.[30] While external controls may be helpful at an early stage of moral development, according to both Ellen White and the research of Lawrence Kohlberg, they are a retarding force at others.[31]

Brad Lau makes the following statement in a study of reasons for student behavior codes:

> "The question is not whether higher education should be in the business of human engineering and social control. It is already in that business.... Every college and university, public or private, church-related or not, is in the business of shaping human lives."[32]

So the question is, What controls are appropriate at a Christian university? Some might suggest that any rules at a university should simply be those that society establishes. The external constraints on behavior should be no more than what society places on students. These are the schools that have abandoned *in loco parentis*. They have accepted that the university-aged students are adults and no longer need any institutional constraints on behavior that would be more restrictive than the law of the land. Issues such as requiring permission for staying out of the dormitory too late, excluding televisions from the residence hall rooms, modesty and neatness in dress, would be considered too inconsequential to be considered.

It was when Mayor Giuliani tackled the supposedly "trivial" things, such as graffiti and street people jumping out into traffic to wash windshields on cars, with his zero tolerance policy that the big social problems in New York were alleviated.

It is through contact on what some might call "trivial" issues that more consequential issues will arise. Under normal circumstances, few students will come to talk about abuse, date rape, or other issues, unless there is a relationship. Relationships can be built through communication on what appear to be minor issues. Some young people in Muslim countries are accepting extreme calls to commitment to giving their lives in suicide bombings. We would do well to issue a call to our young people to reach a high level of commitment that asks not that they give their lives in sacrifice but that they commit themselves to living holy lives in rejection of the perverse sides of their culture. A robust Christianity is a counterculture Christianity.

Our lives are lived immersed in symbols of various types. There is symbolic significance of tattoos; brightly dyed hair; excessive, bizarre makeup; various piercings in unusual places; and clothing that is revealing. The Christian higher education institution is to educate and that includes taking advantage of "teachable moments" that are occasioned by a student acting out in some way that is not appropriate to the culture of the Seventh-day Adventist Christian living-learning environment.

There is a danger, however, of confusing the professor's role as educator with that of enforcer.[33] It is important to be careful not to give students the feeling of constantly being under the scrutiny of professors who are waiting for them to err.[34] Instead, it must be clear to students that faculty and staff are assisting them on their "journey of independence."[35] That is why opportunities of the apparently minor issues can be such a great opportunity for discussion.

The culture of Seventh-day Adventist Christian higher education will not be maintained through a muscular student or faculty handbook that simply raises the punishment for infractions or more narrowly defines the specifics of violations. The Christian university is teaching students principles for life, and while the short-term appearance of using an individualized, gentle, and persuasive approach may seem inefficient, the eternal outcomes will demonstrate that this approach to helping students develop their personal value systems is the preferred approach.

Rules mediated by personal relationships

The development of student personal value systems does not happen without personal contact. Discipline, not in the punitive sense but in the sense of motivating to a higher standard of behavior, only happens through interaction on a personal basis.

Optimally, spiritual safety is mediated by spiritual people connecting with students on a personal level. The more contact there is between students and faculty inside and outside of the classroom, the greater the impact the faculty will have on student lives. Any opportunity for personal discussions about how we relate to the world around us is a good opportunity.

The biblical story of the prodigal son is instructive. The father was not blind or insular. He gave freedom to his prodigal son—not only did he give him freedom but he gave him half the farm. He was no prudish dictator who tried to construct a wall of rules around his son. On the other hand, neither did he go with his son to a far city to waste his money. He stood for what was right even as he let his son pursue his own goals. Neither did he let his son spend his fortune on riotous living while he was home on the farm!

Note that the father in the story of the prodigal son is:

- A man of mature faith, respected in the community but not yielding to community values.
- A man of mature faith who listened to his wayward son but didn't follow him.
- A man of mature faith who listened to his adolescent-thinking older son but didn't cancel the party.

The established mission of Seventh-day Adventist higher education is outlined in more than one place by one founder of the church, and it is to make students more Christlike and to equip them to communicate the message of the Adventist Church to the world.[36] What academic environment makes the best provision to engage the world and the student in a dialogue of faith?

> For the Christian institution, a profound purpose expressed in its institutional mission and ethos is to educate the "character" of students in addition to stretching their minds. It would be irresponsible of such institutions to abdicate their

responsibilities in this area simply because the dialogue is difficult, inconvenient, or uncomfortable. Thoughtful, participatory, and appropriate behavior codes that are tied closely to mission and changed when necessary become an asset, not a liability, for such institutions.[37]

Henry Ward Beecher said, "A nest is good for a robin while it is an egg, but it is bad for a robin when it has got wings. It is a poor place to fly in, but it is a good place to be hatched in."[38] Higher education is a transition point from nest to flight. It is a flight training school. Students are not just kicked out of the nest and told to make it on their own, neither are they to be sheltered in the nest without being allowed to exercise their wings. In aviation, you fly with an instructor; in higher education, you fly with a mentor at your side.

References

[1] John 1:14.

[2] Albert J. Meyer, Mennonite Board of Education, Box 1142, Elkhart, IN 46515. Article "The Church and Higher Education," Monday, November 1, 1993.

[3] "True education is to know and to do the will of God. This education is as lasting as eternity. The Bible is to be our text-book; for true religion is the foundation of all true education. Intellectual training can never safely be disconnected from religion; and with the study of books, manual training is to be combined, that the mind may be correctly balanced, and solidity be given to brain, bone, and muscle. This world is our preparatory school. The school and the college are necessary for the development of the mind and the formation of the character. But the cultivation of the intellect alone, apart from a moral and religious education, has a baleful influence."—*The Youth's Instructor,* August 31, 1899.

[4] Padraic O'Hare, Boston College, Chestnut Hill, MA 02167. The distinction of religion's dual commitment to devotion and inquiry is made by Henry Nelson Wieman, see for example, *Mans Ultimate Commitment,* 1959.

[5] http://www.hcs.harvard.edu/~gsascf/shield.html.

[6] Ibid.

[7] Steven Garber, *The Fabric of Faithfulness: Weaving Together Belief and Behavior During the University Years* (Downers Grove, IL: InterVarsity Press, 1996). Quoted in *Christian Academy,* 112.

[8] Vaclav Havel, in a letter found by Robert Royal; quoted by Martin Marty in *Context* (June 1, 1990), *Christianity Today,* vol. 34, no. 13.

[9] Ellen G. White, *Education* (Nampa, ID: Pacific Press®, 1953), 17.

[10] Arthur F. Holmes, *The Idea of a Christian College,* Kindle Highlight Loc. 453-458.

[11] Oliver O'Donovan, *Begotten or Made?* (Clarendon Press, 1984).

[12] Ellen G. White, *Education,* 17.

[13] Martin Luther (1483-1546) from the *Christianity Today* illustrations Web site.

[14] Stendhal in Fragments, I. *Christianity Today,* vol. 37, no. 14.

[15] "Prayer of a Young Girl," *Leadership* 7, no. 3.

[16] Alexander W. Astin, *What Matters in College? Four Critical Years Revisited* (San Francisco, CA: Jossey-Bass Publishers, 1997), 398.

[17] Astin, *What Matters in College? Four Critical Years Revisited,* 398.

[18] The mission of the Seventh-day Adventist Church is to make disciples of all people, communicating the everlasting gospel in the context of the three angels' messages of Revelation 14:6-12, leading them to accept Jesus as personal Savior and unite with His remnant church, discipling them to serve Him as Lord and preparing them for His soon return.

[19] Rick Rice, *Believing, Behaving, and Belonging.*

[20] Richard Neuhaus, "The Christian University: Eleven Theses," *First Things,* January 1996, 20-22. Quoted in *Christian Academy,* 112.

[21] Luke 7:34.

[22] Matthew 5:14–16.

[23] The only thing I know of that is open to everything is a garbage can.

[24] Following material adapted from an article from Joel Tom Tate, director of Student Activities and the campus minister at the College of St. Joseph in Rutland, Vermont.

[25] Arthur F. Holmes, *The Idea of a Christian College,* Kindle Highlight Loc. 85–88, added on Tuesday, November 24, 2009.

[26] Jean Piaget, *The Moral Judgment of the Child,* 13, quoted in Duska and Whelan, *Moral Development: A Guide to Piaget and Kohlberg,* 8.

[27] Ellen G. White, *Counsels to Parents, Teachers, and Students,* 153.2.

[28] Ellen G. White, *Education,* 290–295. Although Jesus asserted that not "one jot" of Divine law would pass away (Matthew 5:17, 18), His respectful treatment of Mary of Magdala, Judas, the nameless woman caught in the act of adultery, and others, is very instructive of the need to be clear about our ideals, but gracious about how we help people.

[29] M. E. Enzle and S. C. Anderson, "Surveillant Intentions and Intrinsic Motivation," *Journal of Personality and Social Psychology* 64, no. 2 (February 1993): 257–266.

[30] T. D. Wilson and G. D. Lassiter, "Increasing Intrinsic Interest With Superfluous Extrinsic Constraints," *Journal of Personality and Social Psychology* 42, no. 5 (May 1982): 811–819.

[31] L. Kohlberg, C. Levine, and A. Hewer, *Moral Stages: A Current Formulation and a Response to Critics* (Basel, Switzerland: S. Karger AG, 1983).

[32] Cited in D. Guthrie, ed., "Student Affairs Reconsidered: A Christian View of the Profession and Its Contexts," *National Association of Student Personnel Administrators Journal* 42, no. 4 (Lanham, MD: University Press of America, 1997), 42, 549. Brad A. Lau, "Reasons for Student Behavior Codes: A Qualitative Study at Two Christian Liberal Arts Institutions." Brad A. Lau is the vice president for student life at George Fox University in Newberg, Oregon.

[33] Ibid., 287, 288.

[34] Ibid., 289, 290, 291.

[35] This depiction was offered by Tom Gavic, president of Performa, a consulting group, when he was meeting with the Southern Adventist University Strategic Planning Committee on April 28, 2006.

[36] Ellen G. White, *Fundamentals of Education,* 467, and *Testimonies for the Church,* 6, 126.

[37] *National Association of Student Personnel Administrators Journal* 42, no. 4, 549.

[38] Henry Ward Beecher, *Leadership* 4, no. 2.

DAVID THOMAS

Chapter 4

Understanding Christian Education

Christian education today is a massive, complex, and very expensive undertaking. In the Seventh-day Adventist Church, it is, arguably, the single biggest and most expensive church enterprise in existence, hiring more people and spending more money and having more invested in institutions and buildings than any other single church function, pastoral ministry included.[1] In local church settings, when counting local education costs and scholarships offered, it is not uncommon to see as much as 65 percent of local funds being spent on Christian education. At the local conference level, the education budget is often the largest single budget line item. Educational superintendents often oversee more people than do ministerial directors. Such investment of time and resources creates a very high-level mandate toward making sure there is clarity on just what Christian education is and on what it is supposed to be accomplishing. Failure to achieve this will result in the wasting of a whole lot of resources, both financial and human.

The subject of Christian education is a very complicated one. It seems the best place to begin this discussion is with the most foundational of questions: What is Christian education? Foundational questions are very significant ones, for they are both formative, in that they create the ideas we adopt and live by, and normative, in that they make these ideas binding on us. What we establish foundationally has a profound effect on how we envision Christian education, on how we think and expect it to function, on our willingness to keep funding it, and on student willingness to pay the increasingly high costs of obtaining it.

One would think that, after more than a hundred years of significant involvement in Christian education, with perhaps billions spent on the enterprise, and with books and articles galore written on the subject, there would be, by now, a well-known and well-articulated consensus among us as to what Christian education is and what it should be doing. One would think that every student, every teacher, and every professor would be able, on a moment's notice, to explain what Christian education is and what it is to accomplish. Sadly, that is not the case. No consensus has been arrived at. Rather, there are in existence a number of competing ideas that are not at all compatible, often opposing each other and causing their proponents to be at odds. As a result, there are confused and contending voices in the field of Christian education.

This absence of consensus is a significant source of the unrest, unhappiness, and dissatisfaction that one often hears when Christian education is discussed. How many there are, parents in particular, who complain that they paid good money only to realize disappointment as things did not turn out for them or their children as they had expected. It cost them a lot of money, but they did not get the kind of results they were hoping for. And almost always, the "blame" is placed on whatever institution their children went to, or upon one teacher or another. This absence of a clear consensus is clearly highly problematic. Until a consensus is arrived at, this subject must be discussed and agitated still further until one is achieved.

It is helpful to bring to mind that disappointment almost always arises directly from expectations that do not get realized. Whenever we experience disappointment, it is because some expectation we held was not fulfilled. We expected one thing, but ended up with another. Sometimes this is due to failures or inadequacies in the process or mechanism by which we hoped our expectations would be met. At other times, the fault lies with our expectations themselves as they are sometimes simply unrealistic. At still other times, the problem arises because of an undetected difference in expectations between the parties involved in an enterprise. Expectations are present but they were not articulated. The parties involved simply assume that their expectations are similar when, in actuality, they are not. The latter eventuality is very common in the arena of Christian education, parents expecting one thing, the institution another, and the students yet a third. I dare say the bulk of the disappointment and unhappiness people have with Christian education arises from this latter eventuality, the presence of unspoken expectations that, though competing or opposite, remain undeclared so the differences are not discovered until it is too late for any negotiations. Great damage is being done to both people and Christian education itself by this circumstance.

In recent times, nobody has done as fine a job of clarifying these competing and contending interests as Arthur F. Holmes who, in his little book titled *The Idea of a Christian College*,[2] pointed out that there are at least four competing concepts of Christian education over which much misunderstanding occurs. First, and probably foremost, there are those Christian parents who expect college to be a process of thorough and detailed indoctrination for their offspring. The Christian college is supposed to, in their minds, provide the students with the most cogent and powerful justifications for faith along with the most withering arguments against the critics so that when students leave school, they do so with all their doubts banished and a pure faith in place that is strong enough to carry them along for the rest of their lives. The common perception is that if the teachers do a good job, the young people will have all their questions answered and all the critics on the run.[3] As a bonus, any parental failures or inadequacies in matters of faith that might have occurred along the way will be made up for too. These folks view Christian education as a good indoctrination that works for the whole of life.

Holmes notes that there are others who envision Christian higher education as the process of obtaining a good education with the happy little addition of some Bible curriculum. The primary focus here is on getting a top-flight education. The addition of some Bible classes is what makes it Christian. But the Christian "stuff" is clearly in addition to the good education, something added along the way and, while it is a nice addition, the Bible part is not really seen to be at the heart of the educational process.

Still others think of Christian education in terms of the noneducational benefits it can produce, primarily in the form of finding Christian friends and a Christian spouse for students. To some, the prospect of good friends and a spouse is reason enough to pay private college tuition. And how great the disappointment when a spouse is not found!

Lastly, Holmes speaks of those who see Christian education as an educational process charged primarily with the responsibility of providing a continuing supply of people for church employment. In their minds, Christian education consists of a basic training that prepares students to become church workers of various types. Though people in this category may allow for other disciplines to be taught, the primary goal is to provide the church with qualified workers, and other disciplines may be taught as long as they are somehow related to church needs. It is this that churches pay for when they establish and operate educational institutions.

These four concepts Holmes refutes as being less than real Christian education. He holds that Christian education is more than any of these, more even than the sum of all of them together. And I think Holmes is entirely correct. Christian education is vastly more profound and more complex, and vastly more important than this!

The educational component of Christian education

Any comprehensive understanding and appreciation of Christian education has to arise from an understanding and appreciation of the two factors that constitute it, embodied in the words *Christian* and *education.* Though I would not want to cite Wikipedia as a great and authoritative source, the broad and general definition of education given there is helpful as it does explain the features and ideas that make up the common understanding of what education is:

> Education in its broadest sense is any act or experience that has a formative effect on the mind, character, or physical ability of an individual. In its technical sense education is the process by which society deliberately transmits its accumulated knowledge, skills and values from one generation to another through institutions.[4]

Though cobbled together from the various sources that make up Wikipedia, I find this definition refreshingly complete. First, there is mention of education as a process, an experience with "formative effect." There is also mention of the element that involves the deliberate transmission of society's accumulated "knowledge, skills and values from one generation to another . . ." Happily, education is here also defined as involving not only the mind, but also "character" and "physical ability." Education is commonly understood, then, to be a process that conveys information, but also works transformation while, at the same time, affecting students across the full spectrum of experience; involving mind, character, and physical ability. This understanding of education would mitigate against it being something rote or rigid. It is, instead, to be a comprehensive process that involves the growth and transformation of multiple dimensions of a person.

The education element of Christian education is not something different from this. It should participate in this same dynamic, conveying information and, at the same time, working change. In a Christian setting, education is still transformational, still involves mind, character, and physical ability, and it still involves the transmission of accumulated knowledge and skills and values.

It would seem, however, that a Christian education would have more than the usual attention given to the part of education that deals with the formation of the person's "mind, body, and soul," if it may be put that way. Christian education is to be a transformational process that encourages a student to engage with a teacher in a quest to become conversant with many, if not all, fields of knowledge, to develop the mind so it can think with rigor, to aim to understand all that can be understood about life, but to do it in the context of the Christian faith with the intent of developing the person into a thinking, analytical, perceptive, informed, articulate, capable, gracious, intentional person who is, at the same time, devoted to Christ and His teachings and who is committed to expanding the borders of the kingdom on this earth, all the while anticipating the coming of the kingdom in its fullness and reality. Such education should hone, in the student, the ability to gather information, process it, and then draw conclusions that are not at variance with the Christian revelation. I like very much the description Holmes gives of the anticipated product:

> The educated person shows independence and creativity of mind to fashion new skills and techniques, new patterns of thought. She has acquired research ability, the power to gather, sift, and manipulate new facts and materials, and to handle altogether novel situations. The educated Christian exercises critical judgment and manifests the ability to interpret and to evaluate information, particularly in the light of the Christian revelation.[5]

Clearly, Holmes projects that, for the person who experiences Christian education, it will be transformational. More correctly, it will be formational, making them into something more than what they were before they entered the process. They will leave the educational process different from the way they entered upon it. They will end up better informed, better equipped with improved research and analytical skills, able to think their way through issues and problems, and even deal with novel situations, but they will be manifestly Christian, doing all this "particularly in light of the Christian revelation." They will be able to address and work through even new, novel, and unanticipated situations. Such persons will be resilient, able to endure and to make a case for their side.

In the book *The Great Controversy*, there is a cogent but little-known paragraph that, in a wonderful manner, describes Christian education and its outcomes. In this paragraph, there is a description of the education

John Wycliffe received and of what it produced in him, enabling the powerful effect he had on the Reformation.

> Wycliffe received a liberal education, and with him the fear of the Lord was the beginning of wisdom. He was noted at college for his fervent piety as well as for his remarkable talents and sound scholarship. In his thirst for knowledge he sought to become acquainted with every branch of learning. He was educated in the scholastic philosophy, in the canons of the church, and in the civil law, especially that of his own country. In his after labors the value of this early training was apparent. A thorough acquaintance with the speculative philosophy of his time enabled him to expose its errors; and by his study of national and ecclesiastical law he was prepared to engage in the great struggle for civil and religious liberty. While he could wield the weapons drawn from the word of God, he had acquired the intellectual discipline of the schools, and he understood the tactics of the schoolmen. The power of his genius and the extent and thoroughness of his knowledge commanded the respect of both friends and foes. His adherents saw with satisfaction that their champion stood foremost among the leading minds of the nation; and his enemies were prevented from casting contempt upon the cause of reform by exposing the ignorance or weakness of its supporter.[6]

This paragraph is quite engaging in its breadth and vision and in its description of what an education, in the context of faith, did for Wycliffe. It notes that he was schooled across a wide spectrum of subjects—philosophy, canons of the church, civil law, even speculative philosophy! None of this destroyed or damaged his piety or devotion to God. And the outcome of his education was stunning! It transformed him into a formidable contender for right and truth, enabling him to become a history-maker because he understood the meanderings of his time and was able to steer his course in a manifestly Christian way through the confusion and contention of his era. Wycliffe's education set him up to be one of the leading minds of his time and nation, a man with a mind that would be in contention, that could not be ignored or passed by, but a Christian mind no less, devoted to matters of God and faith to the point of death! How interesting and exciting! How worthy of the investment of time and effort, of life itself, even!

The Christian component of Christian education

Though it has been brief, let us leave

off discussion of the education element in Christian education and turn our attention now to the Christian element. Of greater significance in this discussion about Christian education would be the Christian side of the equation. What is the Christian component of Christian education, and what might that involve? This becomes now the pertinent question, one vital to the complex and expensive process of Christian education.

An exploration of what the Christian element of what Christian education consists of is a rather expansive and very interesting task. Most people would simply describe Christianity as a form of religion, one of the many to be found on earth, and leave it at that. But we need to be more descriptive than that. Christianity is, indeed, one of the world's great religions—its largest, if all the variations are considered and counted together. But this assertion does not tell us much. We need to understand more.

A full appreciation of Christianity and what it does in life begins with an appreciation of religion in general, and what it accomplishes in human experience. The best place to start a discussion about the value and role of religion is with the observation that human beings, if they are to live well and purposefully, must have a way of establishing some kind of context for themselves. By context, I have in mind some grand picture of reality into which we can fit ourselves. What I mean here is that we have to find a way of placing ourselves within some grand story from which context we can then derive a sense of place and movement towards some destiny. From these things, we can then derive both meaning and purpose.

Without such a story, we cannot find meaning and purpose in life. Viktor Frankl has made a very strong case, in his book *Man's Search for Meaning*, that finding some kind of meaning in life is, next to those things that make for survival itself, the deepest of human drives. Amidst the horrors of the World War II death camps, Frankl observed that those who had purpose and meaning had much better survival rates than those who had neither. He also observed that the drive for meaning was more enduring than the drive for sex (Freud) or the drive for power (Adler). [7]

And Philip A. Anderson, in a little book on church life, adds the observation that "Man lives in a world of meanings. This world of meanings is an idea structure that helps him make sense out of his world, that influences his decisions, and that is used in helping him understand his experiences and feelings."[8] Expanding on this further are the helpful words of G. Douglass Lewis, who pointed out that

> We constantly try to "make sense" out of reality by shaping our experience and interpreting it to fit into

the scheme we regard as meaningful. . . . As an adult I continue the search for an interpretation of life and experience that "makes sense" to me. For humans such responses come as naturally as breathing, for we are inevitably "meaning makers." If our capacity to "make sense" is impaired, meaningful human life is diminished.[9]

This need to find meaning is true for all humans, even those who are described as postmodernists. To be sure, they differ from others in that they hold that the grand stories by which we understand reality, though not necessarily true, are very important. Postmodernists postulate that all societal stories are manufactured by humans and should not be regarded as telling anything like "Truth," but, nevertheless, they serve a very significant purpose, that of providing context and meaning for life. Even those who deny the prospect of truth claims see the grand stories as vital to good living. It is from them that we derive context, then purpose, and meaning.

Speaking from the context of the current fascination with Celtic Christianity toward the effect of story on human life, Loren Wilkinson of Regent College in Vancouver, B.C., makes this point:

> the other factor that shadows current Celtic Christian enthusiasm is the postmodern conviction that we need to find (or create) stories to live by. True, there is a human need for story. But both neopagans and radical feminists alike are quick to say: "It doesn't really matter whether a useful history [dominated either by magic or by matriarchy] really happened. Too fine a concern for fact and truth is a modern, patriarchal hangup anyway. The important thing is to find stories which nourish us now, and the Celtic past, historical or not, is a rich store of such stories."[10]

Without these, humans simply do not live well.

These powerful stories of context that we encounter are often called *metanarratives,* or *worldviews.* John Fowler defines the term *worldview* as "a construct about the makeup of life as it struggles with the questions of reality, truth, ethics and history. It is a construct that provides a point of departure, a sense of direction, a locus of destination, and a strategy of unity for human thought, life and action."[11] Others have explained worldview as "the pattern of assumptions a people holds about reality that determines what they think, feel and do."[12] Zacchaeus A. Mathema, in a very interesting article on Christianity as it encounters African worldviews, says that worldview "exists at the foundational level of culture and at the core of the same cultural expressions and permeates everything that a people think and do by defining a crucial role in molding individuals and society."[13] Worldview is basically the "control box" of life and culture, it is the place where the code of life is kept, the domain in which "belief-grids"[14] of various levels of importance are assembled by individuals and cultures which are then used in directing life, coming into play every time there is a decision to be made.[15] It is from worldviews that cultures derive the various truths and dictums by which people live. Without them, we simply live in confusion, a condition that is more and more apparent in the Western world as people abandon the worldview that made them and sustained them for nearly two thousand years.[16] And, though slightly parenthetical, is the sad reality that Christians have helped in the creation of the current bout of meaninglessness[17] by disengaging too much from life and culture, and not staying on the intellectual playing field at the level required to affect culture. Once read, these words of Don Eberly are likely to remain in the mind of Christians as rather riveting:

> Christians are understandably dismayed that the culture has become unhitched from its Judeo-Christian roots. What many refuse to acknowledge is that, in a thousand ways, this unhitching was produced by a massive retreat of Christians from the intellectual, cultural, and philanthropic life of the nation. While evangelicals count millions of members among their grassroots political groups and are now, if anything, over-represented in the legislative arena, the number of evangelicals at the top of America's powerful culture-shaping institutions could be seated in a single school bus. The watching world is understandably chagrined by the interest evangelicals have shown in power while simultaneously showing so little interest in the non-coercive arenas of society where one's only weapon is persuasion.[18]

Current circumstances and opinions not withstanding, guiding metanarratives, or worldviews, are found everywhere. Every culture has some story under which it has developed, a whole set of ideas and "truths" that have been assembled into some kind of grand story that is cherished and "worshiped" as the foundation of the community or society. In order to find meaning and significance in life, in order to determine something as important and basic as right and wrong, individuals within a given society consult their worldview.[19] They take the big story and individualize it to themselves, working to find their own place in the grand scheme of things.

One of the great struggles of growing up involves understanding the societal story, testing it to see if it is valid, then adopting its various elements for one's self, thereby finding one's own place within the context provided by the story. The movement from adolescence to adulthood involves, among other things, the testing and adopting of the story, moving its elements from the outside where they consist as something given by parents or leaders, to something inside, internalized where the story and its implications become volitionally owned by one's self. Offspring who end up adopting the same ideas and rubrics as their parents are deemed "good," while those who settle into some other kind of belief-grid that is more at variance are deemed wayward. But those who get to the point of internalizing the elements and dictums of their societal story, owning the story willingly for themselves, become members indeed.

It is important to notice that religion and worldviews are intimately and inextricably intertwined. One way of defining religion is that it is the way we live out our lives under the rubric of our worldview. The various things we do or do not do, or believe or do not believe, the rituals we hold dear and participate in, are expressions that materialize from our living out of our worldview, essentially constituting the elements of our religion. In this sense, all people are religious, even those who proclaim themselves nontheistic. Anyone who has a system of beliefs, a worldview with implications for living, a belief-grid that they use to guide them in their decision-making, has religion. They go through life practicing their "faith" under the rubric of their story.[20] I could argue that even professional sports may amount to a form of religion, loosely defined, providing people with a context and meaning for their living. In sports, after all, there are all the elements of religion. There is a rule book; there are places of worship; there are icons in the form of memorabilia of significance; there are the equivalent of most holy places where the faithful go on pilgrimages to see all the icons and remind themselves of the great deeds of the past. There are even sacraments, beer and peanuts being the ones that traditionally show up at baseball games! All this easily compares with theistic religion in its ability to direct and give purpose and focus to human lives!

Clearly, Christianity participates in this kind of powerful dynamic that is so much a part of religion. Christianity is a movement, an ideology, a religion that has grown up under and around the story of the God of the Bible, particularly as manifest in the person and ministry and teachings of the Man called Jesus Christ. It reveres the acts of God in history as recorded in the Old Testament, but is more clearly defined by the contents of the New Testament. It is arguably more profound a form of religion than sports is in that it includes a supernatural dimension. As Winifred Corduan once observed, religion is "A system of beliefs and practices that provides values to give life meaning and coherence by directing a person toward transcendence."[21] The great American philosopher William James said that religion in the broadest sense "consists of the belief that there is an unseen order, and that our supreme good lies in harmoniously adjusting ourselves thereto."[22] As a theistic religion, Christianity participates in this dynamic, giving deference and preference to the realm of the supernatural, admonishing adherents that "our supreme good lies in harmoniously adjusting ourselves" to it.

Lending more definition to the matter of religion with a particular focus on Christianity and how it fits into this dynamic of religion, are the words of theologian Millard Erickson where he observes:

> The Bible quite clearly affirms a theistic and, specifically, a monotheistic understanding of reality. The supreme reality is a personal, all-powerful, all-knowing, loving, and holy being—God. He has created everything else that is, not by an emanation from his being, but by bringing it all into existence without the use of preexisting materials. Thus the Christian metaphysic is a dualism in which there are two types or levels of reality, the supernatural and the natural, a contingent dualism in which all that is not God has received its existence from him.[23]

Adding still more particulars, Erickson continues:

> How then shall we regard religion? Religion is actually all of these—belief or doctrine, feelings or attitudes, and a way of life or manner of behaving. Christianity fits all these criteria of religion. It is a way of life, a kind of behavior, a style of living. And it is this not in the sense merely of isolated individual experience, but of giving birth to social groups. Christianity also involves certain feelings, such as dependence, love, and fulfillment. And Christianity most certainly involves a set of teachings, a way of viewing reality and oneself, and a perspective from which all of experience makes sense.[24]

Any discussion of Christian education must understand and acknowledge the comprehensive and powerful implications and functions of religion in life, and it must understand the particulars of the Christian faith and the implications they bring for living.

A distinctive feature of Christianity is that it claims to be a religion derived from sources that originate outside the natural world. Pointing to various luminaries who appear in history, Christians pay close attention to their claims that by some means God—who is not bound to the limits of the natural world, who exists outside such limits—came near and opened to them an understanding of a reality grander than what humans could have comprehended on their own, an understanding of the realms beyond, revealing to them a grand reality that is not entirely subject to human derivations, enabling them to define and describe a reality quite different from the one commonly found in the ancient world, to say nothing of the world today. From the writings of these ancient luminaries (usually called prophets), believers have been able to describe a grand and comprehensive worldview that is powerfully capable of giving context and meaning to life and to answer with substantial answers the great questions of life. This worldview enables believers to understand and interpret events in history in a particular and distinctive way.

Christianity dares to claim that the worldview derived from this process, linked to the prophets and to Jesus, approaches more closely to reality, or "Truth," than any other ideological construct available. Precisely because it originates in the Divine, this worldview must be privileged. Gerald Anderson, in his discussion of Christian mission, states this very clearly and succinctly when he says:

> To posit the fact of God ... and to hold that because God is God He can speak to man, and that in Jesus Christ He has done so, is an assumption, but it rests on a possible act of God outside man which, if true, has a greater degree of objectivity than rival assumptions. If this assumption has any validity, the criterion of truth becomes not what one prefers but what God has revealed.

God's self-disclosure, then, is the final truth which is the criterion of all truth.[25]

Quoting Anderson again:

> The fact of such a revelation is an unproved and unprovable assumption, but counter views rest on a similar undemonstrable basis. The assumption of revelation is the only objective criterion of truth which is not at the mercy of human subjectivity.[26]

These are both stirring and challenging. And in a world overtaken by pluralism and relativism, they are not words easily heard, let alone, adopted. But here, Anderson has clearly and succinctly stated what lies at the bottom of the Christian construct, that there is a God who has revealed to humankind something about Himself and about reality. And it is this revelation that is normative and formative.

At the same time, it must be observed and admitted that Anderson does not here address the fact of a human side to this revelation, for God's revelation has still to be reduced to human language by human beings, and there is certainly an element of nuance and subjectivity in that which must be considered. A direct implication of this would be that humility is always appropriate for humans, and a very important ingredient in the Christian faith, something that those on the fundamentalist side easily forget. The fact that there is revelation from God does not mean we have fully, or even rightly, understood it. History is replete with examples of believers in God who went awry, perpetrating all kinds of mayhem, even on fellow human beings, all in the name of God. Of this we must be very aware and ever cautious. We have to live with the reality that our knowledge of God is not exhaustive. At the same time, it is sufficient to be able to proclaim a reality greater than what we might have invented and to have confidence in that proclamation. I like very much the observation of the great teacher of preaching, Fred Craddock, where he so transparently observed of those who believe, the following:

Faith was not the end result of tallying up the evidence. Many did and to this day continue to experience God in the words, deeds, and presence of Jesus, but they did not and do not because God coerced faith as the unavoidable conclusion to divine displays. Whoever has looked upon the crucified Jesus and said, "Son of God," has believed not just because of but also in spite of. The believer has chosen, has taken a risk, has said yes in a world of nos. The believer has leaned forward, heard the whisper, and trusted it to be the voice of God.[27]

Here Craddock envisions revelation from God, not as something powerful enough to be coercive, but as a whisper that we lean forward to hear and then trust to be the voice of God! Here is the reality about revelation, that it is there but, for a number of reasons, it is not coercive. What we are left with is word from God that requires an exercise of faith to hold to and the taking of a risk to believe. Arrogance should never spring from such grounds. But, nevertheless, Anderson's point does prevail, that underneath Christianity, driving it to all parts of this globe, is the belief that there is a God who has made things known to us. This revelation must be given significant play in life. It must be privileged when it comes to knowing. It is because of this that Christianity postulates a story of a reality that is very broad and powerful, quite able to answer most of the great questions of life. It is because of this revelation that the story is distinctive.

Ways of knowing

It seems obvious, then, that education cannot be called Christian unless it facilitates the educational process within the rubric of the basic constructs of Christianity. It must explain the foundations of the Christian faith, helping students learn what "Christian" is, exploring the various beliefs and practices that make up this religion, holding the basic presuppositions of the religion to be normative and formative. It must do its educating with the implications of the Christian faith very much in mind. It must advocate for, and invite and encourage students to become adherents to both the beliefs and practices of the faith, giving the best explanations for what it is that constitutes Christianity. In doing this, it must not be afraid of the hard and challenging things. One of the worst eventualities one can think of is that of masking the challenges and difficulties, shifting education toward some kind of rank indoctrinational model. Indoctrination does not work; it has never worked, except for short periods of time when a people were held captive from information. And, when people eventually discover that they have been merely indoctrinated rather than educated, there is engendered in them a rebellion and hostility fueled by a strong sense of betrayal. Christian education does not need to foster that kind of circumstance.

There is no suggestion here, nor is there an obscuring of the fact, that educating in the context of Christianity is now a very challenging undertaking, especially in current times when the scientific way of knowing is almost universally regarded as being the most reliable, if not the only way, of knowing. There is neither time nor space here to get involved in this crucial discussion, but at least one or two observations should be made. First, we must be careful not to overprivilege the modern way of knowing. It is quite possible, given the passage of another century or so, that we will understand much more clearly than we do now, the frailties of the scientific way of knowing. Certainly, it has brought a great amount of information and knowledge into human experience, some of which has been good, but some of which has been unspeakably bad. Secondly, we must face the fact that science, by its own definition, is focused on the natural world. It, therefore, has nothing to say about any "world" outside the natural one. And it really does not have an explanation for the origins of this world. Something caused the natural world to come into existence. Upon this subject, science can only speculate. It would be inadvisable, then, for Christians to merely capitulate and give away the basic presuppositions upon which faith is built.

Holistic Christian education

This idea of educating in the context of Christianity warrants a little more expansion. Returning once more to the works of theologian Millard Erickson, we should think more about the implications of being a follower of Jesus. Just what does that mean? What is involved in such a process? Certainly, such living involves beliefs. But, as Erickson points out, it involves quite a bit more than just beliefs:

> It seems reasonable, then, to say that holding the beliefs that Jesus held and taught is part of what it means to be Christian or a follower of Christ. . . . Belief is not the whole of Christianity. An experience or set of experiences is involved, including love, humility, adoration, and worship. There are practices, both ethical in nature and ritualistic or devotional. Christianity entails social dimensions, involving relationships both with other Christians in what is usually termed church and with non-Christians in the world as a whole.[28]

Here, Erickson points not just to beliefs, important as they might be, but also to a set of experiences that come along as a result of them, and to a social dimension, too, the beliefs forming the core around which a community rises up. Here, a whole life is described.

Christian education, and those involved in producing it, has to ask not only what education is, but what "Christian" is. I have never read a more precise or focused response to this question than that given by James Orr, where he said, "He who with his whole heart believes in Jesus as the Son of God is thereby committed to much else besides. He is committed to a view of God, to a view of man, to a view of sin, to a view of Redemption, to a view of the purpose of God in creation and history, to a view of human destiny found only in Christianity."[29] All these things go together, part of a comprehensive worldview that provides the context for Christianity.

In light of all of this, the task of providing an education within the context of Christianity is neither simple nor easy. It is, in fact, quite daunting! And it is fraught with enormous implications for both good and bad. This is especially true when we consider the place education and the university have occupied in the Western world for the past several centuries. John North (among others) has pointed out that, in the Western world, the university "has as long and honorable history as Western civilization itself," and, "[it] has become one of the two or three most influential institutions in the world."[30] In other words, it is the process of education and the educational institutions that today describe and determine the tone of society. And, in the words of Nelson Mandela, "Universities are at the same time custodians of tradition and agents central to renewal. They are charged by society with safekeeping the fount of knowledge gained by generations past, while ever exploring new horizons of science and learning. As individual institutions, the great universities are those built on a solid record of achievement and custom, while constantly exploring, creating and adapting to the new."[31] For these reasons, education and the universities are highly prized and they occupy a lofty position in society. Any system of thought, that has no play in the university and in the educational process, simply loses its voice and fades away. It loses its ability to affect and influence the future of human society. As the testimony of one young person reveals, the effects of not doing this job well are significant. Said he:

> I was raised in the church, went three times a week, went to private Christian schools, was active in youth ministry at my church, went to conferences, took nearly ten Bible courses, read my Bible, and attended Bible study regularly for several years, and yet New Atheism sucked me in. As sad as it is, I think that the New Atheists say a whole lot more about the state and culture of modern Christianity than they do about themselves. As crazy as it may sound, the evidence that they put forward (as weak as it is) was intellectually much stronger than anything I had encountered in the Christian church.[32]

Of course, this situation is one linked to a local church more than to an educational institution, but the educational process is still what is here in mind. If Christians fail to provide a cogent basis for Christianity, Christianity will fade.

This all becomes even more sobering when the failure to educate Christianly is viewed on a more global basis. J. P. Moreland and William Lane Craig make a very sobering assessment and projection of what will happen if Christians fail to provide an adequate Christian education, which, in their unvarnished opinion, must include a healthy dose of philosophy. In making a justification for their recent book, Moreland and Craig say:

> Our churches are unfortunately overly-populated with people whose minds, as Christians, are going to waste. As Malik observed, they may be spiritually regenerate, but their minds have not been converted; they still think like nonbelievers. Despite their Christian commitment, they remain largely empty selves. What is an empty self? An empty self is a person who is passive, sensate, busy and hur-

ried, incapable of developing an interior life. Such a person is inordinately individualistic, infantile and narcissistic.[33]

Then Moreland and Craig project something truly alarming, projecting outward to envision or imagine the effect that will accrue to the Christian community at large in the absence of true and effective Christian education. They ask us to imagine what a church filled with "inordinately individualistic, infantile and narcissistic" people might look like. And the picture they portray is grim:

> Such a church will become impotent to stand against the powerful forces of secularism that threaten to wash away Christian ideas in a flood of thoughtless pluralism and misguided scientism. Such a church will be tempted to measure her success largely in terms of numbers—numbers achieved by cultural accommodation to empty selves. In this way, the church will become her own grave digger; for her means of short-term "success" will turn out in the long run to be the very thing that buries her.[34]

The situation found today can be quite well summed up in the words of Dallas Willard, where he said, "The powerful though vague and unsubstantiated presumption is that something has been found out that renders a spiritual understanding of reality in the manner of Jesus simply foolish to those who are 'in the know.' "[35] This "vague and unsubstantiated presumption" is what is driving society today. It is this understanding and circumstance that Christian education must set itself to turn around.

Certainties and complexities

So, the task is large and the implications sobering. And it is precisely the import of this situation that helps drive the various opinions that conflict around Christian education. Everybody understands, to some extent or another, the issues and the urgency. Nobody wants to get this wrong. But, in their intensity, various people take various paths, advocating very different ways. Some, perhaps because of their personalities, strongly advocate for indoctrination. Such people do not have time for nuances nor for process. They want the "enemy" identified, attacked with the best of weapons, and put to rout. They want their children to be given the best explanations to achieve this task, believing that, if it is done well, it will serve for the rest of their lives. And they seem to sense instinctively that there are great efficiencies to be had in authoritarian structures. So they bid for authority-driven indoctrination, and they are not afraid to announce, even in public, that those who do not do what should be done must be summarily dismissed from church employment. This group has no time for nuance or complexity. They like to deal with the "certainties" and drive the enemy from the field, saving the day. People in this category see themselves as warriors of righteousness. What escapes them is the fact that their preferred methodology mitigates against education. It gives to students a narrow slice of information that the critics and scoffers can soon circumvent. It is not uncommon to see people who have received this kind of instruction totally abandoning their faith structures because, for them, religion is an "all-or-nothing" proposition.

There are other people who approach the task of Christian education from a very different angle. This group is far too reflective to engage in indoctrination or anything that looks like it. Daniel Taylor calls this group "reflective" Christians. His description is cogent:

> They have found in God, and in Jesus Christ, a proposed solution to the human dilemma to which they have made, with varying degrees of confidence, a commitment. At the same time they have been blessed and cursed with minds that never rest. They are dissatisfied with superficial answers to difficult questions, willing to defend faith, but not its misuse.
>
> Furthermore, these people find themselves in the church, members of a Christian subculture into which they were either born or later entered. Their relationship to this subculture is complex, and only partly conscious, and they are both indebted to it and victimized by it. At the same time, they are often part of, or heavily influenced by, another subculture which is basically indifferent or hostile to their Christian commitment. This is the secular, intellectual world that deals in the manufacture and propagation of ideas.[36]

Another way of saying this is that these individuals are quite captivated by the "complexities" of life. They are fascinated by the questions, the challenges, the inconsistencies they encounter, wanting to see them resolved. By their natures, they like exploring, trying on new ideas. They do not like to be bound by what is known. They want to be testing to see if there is more than can be known.

If I may risk making a broad generalization here, it seems those Christian institutions that fall into the category commonly known as "Bible colleges," tend toward the first of these categories. They like to focus on the certainties, telling what we know for sure even to the "point of dishonesty, sidestepping genuine difficulties and confusing things."37 Traditional universities, on the other hand, have tended to go toward the second strategy, dismantling truth in search of something more. They have fallen into a vast pluralism that has left the educated human race with little to hold on to in terms of meaning and purpose, so have now come to idolize the notion of tolerance. As S. D. Gaede so astutely observed:

> Why do we who live in the modern world think tolerance is valuable in and of itself, even though it's impossible to live with consistency? The answer is that tolerance is a value that conforms nicely to the world we live in. Having pretty much decided that truth is not attainable, we have made tolerance of a plurality of truths a virtue. Having no truths worth defending, we have made nondefensiveness a mark of distinction.38

This kind of education cannot pass for Christian any more than the previous idea could, for a journey into pluralism eventually destroys the very basis upon which Christianity is built, inconvenient a truth as that might be in today's society.

Surely, there must be a third way, one that should be the stock-in-trade of Seventh-day Adventist Christian education. And that is the idea that arises from pulling both of these ends toward the middle. Christian education done in a Christian institution should involve and promote open investigation of all things, even things that are antithetical to the Christian faith. I do not speak here of advocating such things, but of investigating them. For, if they are not investigated, they will not be understood, and if they are not understood, they cannot be adequately argued against. In other words, Christian education should involve a thorough study of both the "certainties," and the "complexities," even to the point of producing cognitive dissonance, if necessary. But this investigation should be done under the watchful tutelage of Christian professors who do not allow it to go on willy-nilly and without purpose. Students should be "walked through" the issues to the point they understand them. And then, when the issues are known, the Christian professors should help the students settle the matter in a manner that is in harmony with the Christian faith, in this case, Adventism in particular. At some point, it seems, a Christian professor will have to divulge how they have resolved the issue in a way that preserves faith. The goal is tidily summed up in the words of Dr. Steve Pawluk:

> The Seventh-day Adventist college or university seeks to be an organization that provides a safe context for developing adults to test assumptions, ask perplexing questions, try out viewpoints, and do so under the guidance of committed Seventh-day Adventist

Christian professors who honestly, but in a developmentally appropriate way, express what they know, what they are seeking to find out, and what they believe. While there may be a while when cognitive dissonance is utilized, in the end, professors must share with students why they are Seventh-day Adventists and why they choose to believe as they do.[39]

This paragraph, tidy as it is, has one element that I would take slight issue with, and that is the concept of "safe." Given the nature of life today, with all the various and immediate modes of communication, and the Internet with its capacity to freight vast quantities of information into our lives, I am not sure there is anymore a place that can be designated "safe." Perhaps it would be better, and more appropriate, to envision education as teaching that goes on in a dangerous place, teaching students how to process information and live in this dangerous world in a manner that is under the rubric of Christianity! Perhaps, if we undertake the doing of this difficult task, the reaction will be much like the one I had some time ago when, in my office, the parent of a prospective student asked me, "Dr. Thomas, is this a safe place for me to send my child?" That was a poignant moment! If I failed, it would result in the loss of a student to the university where I work. But my own sense of integrity would not allow me to give this mother some platitude. Looking across the desk, I said to her, "Ma'am, given the nature of life and communication, do you think there are any safe places left?" She thought for a moment, then a smile of relief broke over her face. She understood that there really are no safe places anymore, not even our homes. It was then that she understood what we would try to do for her child, help them to learn to live in this dangerous world but to do so under the rubric of all that is Christian. That, I think, should be the real goal of Christian education.

Conclusion

I conclude this chapter with two quotes, which are very valuable to me, both of them speaking in different ways, to the issues raised. The first is from the great New Testament commentator William Barclay. The second is from the notable scholar Elton Trueblood:

> The Christian hope is the hope which has seen everything and endured everything, and has still not despaired, because it believes in God. The Christian hope is not hope in the human spirit, in human goodness, in human endurance, in human achievement; the Christian hope is hope in the power of God.[40]

And the second,

The value of intellectual inquiry lies not in its ability to tell us what we ought to do, but rather in its ability to surmount the barriers that hinder our doing. The careful study of the philosophy of religion is helpful, not because in most instances it brings men to God, but because it fulfils the humbler role of removing barriers to requisite commitment.[41]

Freud once said that dreams are the royal road to the unconscious. This may or may not be the case. But I am convinced that religion is the royal road to the heart of a civilization, the clearest indicator of its hopes and terrors, the surest index of how it is changing. Even that most famous of atheists, Karl Marx, after all, once said that religion is "the heart of a heartless world." As Christian educators, it is our task to help people find their way through the vast mass of information and ideas that exists today, but to do it in a manifestly Christian way. Wherever we take students, we must end with them seeing the value of both "Christian" and "education."[42]

References

[1] This assertion is based on the perusal of conference finance statements where education shows up as the biggest single expense, more than what is spent on pastoring.

[2] Arthur F. Holmes, *The Idea of a Christian College*, rev. ed. (Grand Rapids, MI: Eerdmans, 1987), 4–6.

[3] Holmes correctly points out that all this is not possible because "often there are no ready-made answers, new problems arise constantly, and the critics are perplexingly creative," 4.

[4] http://en.wikipedia.org/wiki/Education.

[5] Holmes, 5.

[6] Ellen G. White, *The Great Controversy* (Mountain View, CA: Pacific Press®, 1889), 80.

[7] Viktor Frankl, *Man's Search for Meaning* (Boston, MA: Beacon Press, 1959).

[8] Philip A. Anderson, *Church Meetings That Matter* (Pilgrim Press, 1965), 86.

[9] G. Douglass Lewis, *Resolving Church Conflicts*, 9.

[10] Taken from an article on Celtic spirituality by Loren Wilkinson, professor of interdisciplinary studies and philosophy at Regent College, Vancouver, B.C., *Christianity Today,* April 24, 2000, 82, 83.

[11] Taken from Zacchaeus A. Mathema, "The African Worldview: A Serious Challenge to Christian Discipleship," *Ministry,* October 2007, 5.

[12] Quote taken from Charles H. Kraft, *Christianity in Culture: A Study in Biblical Theologizing in Cross-Cultural Perspective* (NY: Orbis Book, 2005), 44.

[13] Taken from Zacchaeus A. Mathema, "The African Worldview: A Serious Challenge to Christian Discipleship," *Ministry,* October 2007, 5.

[14] This term, "belief-grid," is one of my own devising.

[15] One little experiment that I often use to illustrate the presence and function of belief-grids is to ask students the question, "How many of you would be willing to accept $500,000.00 after class, with no strings attached?" After overcoming the usual bout of skepticism, a host of hands go up. I then point out that, by raising their hands, they have told me a lot. First, they have taken no vows of poverty; second, that they do not see money as evil; third, that they think such a large sum would benefit their lives. These conclusions were arrived at by filtering the prospect of a gift through their belief grids, something that usually takes just a few seconds to complete.

[16] James Sire makes a very insightful comment when he says, "Christianity had so penetrated the Western world that, whether people believed in Christ or acted as Christians should, they all lived in a context of ideas influenced and informed by the Christian faith. Even those who rejected the faith often lived in the fear of hellfire or the pangs of purgatory. Bad people may have rejected Christian goodness, but they knew themselves to be bad by basically Christian standards. . . . The theistic

presuppositions which lay behind their values came with their mother's milk." James Sire, *The Universe Next Door,* 3rd ed. (Downers Grove, IL: InterVarsity Press, 1997), 22.

[17] Dallas Willard spoke of "the mantle of intellectual meaninglessness [that] shrouds every aspect of our common life. Events, things, and 'information' flood over us, overwhelming us, disorienting us with threats and possibilities we for the most part have no idea what to do about." Dallas Willard, *The Divine Conspiracy* (New York: HarperCollins, 1998), 9.

[18] Don Eberly, "We're Fighting the Wrong Battle," *Christianity Today,* September 6, 1999, 53, 54.

[19] It is a very interesting exercise, particularly for Christians, to think of the role conscience plays in the policing of belief-grids as they are derived from worldviews. And it is also very interesting to contemplate the role and interaction of the Holy Spirit with the making up and functioning of belief-grids.

[20] This point is missed by so many who rail against theistic religion as if they themselves do not have a system of believing that they are bent on foisting upon the world!

[21] Winfried Corduan, *Neighboring Faiths* (Downers Grove, IL: InterVarsity Press, 1998), 21.

[22] William James, *The Varieties of Religious Experience* (New York: Longman, 1902), 53.

[23] Ibid., 57.

[24] Millard Erickson, *Christian Theology,* 2nd ed. (Grand Rapids, MI: Baker Books, 1998), 20.

[25] Gerald Anderson, *The Theology of Christian Mission* (New York: McGraw-Hill, 1961), 77.

[26] Ibid.

[27] Fred Craddock, *Preaching* (Nashville, TN: Abingdon Press, 1985), 57.

[28] Millard Erickson, *Christian Theology,* 2nd ed. (Grand Rapids, MI: Baker Books, 1998), 21.

[29] James Orr, *The Christian View of God and the World* (Grand Rapids, MI: Eerdmans, 1954), 4.

[30] James North, foreword to Charles Habib Malik, *A Christian Critique of the University* (Downers Grove, IL: InterVarsity Press, 1982), 6.

[31] Quoted in Kader Asmal, David Chidester, and Wilmot James, eds., *Nelson Mandela: In His Own Words* (NY: Little, Brown and Company, 2003), 272.

[32] SALVO, no. 7, Winter 2008, 29.

[33] J. P. Moreland and William Lane Craig, *Philosophical Foundations for a Christian Worldview* (Downers Grove, IL: InterVarsity Press, 2003), 5.

[34] Ibid.

[35] Dallas Willard, *The Divine Conspiracy* (San Francisco, CA: Harper, 1998), 92.

[36] Daniel Taylor, *The Myth of Certainty* (TX: Jarrell Word Books, 1986), 11.

[37] This nice little array of descriptors came to me by way of an e-mail from Dr. Steve Pawluk, one of the editors of this book.

[38] S. D. Gaede, *When Tolerance is No Virtue* (Downers Grove, IL: InterVarsity Press, 1993), 27.

[39] Taken from the private e-mail correspondence that led to the creation of this book.

[40] William Barclay, "The Letter to the Romans," *Christianity Today,* October 25, 1999, 96.

[41] Elton Trueblood, *The Validity of Christian Mission* (New York: Harper and Row, 1972), 45.

[42] Harvey Cox, *Harvard Divinity Bulletin,* March 6, 2000, 86.

Section 2

The Value-Added Aspect of Seventh-day Adventist Higher Education

RANDAL WISBEY

Chapter 5

Nurturing the Adventist Mind: What Seventh-day Adventist Education Can Do for the Church

Is the Seventh-day Adventist denomination's historic commitment to operating institutions of higher education worth the investment? Or, could the church use its resources more efficiently?

What would the Seventh-day Adventist Church look like if these universities and colleges did not exist? Would it matter? What does Seventh-day Adventist higher education do for the church? And, more importantly, how is Seventh-day Adventist higher education currently enhancing the church's mission?

In the following pages, I will identify five ways in which Seventh-day Adventist higher education provides an invaluable, essential, and useful resource in supporting the mission of the church.[1]

1. An Adventist window on the world

Neil Postman, in his book *Technopoly: The Surrender of Culture to Technology,* argues that technology has redefined what we mean by religion, art, family, politics, history, truth, privacy, and intelligence—becoming, in effect, a "technopoly." Arguing that education must take up the task of developing "loving resistance fighters," Postman writes:

In consideration of the disintegrative power of technopoly, perhaps the most important contribution schools can make to the education of our youth is to give them a sense of coherence in their studies, a sense of purpose, meaning and interconnectedness in what they learn. Modern secular education is failing . . . because it has no moral, social or intellectual center. . . . It does not even put forward a clear vision of what constitutes an educated person, unless it is a person who possesses "skills." In other words, a technocrat's ideal—a person with no commitment and no point of view but with plenty of marketable skills.[2]

As Postman reminds us, one of the great opportunities given to those who care deeply about Seventh-day Adventist higher education is to provide students a sense of coherence in their studies, a sense of purpose, meaning, and interconnectedness in what they learn. For the church, providing a Seventh-day Adventist education for young members who need an excellent university education ensures that these students will have an opportunity to be mentored by professors who not only understand this need for coherence, but also will focus energy on sharing their discipline from a Christian worldview. In this way, the classroom functions as an Adventist window on the world.

Within our institutions of Seventh-day Adventist higher education, professors focus great attention on the academic development of their students while providing that necessary dialogue with the student's faith experience. And students do well in this caring environment. As Seventh-day Adventist universities and colleges pay attention to the theme of creating coherence between a student's faith journey, their educational pursuits, and participation in a church that encourages them to take an active leadership role, the mission of the Seventh-day Adventist Church is deeply enriched.

2. A clear path through

As students growing up Adventist prepare for their college education, they are met with a vast array of choices. And, if the student has good grades and good test scores, the options are increased dramatically. Over the years, I have been involved in many conversations that remind me of the difficulty of finding a way through the myriad of life choices young adults face. As Dante wrote in the *Divine Comedy:*

> In the middle of this road we call our life,
> I found myself in a dark wood,
> with no clear path through.[3]

In many ways, this struggle to find the path that provides clarity and direction is one in which all of us are constantly involved. This is certainly true for our students as they are increasingly faced with a world that demands the very best of them.

Careful academic preparation is imperative for those who are committed to making a difference through their work and leadership.

For the Seventh-day Adventist Church, it is also clear that we are dependent upon finding properly trained individuals who will guide and support the work of a global community, consistently and ably providing resources in a rapidly changing and challenging environment. We need people who can think with clarity and purpose, whose opinions and commitments are born of a broad understanding of opportunities and challenges. Seventh-day Adventist higher education can help our community navigate these exciting times through our work of properly training the very ones who will one day lead our denomination.

In this vein, Arthur J. De Jong challenges us to faithfully choose the faculty who will serve in our schools: "It is important that enough persons who believe in, exemplify, and articulate ideas, values, worldviews, and belief systems consistent with the college's viewpoint be present on the campus as the students shape their lives. Few tasks are as important as the selection of this total community of persons."[4]

As students come to us in search of meaning and community, it is our privilege, as Seventh-day Adventist educators, to work with determination to ensure that the Adventist culture of our campuses will enable students to experience the value and the quality of our commitment to their overall development as men and women of high morals, great faith, and spirited hopefulness. As they seek for direction, as they work toward their life goals, we are privileged to encourage them to think of their vocation—that work that God calls each of us to do—as the "place where your deep gladness and the world's deep hunger meet."[5]

3. A fitting relationship between self, the church, and the world

For those who question if the investment in Seventh-day Adventist education is worth it, I would point to a challenge made by Sharon Parks in her book *The Critical Years: Young Adults and the Search for Meaning, Faith and Commitment*. Parks argues, "The central task of young adulthood is to discover and compose a faith that can orient the soul to truth and shape a fitting relationship between self and the world." However, when looking across the prevailing North American cultural landscape, she asks a rather significant question, "Can a culture, bereft of a worthy faith and vision, serve the mentoring role upon which the young adult depends?"[6]

Parks calls us to remember that "while the culture seems to sway between nostalgia and faith in technology, young adults stand in need of a mentoring ethos that beckons them to dream, to believe, and to serve."[7]

Preparing members for intellectually competent participation in the mission of the church is imperative if the church is to have a future. The young adults who study on our campuses long to make a difference in the world—and we are privileged to participate as they are properly educated and trained to provide invigorating service and thoughtful witness.

From a purely pragmatic stance, the employment needs of the denomination are immense. Ministry professionals, well-prepared educators, healthcare workers, scientists, attorneys, business leaders, and global agents of transformation are needed. The institutions of the denomination are always hungry for well-prepared leaders who can bring new insights and identify invigorating strategies to support the vast array of Adventist ministry and mission. It is our privilege, as educators working within Seventh-day Adventist higher education, to provide well-educated men and women for the workforce needs of our growing church.

Our campuses also serve, for students and faculty, as a dynamic training ground with which to embrace the surrounding community, bringing recognition to what it truly means to be Adventist and to be a member of the larger human family.

In 2010, La Sierra University, where I serve, was recognized by the Carnegie Foundation for community engagement (the only Seventh-day Adventist institution to be cited among 116 schools nationwide), and was also inducted into the President's Higher Education Community Service Honor Roll—an honor we were delighted to share with Union College and 125 other outstanding institutions in the United States. While honor rolls are important, fulfilling Christ's commission to meet and serve the needs of others around us is what truly matters! On our campus, over the past school year, La Sierra University students logged some forty-five thousand hours of service to benefit others, including ten thousand hours provided through the academic service-learning program. Among those who served were thirty-three faculty who offered service-learning courses, partnering with thirty-two local community organizations—and, in the process, making friends for the Seventh-day Adventist Church and transforming lives in our community. For the students who work in these service programs, they learn that their commitment to service provides a future and a hope.

Seventh-day Adventist higher education offers the incredible energy of committed young adults, full of vigor and vision, who long to share their hopes for their church and their world. Thousands of students give Bible studies, hold evangelistic meetings, go on short-term missions and make year-long service commitments, sit with AIDS victims, and hold the hands of elderly Alzheimer's patients. As a result, the church is better because of their commitment, their desire and willingness to imagine a church that is more embracing and more open to creative expression. Through their service, the members of our learning communities declare to the church, "I will walk alongside you and help you reach your potential."

4. Contributing to the ongoing development of Adventist thinking

Thinking doesn't have to be a barrier to religious belief, and religious belief doesn't have to be a barrier to thinking. One can pray and think at the same time. Thinking is part of our spirituality and spirituality is the most significant element of our core being.

Seventh-day Adventist higher education continues to demonstrate that one can and must be *intelligent,* fully *informed,* and *truly* Adventist at the same time. When we speak about *colleges and universities,* we are focused and intrigued, by definition, with the life of the mind. The question, therefore, is not whether the church's colleges and universities should be intellectually defined, but whether the church wants to have, and is willing to support, these institutions in the first place.

Any complaint that this is all "too intellectual" is analogous to a complaint that a hospital is "too medical." We must never forget that this willingness to focus upon the nurture of the mind is our calling. Ellen G. White says,

God requires the training of the mental faculties. He designs that His [people] shall possess more intelligence and clearer discernment than the worldling, and He is displeased with those who are too careless or too indolent to become efficient, well-informed workers. The Lord bids us love Him with all the heart, and with all the soul, and with all the strength, and with all the mind. This lays upon us the obligation of developing the intellect to its fullest capacity, that with all the mind we may know and love our Creator.

If placed under the control of His Spirit, the more thoroughly the intellect is cultivated, the more effectively it can be used in the service of God. The uneducated [person] who is consecrated to God and who longs to bless others can be, and is, used by the Lord in His service. But those who, with the same spirit of consecration, have had the benefit of a thorough education, can do a much more extensive work for Christ. They stand on vantage ground.[8]

Seventh-day Adventist higher education offers a number of valuable resources to the church as it confronts an ever-changing and challenging postmodern world. On each of our campuses we have dedicated theologians and biblical scholars who continue to shape our understanding of God and of Scripture. For the continuing development of the Seventh-day Adventist Church, our institutions of higher education believe it is imperative that the church turn to these women and men for their insight and guidance. Too often there has been a suspicious glance rather than an embrace, and it is imperative, for the good of the church, that we find a new manner in which to utilize this remarkable resource.

Further, I believe it is imperative that our institutions proclaim our commitment to be a constructive and inquisitive voice for our church, asking appropriate questions and working diligently to find the best, and most powerful, responses. We assert, just as did our early church mothers and fathers, our commitment to be faithful to God and to one another as we participate in the questions and productive debate that ensures that our Adventist faith is strong, yet also rigorous and growing and has every opportunity to be affirmed by the students we serve.

> Long-cherished opinions must not be regarded as infallible.... However long men may have entertained certain views, if they are not clearly sustained by the written word, they should be discarded. Those who sincerely desire truth will not be reluctant to lay open their positions for investigation and criticism, and will not be annoyed if their opinions and ideas are crossed.... We have many lessons to learn, and many, many to unlearn. God and heaven alone are infallible. Those who think that they will never have to give up a cherished view never have occasion to change an opinion, will be disappointed.[9]

There is no excuse for anyone in taking the position that there is no more truth to be revealed, and that all our expositions of Scripture are without an error. The fact that certain doctrines have been held as truth for many years by our people is not a proof that our ideas are infallible. Age will not make error into truth, and truth can afford to be fair. No true doctrine will lose anything by close investigation.[10]

Another way in which we faithfully serve the best interests of our church involves the integration of Adventist thinking with a vast array of intellectual disciplines. How does our faith inform our understanding of the natural, social, and health sciences? What about the humanities? And what of the growing interest in the performing and visual arts—theater, music, and the fine arts? And how will our understanding of current ethical issues—environmental, social, and biomedical—be guided in a uniquely Seventh-day Adventist perspective if we do not rely upon our universities and colleges?[11]

What Seventh-day Adventist colleges and universities can do is to provide a supportive environment and conceptual assistance not only to their students but also to the whole church in addressing these significant issues effectively and with a deep commitment to integrity. In the process, Seventh-day Adventist colleges and universities can be examples of thinking faithfully.

And what happens when members of the educational community seek to identify answers to difficult questions that challenge the general understanding of the church? While Seventh-day Adventist colleges and universities identify their commitment to academic freedom, it is vital that this important value be accompanied by an equally deep commitment to academic responsibility. In the early 1980s, as the Seventh-day Adventist higher education system in North America was needing to identify its commitment to academic freedom to its external accrediting bodies, a committee was formed by the General Conference of Seventh-day Adventists to work through this topic. Eventually, the work of this committee was adopted at the 1984 Annual Council, and it became the foundation for many of the colleges' and universities' academic freedom statements. In one section of the paper, the subject of shared responsibility was discussed:

> Just as the need for academic freedom has a special significance in a church institution, so do the limitations placed on it reflect the special concerns of such an institution. The first responsibility of the teacher and leaders of the institution, and of the Church, is to seek for and to disseminate truth. The second responsibility is the obligation of teachers and leaders of the institution and the Church to counsel together when scholarly findings have a bearing on the message and mission of the Church.
>
> The true scholar, humble in his quest for truth, will not refuse to listen to the findings and the advice of others. He recognizes that others also have discovered and are discovering truth. He will learn from them and actively seek their counsel regarding the expression of views inconsistent with those generally taught by his Church, for his concern is for the harmony of the Church community.
>
> On the other hand, church leaders are expected to foster an atmosphere of Christian cordiality within which the scholar will not feel threatened if his findings differ from traditionally held views. Since

the dynamic development of the Church depends on the continuing study of dedicated scholars, the president, board of trustees, and Church leaders will protect the scholar, not only for his sake but also for the cause of truth and the welfare of the Church.[12]

This is a significant and profound ideal to strive for and it is, by its nature, always going to be a work in progress for all parties involved. However, with mutual encouragement and support, we will continue to come closer to meeting this ideal for the future benefit of our students, our schools, our church, and the truth we mutually seek to better understand.

5. Helping the church to communicate Adventist faith to the world

One of the more important contributions the Seventh-day Adventist learning community provides on behalf of the denomination is in establishing Seventh-day Adventist credibility through participation in external academic communities and conducting research that increases the sum of human knowledge. When demonstrating the intellectual soundness of Adventist faith, our professors contribute to current theological, scientific, and ethical conversations.

As Arthur J. De Jong reminds us,

The church-related college should pursue excellence for many reasons. Let me cite just one. In our secular, pluralistic society, the Christian faith is just one alternative, and it no longer holds a favored position. Church-related colleges must shape their learning program into the best possible program, and they must develop their students with the utmost vigor so that an educational program which integrates faith and learning will stand out in our society as the best educational process. It must also be the best to insure that the graduates of the church-related college rise to positions of leadership in our society and in our world.[13]

Few challenges are more daunting to the Seventh-day Adventist Church than the task of clearly understanding the world we are today called to serve. As members of the Seventh-day Adventist learning community, we long for our church to work with us in identifying ways in which the amazing resources of intellect and determined energy on our campuses can be utilized to not only better understand the world we long to minister to, but to develop new and effective ways with which to proclaim the message of a soon-coming Savior to a world that is often stranded in a postmodern morass of ineffectual human experience lacking absolutes in the areas of truth and meaning.

Today, this way of understanding the world impacts our literature, our dress, our art, our music, our sense of right and wrong, our self-identity, and our understanding of God. And because we live in a global community—connected by the Internet and by satellite television—we listen to the same songs, wear the same clothing, watch the same movies, and give adoration to the same actors and athletes. This is the world our church must address, and our faculty and students have much to offer to this intriguing, and daunting, work.

A valuable resource that Seventh-day Adventist higher education offers the church is research that enables the denomination to better understand itself.[14] Likewise, the development of much needed church resources are often spearheaded by those who serve as faculty on our campuses.[15] To the church we declare, "We love doing this work!" We know that this is one of the best ways we can continue to give back to our sponsoring church, and we are grateful for the opportunity to help the church communicate its mission to the world.

As Seventh-day Adventist educators, we also recognize that our institutions of higher education nurture Adventist culture and help to shepherd it. Our universities and colleges continue to be the place where communities gather, and campuses are alive with activity and worship and music and art and theater. Our institutional churches likewise benefit this work of keeping our culture alive, as they utilize the resources of the campus to provide excellence in Adventist preaching and music, and serve as an embodiment of our institutional commitment to be a progressive role model and voice for the denomination.

A call to dream

I am convinced that the church and the learning institutions we represent must more fully enter into partnership with one another. We must believe the best of one another. While we both at times make mistakes, I am convinced that the church would be well advised to see higher education as a friend—not to be feared because of the questions that we at times ask, but embraced because we are willing to ask these very questions.

The church has every right to expect much from the system they so heavily invest in. We must, in turn, expect much from our church—far more than financial support. We hope that the church will always believe the best about the people who have given their lives to the mission of Seventh-day Adventist education, who stand before the young of the church, and who know—deep within their souls—that they are making a difference.

As members of the Seventh-day Adventist learning community, we must help our students, faculty, staff, and yes, even the wider church that supports us, to dream. We must imagine—and work toward a future—in which our community is ever-increasingly characterized by grace, a community committed to serving God and our fellow humans; a place where legalism is replaced with freedom, fear with love, cynicism with hope, performance with acceptance, indifference with passion, conformity with conviction, pride with humility, exclusiveness with inclusiveness, and the letter of the law with its spirit if we are to re-envision and invigorate Adventist faith.

If we do this work well, it may be our greatest gift to our church.

References

[1] I wish to acknowledge my colleagues in the H. M. S. Richards Divinity School at La Sierra University who have generously dialogued with me in preparation for the writing of this paper. I have also been encouraged by conversations with members of the Association of Adventist Colleges and Universities who heard an earlier version of this paper presented during its 2008 Mission Conference.

[2] Neil Postman, *Technopoly: The Surrender of Culture to Technology* (New York: Vintage Books, 1993), 185, 186.

[3] Dante Alighieri, *The Divine Comedy—Inferno*: canto 1.

[4] Arthur J. De Jong, *Reclaiming a Mission: New Direction for the Church-Related College* (Grand Rapids, MI: William B. Eerdmans Publishing Company, 1990), 133.

[5] Ellen G. White, *Christ's Object Lessons*, 333, 334.

[6] Frederick Buechner, *Wishful Thinking: A Theological ABC* (San Francisco: Harper and Row, 1973), 95.

[7] Sharon Parks, *The Critical Years: Young Adults and the Search for Meaning, Faith and Commitment* (San Francisco: Harper and Row, 1986), 177.

[8] Ibid., 184.

[9] "Search the Scriptures," *Advent Review and Sabbath Herald,* July 26, 1892, 465; repr. *Counsels to Writers and Editors,* 36, 37; and, in part, in *Selected Messages From the Writings of Ellen G. White* (Washington, DC: Review and Herald®, 1958–1980), 1:37.

[10] "Christ Our Hope," *Advent Review and Sabbath Herald,* December 20, 1892, 785; repr. *Counsels to Writers and Editors,* 35.

[11] One example of how the church needs this integration is in the vexing issue of the relation of Adventist thinking to the natural sciences as pertains to the history of life on planet Earth. On the one hand, for more than a hundred years Adventists have believed that "the book of nature and the written word shed light upon each other. They make us acquainted with God by teaching us something of the laws through which He works." Ellen G. White, *Education* (Mountain View, CA: Pacific Press®, 1903), 128. On the other hand, as James Gibson of the Adventist Church's Geoscience Research Institute notes, "creationists do not have an adequate explanation" for "radiometric dates of many millions of years. . . . The most difficult question is probably the apparent sequence of radiometric dates, giving older dates for lower layers in the geologic column and younger dates for upper layers." James Gibson, "Frequently Asked Questions," Geoscience Research Institute, www.grisda.org/teachers, accessed March 5, 2002.

[12] W. O. Coe, chairman, Leo Ranzolin, secretary, *Academic Freedom in Seventh-day Adventist Institutions of Higher Education* (voted at the General Conference Annual Council, October 16, 1984).

[13] Arthur J. De Jong, *Reclaiming a Mission: New Direction for the Church-Related College* (Grand Rapids, MI: William B. Eerdmans Publishing Company, 1990), 148.

[14] For example, the Valuegenesis and CognitiveGenesis studies, based at La Sierra University, have been the largest studies of any denomination's youth and K–8 elementary students, while the Adventist Health Study, based at Loma Linda University, continues to provide keen insights for researchers intrigued by the effects of a plant-based diet and healthy lifestyle.

[15] One thinks of the multitude of resources that have been created by the Center for Youth Evangelism and the North American Division Evangelism Institute based at Andrews University.

HEATHER J. KNIGHT

Chapter 6

The Adventist Advantage

Since my arrival at Pacific Union College (PUC) in the fall of 2009, I have been sharing a new platform or concept, which I have entitled the "Adventist Advantage." In essence, the "Adventist Advantage" is a set of seven principles and assets, which I believe give Adventist education its exceptional value and significance in a twenty-first-century world fraught with complexity and confusion. In a world where truth claims are often dismissed as naive or merely irrelevant, why should our students commit to Adventism? Furthermore, in the context of Christian education, why invest in attending an Adventist institution of higher learning at all? What significant difference will this decision make, if any?

1. It is my strong belief that the "Adventist Advantage" assists our students in their quest for meaning and purpose in life by providing them with multiple opportunities to connect with Jesus Christ as their personal Savior. In fact, it is only through this critical life-saving connection that our students can truly develop a meaningful and fulfilling philosophy of life, which will guide them successfully through and around the mountains and valleys that characterize every human life. The importance of providing a meaningful response to this quest for meaning and purpose in the lives of today's college students has been further highlighted in the Spirituality in Higher Education project, a multiyear initiative housed at

UCLA's Higher Education Research Institute (HERI), in which PUC was a participating institution.

In this groundbreaking study, which was initiated in 2003 by Alexander W. Astin, the most oft-quoted researcher in American higher education, researchers discovered that by their third year in college, students are quite likely to be involved in a spiritual quest and have a strong interest in spirituality and religion. Seventy-four percent of these college students had discussions about the meaning of life with their friends, and three out of four indicated that they were seeking for meaning and purpose in their lives. "In addition, they exhibit a stronger ethic of caring, show higher levels of equanimity, and are more likely to embrace an ecumenical worldview" (Spirituality in Higher Education brochure). Thus, this is a particularly relevant time for colleges to explore how to assist students in their spiritual development and formation, and every Seventh-day Adventist college and university should have a systematic and intentional plan for the spiritual development of its students characterized by the intentional integration of faith and learning in *every* classroom, as well as partnerships with their college and university churches and chaplain's offices toward this important outcome for Christian colleges and universities.

Furthermore, higher education, itself, seems to have experienced a religious renaissance in 2005 wherein the initial results from the Spirituality in Higher Education study were first reported, the Society for Values in Higher Education convened a Wingspread Conference in Wisconsin sponsored by the Johnson Foundation, which yielded the *Wingspread Declaration on Religion and Public Life: Engaging Higher Education,* itself a clarion call for the teaching of religious literacy on all college campuses, the establishment of ground rules for civic discourse on matters of religion and public life, as well as inquiry regarding the responsibility of colleges and universities to respond to growing spiritual concerns among students. It was also in 2005 that the Carnegie Foundation for the Advancement of Teaching published the first text in its Preparation for the Professions series, *Educating Clergy: Teaching Practices and the Pastoral Imagination*. It was no coincidence that the first text in this prestigious series focused on the education of clergy, for as then Carnegie Foundation President Lee Shulman indicated in his foreword to the text, "we entrust our very souls to them."

This same watershed year also saw the publication of *Spirituality in Higher Education* by Speck and Hoppe and *Encouraging Authenticity and Spirituality in Higher Education* by legendary student development theorist Arthur Chickering, characterized as "a comprehensive resource that addresses the growing movement for incorporating spirituality as an important aspect of the meaning and purpose of higher education." Other texts such as *Searching for Spirituality in Higher Education,* also by Speck and Hoppe (2007), *Encountering Faith in the Classroom: Turning Difficult Discussions Into Constructive Engagement,* by Miriam Rosalyn Diamond (2008), further testify to the fact that a religious renaissance is taking place in secular higher education with students and major thought-leaders alike expressing a renewed interest in spiritual concerns. Surely, Seventh-day Adventist higher education should be at the forefront of this movement dialoguing about pedagogical best practices in meeting students' needs for finding and maintaining meaning and purpose in their lives as higher education is issued a call back to its historic roots.

2. The "Adventist Advantage" foregrounds our church's historical focus on health, wellness, and a wholesome lifestyle, an emphasis which has garnered national and international recognition for our church whether through the vehicle of Loma Linda's distinction as a "blue zone," in several documentaries, as well as *National Geographic,* or the advice, inscribed in the February 20, 2009, issue of *U.S. News and World Report,* in an article by Deborah Kotz entitled "10 Health Habits That Will Help You Live to 100" to "live like a Seventh-day Adventist" if one desires to emulate the health habits that can provide the best opportunity to live to be one hundred (health habit 8). "Americans who define themselves as Seventh-day Adventists have an average life expectancy of 89, about a decade longer than the average American." The article further highlights the church's tenets to regard the body as the temple of God, refrain from drug and alcohol abuse or overindulging in sweets, as well as the promotion of a diet based on fruits, vegetables, beans, and nuts, not to mention the Adventist focus on family and community as reasons for its high number of centenarians. What a powerful witness!

Although we sometimes dismiss the value of a wholesome lifestyle in our contemporary and sophisticated world, I still believe that it is an important aspect of the "Adventist Advantage." After all, no one really starts out planning to become an alcoholic or drug addict, but all too often social drinking, recreational drug use, illicit sexual relations, as well as that first cigarette just to "fit in" can result in dangerous and gripping addictions that ruin families and individual lives. Today's reality show obsessed world is anything but the kind of reality that we want our young people to experience. Dysfunctional relationships seem to rule the day, and so it is well worth the reminder that a wholesome lifestyle can really help to keep us safe, well-adjusted, and happy in a world where danger is certainly not a stranger.

3. The "Adventist Advantage" highlights

our commitment to education and lifelong learning extending into eternity. Wherever we go, Adventists establish churches, hospitals, and schools. This commitment to an educated clergy and laity is certainly an element that has contributed to creative and critical thinking and a broad range of perspectives on various issues within our society and our church—a contributor to civility, as well as to healthy debate and dialogue. This commitment has also been a tool for social and economic upward mobility within our church resulting in a church of exceptional professionals across the globe. I am always amazed at the number of educational institutions that Adventists have around the world, extending from preschool to graduate and professional, programs resulting in the largest Protestant educational system in the world. This commitment to developing the mind in the image of God, through the vehicle of Christian education, in such a wide variety of fields, says much about our desire to intentionally integrate our faith and our learning, to see our world through the lens of our faith and to truly create a distinctive Adventist worldview focused on love, longevity, and literacy.

4. The "Adventist Advantage" provides a values-driven education well recognized for equipping our students with a moral and ethical compass, an MPS if you will, a moral positioning system, as the authors Lennick and Kiel, of the recent text *Moral Intelligence,* remind us. In an age characterized by greed and selfishness, as well as ethical failures of the type seen in the recent Enron and Wall Street scandals, it is imperative that our students are taught to live lives of moral integrity as they navigate the murky waters of today's provocative moral and ethical dilemmas. More and more, higher education is being challenged by employers to produce graduates who truly embody the skill sets that a twenty-first-century college degree should represent. Among these skill sets are the skills of moral leadership, integrity, responsibility, and, interestingly enough, Lennick and Kiel also mention forgiveness as one of the traits of character of the morally grounded. Imagine that—workplaces characterized by forgiveness and, perhaps, even wisdom? Another one of my favorite authors, Jim Collins, in his best-selling business text *Good to Great,* also highlights humility as a necessary characteristic of the Level 5 leader, the type of leader who, ironically, can lead an institution from good to great. Certainly, then, the Adventist emphasis on inculcating morals and ethics can only serve to set our students apart in a positive way and give them a much needed edge or advantage in the world of work and society at large.

5. The "Adventist Advantage" has always emphasized and highly prized an ethos of Christian service leading to organizations such as the Dorcas Society,

Adventist Development and Relief Agency, and PUC's own REVO (a student social action group, REVO is short for *revolution*). This type of involvement has now morphed and is now manifest in higher education through the Service Learning Movement and students' interest in participating in the public square in terms of more active civic engagement. In today's crisis-ridden world, it has become increasingly apparent that governments alone cannot provide either the human or financial capital to even begin to cure all of the world's ills. Therefore, it has become incumbent upon an engaged citizenry to "change the world." As a global church, 16.8 million strong, we have the human power to be spiritual catalysts, empowered to live out the change that we want to see in the world, as Mahatma Gandhi reminded us all in his famous call to action. It is also important to note that even when many of today's youth are turned off to organized religion, they are turned on to service. Thus, enacting Christ's ethos of service can be a powerful linchpin in connecting committed young citizen-leaders to Christ.

6. The "Adventist Advantage" helps us to foreground, articulate, and maximize the educational, spiritual, and social benefits of diversity with a global church filled with rich potential for teaching intercultural competence and global understanding—two skills vitally necessary for surviving and thriving in a new global society where together we inhabit Thomas Friedman's "flat world." Indeed, our Adventist faith becomes the common glue that binds us together as we embody and enact the beloved community. Being part of a world church also reminds us that the gospel and the Adventist articulation of it is still relevant to humanity regardless of country, color, class, or creed. In the context of higher education today, many American colleges and universities are investing many of their resources to enhance diversity on their campuses. Because of the rich cultural and ethnic diversity in the Adventist Church, most of our college campuses are achieving a multicultural dimension without much effort. As I often tell individuals who ask me how they can replicate the rich diversity of our Adventist higher educational institutions, "Our schools are diverse because our church is diverse, and our church is diverse because we have heeded Christ's injunction in the Gospel of Matthew to 'Go ye therefore and teach all nations.' " Therefore, the real question for us now is, "Now that we have diversity, what are we going to do with it?" As Adventists, we are uniquely positioned to live out transformative diversity—that is, to showcase how diversity can serve as a powerful lever for true inclusion and excellence in our personal lives, as well as our Adventist institutions.

7. The "Adventist Advantage" requires active stewardship of the earth, which our loving Creator God created in six days

while reminding us to rest on the seventh day, a memorial of His creative powers and our need for re-creation in Him. In granting humankind dominion of the earth, He has made us stewards and caretakers of the highest order. This focus on stewardship and sustainabilty is also an important aspect of our signature worldview, which aligns very nicely with positive aspects of the conservation and environmental movements.

Finally, at our Seventh-day Adventist colleges and universities, our highest goal is to transform our students by means of the "Adventist Advantage" by highlighting for our students the truth that knowledge alone is not power. Rather, "Joyful is the person who finds *wisdom,* the one who gains understanding" (Proverbs 3:13; emphasis added). Wisdom is the true learning outcome that we highly prize in our distinctive learning communities. At Seventh-day Adventist institutions of higher learning, we want to provide positive peer-pressure. At Seventh-day Adventist institutions of higher learning, we want to help our students to cultivate and foster a commitment to our Lord and a commitment to our church. Taken altogether, what could be of higher value than the "Adventist Advantage"?

Bibliography

Astin, Alexander W. *Spirituality in Higher Education: A National Study of College Students' Search for Meaning and Purpose.* www.spirituality.ucla.edu.

Collins, Jim. *Good to Great.* New York, NY: HarperCollins Publishers, Inc., 2001.

Foster, Charles R., Lisa E. Dahill, Lawrence A. Goleman, and Barbara Wang Tolentino. *Educating Clergy: Teaching Practices and the Pastoral Imagination.* Stanford, CA: The Carnegie Foundation for the Advancement of Teaching, 2005.

Kotz, Deborah. "10 Health Habits That Will Help You Live to 100." *U.S. News and World Report.* www.usnews.com/health/family-health/articles/2009/2/20/10.

Lennick, Doug and Fred Kiel. *Moral Intelligence.* NJ: Wharton School Publishing, 2008.

Wingspread Declaration on Religion and Public Life: Engaging Higher Education. Compiled on behalf of participants in a Wingspread Conference by the Society for Values in Higher Education, 2005.

DON WILLIAMS

Chapter 7

A New Mission School Model: How Adventist Colleges and Universities Can Thrive and Fulfill Their Mission in the Twenty-First Century

A man never goes so far as when he does not know whither he is going.
—Eric Hofer

I begin this chapter with a personal experience that has influenced my thoughts about Adventist higher education in the North American Division (NAD). The heart of the chapter will explore the adaptation of an old, but effective, approach to Seventh-day Adventist education that may help us with challenges it faces in the NAD. It will end with an examination of the potential pitfalls of this new model and suggested pathways through them.

During the summer of 1992, my family and I moved to Florida to help start a new Adventist college of nursing and allied health. At that time, my daughter decided to move into the girl's dormitory at Indiana Academy where she had been attending as a village student. My son moved with us to Orlando and enrolled as a sophomore at Forest Lake Academy.

Within a year, my daughter graduated and moved home to start her freshman year at Florida Hospital College of Health Sciences (FHCHS) where the tuition was free because of my faculty status. By the end of that school year, however, she decided to transfer to Southern Adventist University (SAU) where she could find a more traditional campus life.

That same year, my son began a journey that would first lead him away from Adventist education and, eventually, the church. By the fall of 1994, I found both of my children on educational trajectories different from the one I was helping to shape.

The reality of these distinct paths challenged my thinking about Adventist education. I was working at a school whose standing as a "real" Seventh-day Adventist institution was being questioned because of its low Seventh-day Adventist enrollment. My daughter's successful transition to SAU forced me to ask whether its homogeneous, conservative atmosphere had captured what was best in Adventist education. At the same time, my son's choices made me wonder whether there was a place for nontraditional, perhaps even nonbelieving, students in Seventh-day Adventist schools.

Seventeen years later, I'm still working at the same institution and my children have continued on the paths they started years before. My quest for an answer about what constitutes genuine Adventist education has led me to this conviction—the church must provide philosophical frameworks that help institutions and individuals who do not fit the traditional mold. Fortunately, there is a well-known approach that can be adapted to meet this challenge.

Development of mission schools

Most of us are aware of the Seventh-day Adventist schools around the globe whose enrollment, and perhaps even survival, depends on matriculating students who do not come from Seventh-day Adventist backgrounds. Through the years, church members have been supportive of those institutions with their tithe and mission offerings.

My first exposure to this type of school came in 1971 when my wife and I went to New Guinea as student missionaries. There we found an educational system from primary school through college where many, if not most, of the students came from animist homes. Later we spent eight years working in the Far East. Most summers, I taught at the Seventh-day Adventist college in Singapore where a significant number of the students represented a variety of belief systems. One term I even taught a class designed specifically to teach non-Christian students about Christianity. I also became friends with the chaplain at the Chinese Seventh-day Adventist high school whose enrollment of church members' children never exceeded 5 percent of the total and who baptized between thirty and forty students each year.

In each of these cases, institutions built on the Mission School Model proved to be the most effective evangelistic outreach in those countries. Years later, while manning the Florida Hospital College booth at a General Conference session, I visited with a worker from New Guinea who shared that a number of members of Parliament and government leaders in his home country were Seventh-day Adventists. He attributed this to the mission schools scattered throughout the villages and towns across his nation.

Floyd Greenleaf, in his work *In Passion for the World: A History of Seventh-day Adventist Education* (2005), tells the story of the development of mission school education in Africa. Solusi is, for him, the model of the Seventh-day Adventist mission school. Started on a twelve-thousand-acre gift from Cecil Rhodes, head of the British South Africa Company, Solusi became a center for the spread of the gospel in that part of Africa (177). Converting, and then training, the future teachers of the Seventh-day Adventist Church in Africa, Solusi developed a system of smaller outlying schools that, by the second decade of the twentieth century, enrolled over three thousand students (176). Solusi also became an Ellen G. White approved model of when it was appropriate to accept government largess at a Seventh-day Adventist educational institution (190).

In India, as the Adventist work spread, so did the mission school concept. "Similar to Adventist schools in Africa, the original purpose of Adventist schools [in India] was to convert students to Adventism rather than preserving Adventist children to the church—at first there were no Adventist children to preserve—but they also prepared workers. . . . It was from the elementary and mission schools that the church realized membership gains" (Greenleaf, 2005, 182).

In a country with strong Hindu and Buddhist traditions, Seventh-day Adventist education became a critical evangelistic tool. "As G. G. Lowry envisioned it, the mission school was the most important vehicle to carry the gospel to the Indian masses" (Greenleaf, 2005, 268).

Seventh-day Adventist education in China developed a more complex model. There Fredrick Griggs envisioned four categories of institutions, "Schools for the children of missionaries and English members, training schools for nationals, elementary schools conducted by church members for native children, and mission schools for the public" (Greenleaf, 2005, 183). The approach was successful. By the beginning of the third decade of the twentieth century, the Seventh-day Adventist educational system in China was the largest outside of the North American Division (Greenleaf, 2005, 184).

The history of those mission schools belies the "one blueprint" misconception identified by George Knight in *Myths in Adventism* (1985). His contention is that there has never been a single blueprint for Adventist education. Quoting Ellen G. White concerning this, Knight says,

"Again in 1907 she wrote regarding the Madison School which was doing its best to follow the 'pattern' under Adventism's most zealous educational reformers, that 'no exact picture can be given for the establishment of schools in new fields. The climate, the surroundings, the condition of the country, and the means at hand with which to work must all bear a part in shaping the work' (CT, p. 531)" (1985, 18, 19).

Clearly the Adventist Church developed several models of education even in its earliest years. From the implementation of the classical model of education at Battle Creek College, to the establishment of the Avondale Model endorsed by Ellen G. White, to the establishment of the schools in Africa, India, and China, Adventist education adapted to fit the time, place, and needs of the surrounding population.

So what does this all have to say to twenty-first-century Seventh-day Adventist education in North America? Let us begin with some basic facts. The North American Division has thirteen colleges and universities ranging in size from small (under four hundred) to medium (four thousand plus) when compared to other private institutions of higher education. Their educational offerings fall into two broad categories, liberal arts and health professions. The makeup of their student bodies divide along these lines as well. The ten liberal arts colleges cater largely to members of the Seventh-day Adventist Church. The three health professions schools, Loma Linda University, Kettering College of Medical Arts, and Florida Hospital College of Health Sciences, enroll students from within the church as well as significant numbers from the larger community. The number of students representing a variety of belief systems in the former group range from 4 percent to 30 percent. The latter three institutions have enrollments of the same demographic, ranging from 50 percent to 90 percent (*World Report 2007,* 55).

While the health sciences schools might seem to fit the Mission School Model, it would be inaccurate to give them that label. The traditional mission schools had certain aspects in common:

1. They were established in developing countries where the number of Adventists was low—too low, in most cases to support a school for the children of church members only.
2. Typically, the government educational system was nascent or nonexistent (Greenleaf, 2005, 270).
3. Other, more traditional, means of evangelism were challenging, at best.
4. Within the family and the

culture at large, education was seen as an important avenue to a better life.
5. While there were various times and places where the colonial link with mission endeavors was seen as a negative factor, in many cases the idea of a foreign sponsored school had built-in appeal, especially to the elite.

While Loma Linda, Kettering, and Florida Hospital College do not share most of the above factors, they do share one central characteristic with the traditional mission school—they have reached beyond the church rolls to define their circle of influence on a much broader scale. Because their parent medical institutions cannot conduct business with only the number of Adventist healthcare professionals available, each of these educational institutions has purposefully reached beyond the church for students, faculty, and staff. Depending on one's point of view, the result has been either a breach in the wall defending the denomination's youth or an opportunity to impact the world for good.

A new model

To provide a framework to guide those institutions with a significant number of students representing a variety of belief systems, I am proposing the New Mission School Model. It is an approach that addresses the contextual issues identified by Ellen G. White as critical in developing effective educational institutions—"the climate, the surroundings, the condition of the country, and the means at hand with which to work" (1943, 531).

The New Mission School Model provides a way of dealing with these factors in a principled, rather than a pragmatic, way. This model does not replace the original Mission School Model, which is still an effective educational and evangelistic approach in many parts of the world. It builds in a mission approach that will help them address the unique challenges faced by the growing number of students, faculty, and staff representing a variety of belief systems.

A critical component of this model is based upon the concept of the centered set. Centered sets and their converse, bounded sets, are sociological models that identify the organizing principles used to define group membership. Frost and Hirsch, in their book *The Shaping of Things to Come* (2003), use the agricultural metaphor of wells and fences to illustrate their understanding of centered and bounded sets. In their native Australia, water wells, rather than barbwire fences, are used to control herds of livestock. Providing a source of water keeps the animals centered geographically. In America, ranches are more likely to use fences to corral their herds. The Australian way could be considered

115

a centered set and the American way a bounded one (47).

And so with the church, if Christ is at the center, individuals are drawn to Him as the source of living water (John 3:14, 15). Centered set institutions identify an individual's movement toward or away from Christ as the defining principle for "membership." In contrast, bounded sets have criteria such as doctrines or religious practices that help a church know who is in or out of their group.

Bruce Bauer (2008), an Adventist missiologist, sees the centered set church placing Jesus at its heart. While baptism (and therefore church membership) still plays an important role at the beginning of the Christian life, discipleship, with its goal of moving people toward the center, is the end. In contrast, he identifies three characteristics of bounded sets. One, they are created by "listing essential characteristics." Two, "objects inside the set share [common] characteristics." And three, these sets identify who is either inside or outside of their boundaries.

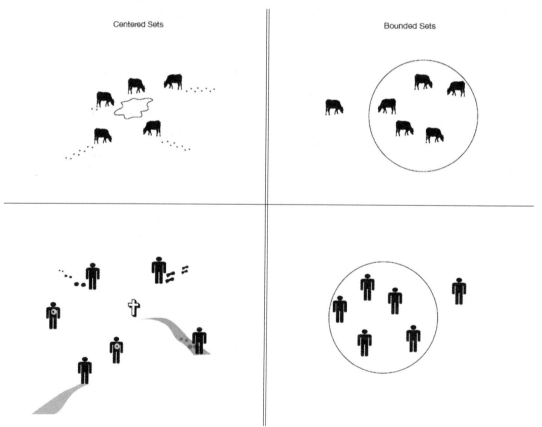

Figure 1: Centered and Bounded Sets (Artwork by Paul Martin)

The adoption of the centered set within an educational model has important implications. Institutions using this approach view their students, not in terms of whether they are in or out of the church, but whether they want to move closer in their relationship with God.

My experience at Florida Hospital College is indicative of what I know has happened many times at each of the health sciences schools. The opportunity to teach hundreds of non-Adventist students in the religion courses at FHCHS has been one of the great joys of my life. When asked by church members whether I was teaching Adventist truths, I replied that I always taught the Bible from an Adventist perspective. The centered set approach brought in students who wanted an education in a faith-based environment and did not preclude the teaching of Adventist doctrine. In fact, it ensured that the Christ-centered basis for each of these doctrines was what was being taught.

Thus, within the context of the New Mission School Model, students who are not members of the Seventh-day Adventist Church should be considered part of the marketing mix. If an institution has made its faith orientation clear, any student interested in growing within that environment should be considered for admission. Both Loma Linda and Florida Hospital College have their statements of mission on their recommendation forms. Individuals asked to complete those forms are encouraged to give their feedback on whether that prospect is a good fit in light of the school's orientation.

The inclusion of these students can help schools fulfill their evangelistic mission (Ellen G. White, *Education*, 30). When criticized by others for having a "mixed multitude" at Florida Hospital College, I always respond by asking which of those students would they not want sitting in Bible class. Many stories could be told of students who have never entered a church before but who found Christ as a result of going to school in that environment. The FHCHS student from Communist China who became a Christian and the Hindu student who was baptized several years ago quickly come to mind.

One might ask what the presence of this type of individual has on the Adventist students. I believe institutions with this mix provide a healthy, real-world environment for Seventh-day Adventist students preparing for their lives and careers. Rather than bringing distractions or temptations they may not otherwise be exposed to, rubbing shoulders with peers of different persuasions can actually strengthen and clarify their own faith. Students who have grown up within the Adventist educational system are challenged to not only stake out their spiritual turf, but also to explain it to others. A number of students I have worked with at Florida Hospital College have stated that this environment has helped make their faith real.

At the same time, this approach can help ensure the economic viability of institutions designed for the education of the church's children. Sadly, if the financial rationale for admitting non-Seventh-day Adventists is placed first, the mission/evangelistic goal may be watered down or missed altogether. However, kept in its appropriate place, the financial benefits can be significant.

This means that institutions using the New Mission School Model must be very purposeful in their mission emphasis. This is critical, not only for the success of this approach, but for the true success of the institution. For example, at FHCHS, each academic department has committed to having prayer and a devotional thought before each class period. Even online course chats begin with prayer requests and prayer. Sadly, in my undergraduate experience at another Seventh-day Adventist college, only the religion teachers regularly had prayer in class. In my major field of study, psychology, no attempt was made on the part of my professors to give me an Adventist, or even Christian, perspective in a very secular field. I tell myself that I should have figured it out on my own, but speaking as one who found Christ in college, I didn't know anyone who could guide me in the process. Perhaps my teachers assumed or presumed too much because of the homogeneous makeup of the student body.

With the presence of students from a wide variety of backgrounds in the health sciences schools, no assumptions can be made about what the students already know or believe. In the New Mission School Model, no aspect of school life is left unaffected by the overall spiritual mission of the College. Every employee hired is screened for mission fit, not just for church affiliation. Every course is designed with the spiritual, moral, and ethical development of the student in mind.

In reality, the New Mission School Model is a framework that can address what is already happening at all of our colleges and universities. As seen from the enrollment statistics above, students representing a variety of belief systems are already on our campuses and in growing numbers. Many are in graduate and evening adult education programs. One institution is contemplating a partnership with the local community college. Others are opening programs in response to needs in their state rather than just in their Adventist constituency.

It is not that the more traditional Seventh-day Adventist institutions don't care about the mission impact of these trends. They do. What I am concerned about is that, as a church, we have no model to guide the demographic changes taking place to ensure their fit to mission. Perhaps we have even been guilty of downplaying these changes because they have not been mission driven. In some cases, I fear we have slid into these trends and programs for financial reasons. Thus, spiritual opportunities may be missed and important services neglected. For example, what should the chaplain's office, student services, or residence halls look like with a significant number of students representing a broad variety of belief systems?

What strikes me is that while some may recognize that there is more than one model operating in North America (e.g., Loma Linda), even this institution is frequently criticized *sotto voce* for not fitting the traditional model. In Floyd Greenleaf's (2005) comprehensive history of Adventist higher education, I find no mention of either Kettering or Florida Hospital College. Clearly, these institutions do not meet what might be considered the traditional model or blueprint for Adventist higher education. A recent article on Seventh-day Adventist education in a church paper, where one of the above institutions resides, did not mention the nontraditional college within its territory, while fairly extensive coverage was given to both the traditional institutions as well as the nontraditional high schools and homeschools.

I propose that, rather than ignore (as in the case of Kettering and Florida) or criticize (as in the case of Loma Linda), the church should learn from the approaches these institutions are pioneering, and, where appropriate, embrace them. There is no doubt that seeking a heterogeneous environment presents significant challenges and that these institutions have fallen short many times of their own goals. However, in spite of the challenges, much good has been done by these schools and lives have been changed which might not have been if it had not been for their efforts.

An additional benefit of the New Mission School Model is that many students from Seventh-day Adventist homes who are not choosing Adventist schools may give this type of education a second look. With a larger pool of applicants to choose from, these schools may be able to offer their education at a lower tuition level. A significant part of church growth in the North American Division in recent years has been coming from first generation immigrant communities. These families may not have yet reached the median income levels found in the general population. Their children might be better able to afford this option.

Looking at the benefits from the perspective of the students who do not fit into a traditional Adventist environment, the New Mission School Model institution may provide an attractive option. With its centered set approach that looks at one's openness to spiritual matters rather than behavioral or doctrinal ones, this model may provide an attractive atmosphere for these nontraditional students. It is not that the spirituality is a soft sell in this new model; it is simply presented in ways that may appeal to them.

Caveats

Up until now, I have identified the benefits of the New Mission School Model. There are weaknesses and dangers inherent in it as well. One of the most obvious is the fact that parents send their children to Seventh-day Adventist colleges not only to find a career, but to potentially find a life partner. At a school where there are a significant number of students not of our faith, the odds increase that those students might fall in love with someone outside that circle.

With that reality in mind, several countervailing factors must also be noted. If this type of school is able to attract Adventist students who might have ended up at a public institution, they will at least have greater odds of meeting an Adventist mate in one of these schools than in the public sector.

Also, one of the realities of Adventist students living in this more diverse environment is that they have the potential of ending up with a stronger, clearer sense of their own spiritual values. As a result, I believe those solidified spiritual values will help them choose mates with greater discernment. For example, while the single Seventh-day Adventist students at FHCHS have individuals from many faith backgrounds to choose a mate from, to my knowledge (and this is certainly not a scientific study), I am not aware of one Seventh-day Adventist student at FHCHS who has married outside their faith as a result of attending FHCHS. While that does not mean it won't happen, it does indicate the risk of poor choices may not be as high as feared.

A concern often expressed by the church organization is the creeping compromise that, it is assumed, will accompany the trend of accepting more students representing a variety of belief systems. There is no doubt that this is a possibility if this direction is chosen for the wrong reason or without a clear mission in mind. That has not been the case with the traditional mission schools when they have stayed true to their mission mentality.

The works of two men are often cited when raising this concern: George Marsden in his study of the drift to secularism in the Ivy League schools in *The Soul of the American University* (1994), and James Burtchaell's similar study of smaller denominationally related schools in his work *The Dying of the Light* (1998). Both authors document the drift away from spiritual mission and denominational orientation by many well-known and respected schools such as Harvard, Princeton, Yale, Duke, and Wake Forest. Their analysis should act as a cautionary tale for Seventh-day Adventist education. The factors identified by these authors as leading these institutions toward secularism are as follows:

1. Weak or tangential denominational linkage from the beginning of the school
2. Spiritual matters relegated to the religion department or the service sectors on campus
3. A clear identification by the faculty with larger trends in society, such as evolution in the sciences and postmodernism in the humanities
4. A decline and disappearance of financial and leadership support from the founding denomination
5. A desire to be open and tolerant of all points of view—a movement away from the truths and absolutes identifiable at the founding of these institutions.

The trends identified by these authors are real and must be addressed, but they are not inevitable. For example, there is a difference between intellectual drift toward a particular position (or for that matter away from one), and a well-thought-out decision to take a particular position and provide the support to make it happen. In the case of the New Mission School Model, a conscious choice is made to diversify the student body. That need not mean a corresponding watering down of beliefs or mission. In fact, as stated earlier, it may mean a more intentional mission, and more clearly chosen theological positions.

I believe that there is an important distinction between a drift or slide and a carefully embraced approach to Christian education. One may not agree with those choices, but the fact that they are well-thought-out and have a clear basis in mission can make a big difference in the final outcome.

A related issue is that of hiring faculty members who are not members of the Seventh-day Adventist Church. Does the embracing of the New Mission School Model result in a corresponding increase in the number of teachers who are not Adventist? Not necessarily. With the three healthcare institutions, it would appear to be the case. These schools not only have the highest percentage of students representing a variety of belief systems but they also have the highest number of teachers representing a diversity of faith traditions. According to the *World Report 2007*, the percentage of teachers representing a diversity of faith traditions at these three schools is as follows: Loma Linda—35 percent; Florida Hospital College—40 percent; Kettering—69 percent. The percentage for the liberal arts institutions ranges from almost nil to 17.5 percent (55).

Since mission is lived out by faculty members (and staff as well), does the presence of those who may not embrace all of the fundamental tenets of the Seventh-day Adventist Church inhibit the accomplishment of that mission? Though Andringa (2009, 173) identifies a strong president as one of three recommended best practices for Christian colleges, he also says, "if a campus wants to position itself as a distinctly religious institution, one key is to hire faculty who see faith not just as a private matter but as one central to the development of the whole person" (178).

Both Burtchaell (1998) and Marsden (1994) attribute the drift in the schools they studied at least in part to the hiring of faculty with different spiritual values and beliefs. Burtchaell (1998) states,

> Whatever presidents and trustees do, whatever be the market forces imposed by those who pay (students and benefactors), the inertial force of these institutions is in their faculties. And in our saga, the faculty was the first constituency to lose interest in their colleges being Lutheran or Catholic or Congregational. The faculty shifted from clerical to lay status before the presidency did. The faculty resided farther from their students [colonial institutions had students living with faculty], became dissociated from responsibility for their moral discipline and from partnership in their piety (828, 829).

In his "Concluding Unscientific Postscript," Marsden (1994) addresses this issue in particular for the liberal Protestant institutions he was studying.

> Throughout the first sixty years of the twentieth century, as prevailing intellectual ideals became less friendly to religious concerns and the dominance of the mainline Protestant ethos receded, Protestant leaders became increasingly uneasy with this original arrangement [the exclusion of religion from the core business of their universities]. They realized that in academic life itself it favored purely naturalistic and materialistic worldviews. In response, they added campus ministries, schools of religion, chaplains, impressive chapel buildings, student programs, and literature to promote religious concerns. They had limited success, however, in challenging the original definitions of academic life, and with the cultural upheavals of the 1960's, such efforts declined as well. Academic life remained a haven largely freed from religious perspectives (430).

In thinking about this issue, several factors must be taken into account before any conclusions can be reached. The first is that membership in the Seventh-day Adventist Church does not guarantee either doctrinal buy-in or spiritual commitment. A look at the history of any of the institutions of higher education in the North American Division of Seventh-day Adventists would reveal action on the part of administration to reform or remove Seventh-day Adventist faculty members who do not meet institutional spiritual *bona fides*. Certainly, the movement on the part of the General Conference to institute the International Board of Ministerial and Theological Education attests to these concerns relative to faculty in the religion departments. And there has been informal discussion at various levels within the church as to whether a statement of faith in young earth creationism on the part of science teachers is also warranted.

Another factor to consider is the challenge that the health professions schools face in recruiting and retaining Adventist faculty. Even when there is a preference for Seventh-day Adventist educators, if a position comes open in a professional program and no Adventist accepts, should the school close down the program? Large programs such as nursing present less of a problem than allied health, but even if there is a policy to search for Adventists first, I'm sure that each of the three schools in North America have had to make strategic choices to get the best candidate available.

Since faculty members play such a critical role in mission, there are several strategies used by Seventh-day Adventist healthcare institutions and the schools they run. One, hire a Seventh-day Adventist first if he or she is qualified. Two, keep Seventh-day Adventists in institutional leadership positions. Three, core areas of mission delivery must have qualified Seventh-day Adventists or no one. Four, no matter who is hired for whatever position, the institution should never compromise on mission. Each person hired at FHCHS is interviewed by the president for mission fit.

Would the ideal be to have a faculty of academically qualified, Seventh-day Adventist teachers? Perhaps. But there are two problems with that. One, some employees from other faiths may have as much or more of a commitment to the Christ-centered approach we are striving for. It was a faculty member from another Christian faith tradition who proposed the pre-chat prayer sessions for our online classes. Two, it is unlikely to happen at the health science schools for the reasons stated above.

In fact, as counterintuitive as it may seem to some, the presence of teachers representing a diversity of faith traditions keeps us from falling into the trap of assuming we are all on the same page when, in fact, we almost never are. That has benefits for both employees and students.

One of the trends identified by Marsden (1994, 317–331) is the influence of fundamentalism on the devolution of the institutions he studied. As a reaction to biblical higher criticism and evolution during the early part of the twentieth century, the fundamentalist movement played a major role in driving a wedge between the denominations and the educational institutions they had founded.

There appears to be a similar trend taking place in Adventism today. The development of Weimar and Heartland a generation ago and the more recent development of the ministerial training centers, such as the Black Hills institute, are an indication of the split between the traditional colleges and universities within Adventism and those members who believe the drift mentioned above has already taken place. These feelings are strong enough that some conferences are reluctant to hire ministerial graduates unless they have come from either Southern Adventist University or the Black Hills. Several years ago, the academic deans at two Seventh-day Adventist colleges reported at a meeting of the Association of Adventist Academic Administrators that they each had only one ministerial graduate hired as pastors by the local conferences. At the same time, a number of those completing a ministerial program at self-supporting ministerial institutes had been hired as pastors in the same conferences.

What does this trend have to do with the New Mission School Model? First of all it is a recognition that there is in fact more than one blueprint for Adventist education already operating in the North American Division. Two, the needs of a wide variety of homes and students must be met and the traditional campuses may not be able to be all things to all people. Three, in their own way, and from a more fundamentalist approach, these new institutions are as sincere in their attempt to accomplish mission-driven goals as are Loma Linda and Florida Hospital College. I believe the church is a healthier place, not only for having this wide variety of institutions, but the competition and dialog between these entities will make all of them stronger. As in the case of my daughter, not all institutions will be a good fit for all students. Options should be available so students can choose.

Conclusion

The New Mission School Model with the centered set paradigm provides a philosophical framework for recruiting students from outside the fold, and growing them spiritually in ways that are consistent with the overarching purpose for Adventist education. While there are challenges inherent in the model, I believe the benefits outweigh the potential harm.

Does Adventism need another model of higher education? I believe one is needed. The downward trend in enrollment, the increased number of students from other faiths at our institutions of higher education, and the fundamentalist divide all demand we look at education in new ways.

Bibliography

Andringa, R. C. "Keeping the Faith: Leadership Challenges Unique to Religiously Affiliated Colleges and Universities." In Martin, J., J. E. Samels, and Associates, eds. *Turnaround: Leading Stressed Colleges and Universities to Excellence.* Baltimore: Johns Hopkins University Press, 2009.

Bauer, B. L. www.aup.edu.ph/software/bruce_bauer_02_bounded_n_centered_sets_slides.pdf.

Burtchaell, J. T. *The Dying of the Light: The Disengagement of Colleges and Universities From Their Christian Churches.* Grand Rapids: William B. Eerdmans Publishing Company, 1998.

Frost, M. and A. Hirsch. *The Shaping of Things to Come.* Peabody, MA: Hendrickson Publishers, 2003.

Greenleaf, F. *In Passion for the World: A History of Seventh-day Adventist Education.* Nampa, Idaho: Pacific Press® Publishing Association, 2005.

Hofer, E. *The True Believer: Thoughts on the Nature of Mass Movements.* New York: Harper and Row Publishers, 1951.

Knight, G. R. *Myths in Adventism.* Washington, DC: Review and Herald® Publishing Association, 1985.

Marsden, G. M. *The Soul of the American University: From Protestant Establishment to Established Nonbelief.* New York: Oxford University Press, 1994.

Osborn, R. "Identifying the Challenges Facing Adventist K–12 Education." Keynote speech at the Renaissance Adventist Education Forum, Lake Mary, FL, February 27, 2010.

White, Ellen G. *Counsels to Parents, Teachers, and Students.* Mountain View, CA: Pacific Press® Publishing Association, 1943.

_____. *Education.* Mountain View: CA: Pacific Press® Publishing Association, 1952.

World Report 2007: Adventist Education Around the World. General Conference of Seventh-day Adventists, Department of Education, December 31, 2007.

V. BAILEY GILLESPIE

Chapter 8

Faith, Young Adults, and the Campus Experience

I am intrigued by a statement of Christ found in Luke 18:8. It seems that Jesus was walking toward Jerusalem at the end of His ministry. He had provided His disciples a curriculum of action, reflection, and theological thinking—not a bad curriculum plan for spiritual growth. He had used the best methods known to the rabbis to communicate truth—parables, illustrations, repetition, rhetorical questions. In His closing pilgrimage, He shares the goodness and hopefulness of God for His people. In a rather pensive moment, He refocuses priorities.

In the midst of a discussion of justice, He interjects, "When the Son of Man comes, will He find faith on the earth?" After a number of years, His students were faced with a question that is at the core of the gospel message. His lament points to the major mission of Christian higher education throughout our modern centuries too. His objective is our goal, our direction, and our focus also. Faith on the earth is a priority issue. This aspiration through the centuries has been implemented in a number of ways in Christian higher education.

In the early nineteenth century, small denominational colleges participated in the shaping of faith in three ways:

- First, denominational colleges consciously promoted common social values which had religious roots, which, in part, grew to form American "civil religion." This was done with the "externals" of religious life—chapels, dormitory worships, religion classes, and morning and evening prayers. These behaviors were the "models" of spiritual life. Observing them meant that your college or university was on the right path, observant, reflective, and obedient.

- Second, graduates of these colleges were expected to make a difference in society—as evidenced by the titles of the sermons at commencement and the class aims and mottos of bygone days.[1] They reflected the gravitas of Christian education. Hope. Joy. Fulfillment. Mission.
- Third, the college president usually taught a moral philosophy course to the seniors, which sought to help them integrate curriculum learning and provided a guide for the ethical application of that knowledge. We don't have much information as to how popular this course was!

Since then, not much else has happened to creatively critique or reconstruct college religious life during the last century, except for the fact that the college presidents have become too busy to teach this vital course. While this is a minor thing, to a large extent, the loss of trust and respect for reason and the subsequent movement towards experience as a norm in approaches to learning in this century has eroded the confidence of students in the educational system as they navigate their way through the myriad values they experience in higher education.

Church-related colleges, early on, gave up religious formalism such as chapels and devotional periods because students were more interested in writing obscene doggerel in the front of hymnbooks than in worship. The church of football then replaced religious values and congregational assembly on Sunday morning in American educational systems.

Seventh-day Adventist education was not without its own shifts in emphasis, focus, and practice over time. Our youth criticize our religious externals too. We have to, more and more, ask them to be quiet in chapel in order to set their religious focus anew. What is next? One is inclined to wonder when these forms of religiousness might disappear from our ranks altogether, or in the least, we are forced to ask if they serve a significant purpose any longer in the Christian higher education market in Adventism.

The religious self

It goes without saying that the religious self of a person, be he or she young or old, is composed of feelings, aspirations, and thoughts all influenced by myriad factors. If we agree with this brief description of what makes a religious person, we might conclude that one's worldview has a great deal to do with how a person perceives religion in his or her life. Looking back is often a good guide to understanding the present. So allow me a moment of reflection on what was, is, and might be, as we try to sort out the influences that impact college and university students today.

Modernity, or the modern person, as depicted by Heath White, a philosophy professor at the University of North Carolina, describes one who,

> tries to live his life autonomously, controlling it through the exercise of his reason. . . . Rational thinking proceeds according to rules and principles, where the paradigm is step-by-step logic. Thus, modernism respects whatever influences on the mind are logical, rational, and rule-bound; it denigrates whatever influences are not. Emotion, being illogical and unruly, is a distraction and a potential trap so the modern person tries not to let emotion influence his decisions.[2]

Postmodernism has arrived, however. Modernism rules the past. We often say that our young people today are products of a postmodern world, whether they buy into its pragmatism or not. I saw a cartoon the other day describing commitment in this century by its young. One young person is confronting another about what he believes. The other says, "Consider me an emergent, purpose-driven meta-seeker with a moderate, postmodern, freethinker-based worldview . . . I'm not sure what I believe yet, but I certainly nailed my label!"[3]

It is said, "The notion of postmodernism is invoked as both poison and cure within the contemporary church. To some, postmodernity is the bane of Christian faith, the new enemy taking over the role of secular humanism as an object of fear and a primary target of demonization. Others see postmodernism as a fresh wind of the Spirit sent to revitalize the dry bones of the church."[4]

Today, postmodern students caught in the midst of their religious self-identity process seem to have lost faith in the process of reason and don't appear to have a stake in step-by-step, logical rule-bound procedures, or in general, what the modern would call rational thinking. Now, they don't oppose it entirely; however, it is only one singular thing in a multiplicity of various experiences that makes up their self-understanding and informs their religious lives. I believe that no one is purely modern or purely postmodern. We all probably tend to be eclectic. A balanced view of the world almost demands it, but college and university students live much of what is postmodern in a particularly real way because the culture is postmodern, their lives are surrounded by, infiltrated with, and bound by postmodern thinking, people, and culture.

As an illustration of this, Sharon Parks, professor at Harvard Divinity School, describes a young woman in her senior year of college who was reflecting on her faith journey and the contribution that college life had made to it. The girl's story was one of a rocky voyage from freshman year through her senior year. Her turbulence had swirled around the issues of individuation from family and the cognitive dissonance between traditional religious knowing and academic study—all cast in a series of romances that raised further questions regarding role definitions for herself as a woman. Seeming to have arrived at some new shore of understanding and anticipating entering graduate studies at a prestigious university, she says of her sense of present and future faith experience:

> I'm open to being a believer, but . . . I'm comfortable and aware now that whatever I come up with will not be the traditional and that's OK. It can still be bona fide even though I know everyone doesn't have to fit into a niche. So I'm working it through and it feels comfortable and it feels like it'll come.[5]

In a journal entry from an Adventist student working through the struggles of college and religious experience, we see similar struggles:

> I do a lot of things that I hate. Being a hypocrite is not what I want to be and not what I want to do. . . . There are some days when I catch myself. I try not to gossip, complain, and put people down, but I have a terrible inferiority complex. As a whole, there are so many things that you have to have blind feelings about if you believe in the Bible, Jesus, and the end of the world. Then there are the facts that are supposed to be true about evolution and everything like that. I am not really sure what I believe. Church has not been any big help. I don't like religion. . . . I know there is a God, but where? If I can't see God then how am I supposed to know if God is going to help me; and if God will, then how am I going to know? How am I to understand what is best for me?[6]

This seeming lack of commitment may make some a bit squeamish, observing a student in a Seventh-day Adventist setting, not knowing what most assume. But it points out the significance of transitions in the faith development of young people today. Movement from what was somebody else's faith now is becoming personalized, now becoming established. And solving the "big" questions becomes a process most don't have the luxury of clarifying during their high school days or their summertime schedules. College and university life offers students a moratorium, much like Erik Erikson's moratorium on life suggests.[7]

A few summers ago, while leading a study tour which included Italy, in a hotel lobby in Rome, a colleague and I had an opportunity to talk with a Seventh-day Adventist student—a bit distant from her own church now—who was then attending a secular university. She reflected on her college educational experience within and without the Seventh-day Adventist system in this way:

> I believe that that narrow approach to the church presented by my parents and school has forever damaged my view of religion. Whenever I am home my folks ask if I am going to church. During meals my mother reads the scripture to the family, and each week at the university when they visit I am asked if I have attended the local church. I just want some freedom. I want to understand religion for myself. I am a member of a sorority at the university now. It provides philanthropic service for the community, a sisterhood and loyalty to community, and ritual. This gives me all I need from people that really care about me. Why do I need the church? This is church for me.

It seems that postmodern Adventist Christians see things a bit differently. Many young adults see no particularly good reason to believe that church services, for example, should remain the way they have always been. They see a more relevant approach when the new and old are in juxtaposition—taking the best of the old, but always adding the new, reaching into the past and the future without fear of either. Worship, in the near future, may not look like anything we have seen before. Yet, sorting out how to worship is only one of the issues for young Christians.

Young adults now are more open to different kinds of influences on their religious life. Emotions play a more central role, and the media—where pictures, stories, poems, art, films, and music reside—are tangible ways in which they find God real in their lives. Their worldview demands a more creative approach to finding and growing with God for this age's young person.

Community is an important experience that young people today need now during their higher educational sojourn. For some, it may be a new experience. While it is true that church can be that community—one where sharing of insights, social contacts, service, and questions of faith and personal growth might occur—the young don't see community happening in many of their home churches. In their world, constant communication is an identity tag of the young. Unless you can use social networking as a means of building community, you are simply old-fashioned, and many churches have not quite arrived in the twenty-first century as their needed community home. The higher educational experience, if creative and up-to-date in approach, could be a rich community experience.

What are the frustrations?

Over the past years, working on the Valuegenesis 1, 2, and now 3, research project for the North American Division of Seventh-day Adventists, I often get letters from ex-Adventists who hear about the research on Adventist young people and who want to share their frustrations about the Seventh-day Adventist Church and about their religious experiences. Their frustrations can be content analyzed around three areas:

1. *Feelings that the church does not care deeply for important things. It is caught up in endless discussions about doctrinal issues, which, for the young and many adult church members, too, no longer seems central to Seventh-day Adventists in the church. Couple this attitude about overwhelming propositional truth with behavioral issues that for young adults no longer are practiced or seem central to their relationship with God, and you can see why some call our churches "revolving doors."* Many of these behaviors are seen, in contemporary sociology, as cultural lags.

2. *Feelings that their educational experience in the lower grades and high school was inferior, or that their religious education was not much different from public education.* For some, the only difference they found in religious education was that they had to spend a lot of money for a Bible class. While this challenge has not been proven, and in fact the opposite seems true, based on the CognitiveGenesis research on the quality of Adventist education, the perception still persists.

3. *Recognition that the church now has new meaning for them since they have been able to define Adventism for themselves.* This must be viewed as a positive outcome. They have decided what

is important or core in their experience, and it might not often jibe with traditional norms expressed on their baptismal certificate.

These examples, and others that I could cite, are typical, standard responses from college and university-age youth regarding their faith journey as it is experienced in the midst of the sea of frustrations that college often bequeaths.

What does the research say?

In my book *The Dynamics of Change*, I have noted several such experiences of youth. What is seen is the *ambivalence* and *changing commitment* to religious life that college students seem to both demonstrate and share. It is out of these observations and research over two decades with Adventist generations that I want to address the following issues:

First, to briefly review young adult faith development and to suggest that the movement from *tacit* to *explicit* knowing and from *outside* to *inner* authority may appear to best describe one dimension of the faith experience of youth of college age. And it may be the best practical help to university educators as we seek to develop a model for faithfulness in teaching values and commitment to college- and university-age youth.

Second, to explore a research-based portrait of Adventist college-age youth in order to understand their priorities and their vulnerability to ideological interpretations of self, world, and God, in light of traditional understandings of religious education at the college level in the midst of a postmodern culture that permeates all our lives.

And finally, third, to suggest some directions for change in Seventh-day Adventist institutions of higher learning, which may help to nurture the faith experience of young adults.

Becoming adult and becoming religious

Becoming *adult* and becoming *religious* is a complex process. Simple attendance at church worship services, required worships in dormitories, required religion classes, and an occasional outreach program do not constitute the whole of the faith experience for young adults and has shown not to be the only method of religious instruction that makes a difference in young lives.

The multidisciplinary study of faith development is informed by our understanding of the phenomenology of faith experience itself. Faith is central in the spiritual development of the young. In short, faith is more than simple belief. The work of such individuals as theologians Leonardo Boff, Willfred Cantwell Smith, H. R. Niebuhr, and Richard Rice have helped us to conceptualize and balance faith as a more dynamic, ongoing, composing activity—the activity of meaning-making and seeking of patterns and order in the chaos of life—the cognitive, intellectual, affective, and emotional together in light of the personal complexity of each individual. Faith is not simply a matter of knowing the right beliefs, doctrines, or propositions anymore. Faithfulness is not restricted to making good choices—life-affirming choices. Faith, while it encompasses what one knows, also has a great deal to do with how one feels and responds to these facts in a dynamic texture of friends, institutions, priorities, tensions, growth, and new challenges.

Faith must be thought of as more than belief. It describes a relationship that is fluid and active. "The faith that you have," Paul said, "keep between yourself and God" (Romans 14:22). C. Ellis Nelson says, "Faith is not something to be displayed or measured, for it describes a relationship. Because of the nature of God, the relationship will take on different qualities according to the circumstances the person is facing."[8]

Faith is now more often understood to have certain qualities: struggle, acceptance, obedience, responsibility, confidence, and serenity are some of the objective mirrors used to enrich our understanding of faith and stress its individual texture and character. If we are working and praying for a mature faith, these qualities should be evident and our instruction, environments, attitudes, relationships, communication, and assessments should verify that these qualities can be seen as outcomes.

Faith not only creates beliefs, it re-creates beliefs. A personal faith allows for the possibility of new beliefs and for a fresh or different way of interpreting old ones. We must remember, "Although faith may live in the realm of the affections, it operates in our lives through our perceptive system. The person of faith sees things and evaluates the forces in human situations differently from a person with no trust in God."[9] Faith is dynamic and therefore demands dynamic experiences to nurture it. Staid, oft-repeated formalism just does not re-create religious experience any longer. Conformity to rules and regulations, standards and selected obedience do not re-create value-laden choices.

From this perspective of faith, the concept becomes as much a verb as a noun. Faith is the activity of "composing our convictions of value and trustworthiness. Faith is the patterning activity that orders our sense of the ultimate nature of the cosmos of being."[10]

When faith is defined this way, one is thrust into one of the first problems facing young adults when they try to understand their faith.

1. Faith and life are closely related. Just as faith must be understood as multifaceted, so must the religious educational programming of the university learn to take such a multifaceted approach through both a *listening* and *pro-active* stance.

Religious education in the university must look for points of interaction with other disciplines at their cutting edges and see, too, the cutting edges of present-day forms of Christianity. In short, religious education is everyone's job. All professors are pastors in a sense and everyone contributes to the student's picture of God. No one is exempt, since the student is thrust into this environment where God is supposed to be seen, felt, and understood.

The departments of religion in our colleges cannot do it all, nor can the schools of religion in our universities. And certainly, the seminaries in our church can't believe that pastors know or do it all. In fact, we may actually be at a disadvantage due to the baggage that "preachers" of religion carry. Religion is "taught," in the institutional setting, by each employee, from the friendly helpfulness of the advisor in the student finance office to the gentleness of the professor's response when a student fails an assignment or course. It includes the modeling of faithful church attendance by the faculty, and personal growth and questioning by faculty committed to understand truth for truth's sake: truth in light of the changing world, and new truth because of the changing world. It includes such experiences as the discussions that take place in the shade of the trees or during luncheons with majors. It involves regular faith talk of sharing God's work in our lives as well as probing how God works in theirs.

Faith moves from the students' experiences through our experiences to biblical exposition if relevance is to be achieved, rather than from the text to experience, as we have often argued in the past. While the discipline of philosophical exploration provides reflection on faithfulness, understanding faith requires life-situation inquiry as a priority. This way, one is driven to the texts of the Bible because of the experiences we seek to understand and foster rather than from the text to action inductively, and involvement with those for whom the texts of Scripture are written.

In times of perceived threat or danger, social sentiments intensify and social symbols gain new sacredness. "In times of perceived national crisis, nationalistic symbols and norms take on such sanctity that their violation is greeted with public outrage and repressiveness."[11] We need to look at the direct impact of events on the personal commitments of college students if we are to be significantly oriented to reaching their faith commitments. Religious experience for youth, as well as for all of us, is rooted and grounded in the personal life experiences of the individuals. Religious instruction must proceed from that center if it is to be "faithful."

Historical and personal events may impinge directly on strongly held sentiments and ideas. Religion classes, and any classes that stress values in education, that do not take that into consideration are doomed for failure. When the church fails to deal with such issues, either in curriculum choices or social action, it fails in the sphere of relevance and meaningfulness for the sake of the status quo. In times of war, we are challenged to explore our relationship to violence in all aspects of life. In times of economic hardship, we are encouraged to talk of the compassion and care of our God in former times of trial. And in moments of political turmoil, we are then driven to the passages of God's appointed leaders and their role in following God's values in spite of the world's pressure.

So now what about life stages?

Briefly, James Fowler, the primary pioneer in the research on faith growth, has identified a sequence of six "stages" in the development of faith. While the stages are rather complex, the third stage is of special importance to us in looking at these young adult years. The faith pattern during this age is referred to as the "conventional" stage and is evidenced by the "tacit" character of its faith-knowing. This "tacit" or intuitive way of knowing becomes a more "explicit" way of knowing as ideas are formed and tested in young adulthood.

In my own theory of faith growth, the situation young adults find themselves in is that of an "established" stage, which then moves to a "reordered" faith, one that has been found, yet is constantly being revised. Later Fowler argues that the way of knowing becomes "explicit" where pragmatic experience dictates the interpretation of knowledge. This movement is crucial in understanding young adult faith. What is true is true not because they have thought it to be and have heard it to be, but because they have experienced it as so.

2. Faith and taking responsibility for one's self are closely related. In other words, this is the beginning of taking one's own responsibility for one's religious growth. The concept of developing a distinct personalization of faith becomes significant now. It is the shifting of the locus of authority that is significant here in the formulation of one's faith life.

Sharon Parks argues that one of the most significant aspects of faith structure is what Fowler terms the "locus of authority." This dimension of faith describes the manner in which we "interpret and rely upon sources of authoritative insight or truth."[12] So what does this mean when we consider the students we teach? What can we say about our young lady in the introduction? The college years served to enable the voyage from her conventional faith through her own personal faith understanding. She has rejected some family and societal values, she has re-created, yes, reordered what is her faith; she has arrived on a new shore, so to speak, in that she now feels comfortable with her lack of faith, knowing that she will not be traditional, yet more is still coming that will formulate her belief system and faith structure. She is self-aware, fragile, and full of promise, developing, dynamic, and reflective.[13] She will not be considered "Adventist" by her family or church, but she sees herself as "religious" in a deeply personal way. And now, since she is in charge, she is quite content with her commitment and can build through her own life experiences. And, if inconsistent in her appraisal of what should be central to faith life, she is not troubled, nor worried, because she knows she is on the journey of faith. This faith-knowing is important. We need to learn to do what we can to make sure college and university young adults know that they are on the journey, and that is most important. Arrival will come, but perhaps not yet. We want to be the mentors, the guarantors of that journey.

In addition to Fowler's contribution to faith staging, what is becoming an important resource for those interested in facilitating positive youth development is a focus on spiritual development, an understudied, complex, and multifaceted subject, yet a process grounded in a human propensity, overlapping religious development, shaped by individual capacities and ecological influences, and which has potential to be an important resource for positive human development.[14]

3. Aiding young adults to think seriously about positive developmental outcomes and their connection to a community of believers is a priority now. The most prominent current theories suggest that positive developmental outcomes are associated with religious involvement. Several studies associating religious or spiritual involvement with positive developmental outcomes such as health, academic achievement, civic engagement, developmental assets, the resolution of identity, and finding meaning and purpose in life are identified as having a relationship with spiritual development and thriving in young people.[15]

4. Regular involvement in the lives of others provides a significant motivation to grow in spiritual commitments and church attendance. We can't assert strongly enough the relationship of involvement and community service projects in the development of a clear religious worldview. Judging by the current knowledge, including the findings that youth who are active in a faith community are almost twice as likely as their nonreligious peers to be involved in service, it seems that congregational life plays an important role in motivating and involving young adults in service and service learning.[16] Correlations of other research suggest that release of creativity becomes most potent through participation in the arts or through community service activities.[17] How can such participation become an integral part of religious college education?

Faith communities have embraced principles and practices of learning through helping others, and this aspect of maturing faith cannot be overlooked in curriculum planning and course requirements.[18]

Valuegenesis and the college student

There have been many studies that reflect the trends among college students as they relate to religion and their personal commitments. Valuegenesis research is but one type of research provided by the North American Division of Seventh-day Adventists. The study was begun in 1990 and Valuegenesis 2 was completed in 2000. The students studied in the Valuegenesis 2 research are now college and university age at the writing of this book. A third study, Valuegenesis 3, in 2010, provides three data sets for analysis that impact student life in the next decade.

The research regarding the college influence on faith life is particularly interesting, and Valuegenesis research has gathered a number of Seventh-day Adventist college and university students in data sets that explore these concepts. The following conclusions are statistically important and provide insight into the religious exploration of youth and young adults.

1. First, there is a long and gradual decline in church attendance among young adults, and we often blame modernization and secularization as the reasons. Roger Dudley, in his longitudinal study of Adventist high school seniors, discovered that 48 percent were distant from the church after ten years from graduation.[19] If the research is correct, there are important reasons. Young people are more likely to attend church less, not just to challenge their parents' belief system, but because there is a movement from a theology of traditional beliefs to one of keen social involvement, as evidenced by their utilization of Internet social networking sites, which moves young people toward a concern for a more immediate, relevant, and personal faith experience. This may have the effect of lowering corporate worship involvement. The new emphasis for young adult spiritual experience is on the *personal, experiential,* and what we might call the *mystical* rather than corporate worship experience.

Churches that continue to plan worship at the "regular" time, with "traditional" patterns of liturgy, may find young adults getting their experience with God somewhere else than the local sanctuary. Something as simple as changing the time when worship meets is a small beginning, but reflects concern for the individual young adult just beginning to establish his or her own habit patterns that build their spiritual lives and mature their faith choices.

Collegiate data of Valuegenesis illustrates this personal experiential movement too. Some of the information is cause to rejoice about our collegiate charges. Valuegenesis uses a scale that provides an average score for faith development. Originally using a complex scale of some thirty-eight items, and now using a shorter scale with the same reliabilty, we can paint a picture of a typical youth's faith in a number of dimensions.

Valuegenesis suggests that college students are more mature in their faith than their high school counterparts. The North American Division of Seventh-day Adventist averages for mature faith were at 44 percent in the year 2000 for high school twelfth-graders, while the college students, in the sample of over twenty-one hundred students, showed that 64 percent of the students surveyed showed maturity and a balance between horizontal (compassionate involvement with others) and vertical faith (devotional aspects of experience) scores. Seventh-day Adventist college students agree that faith shapes their thoughts and actions every day as well. Seventy-eight percent believe that this is so. College students we have surveyed have higher percentages (70 percent) on our loyalty to the church scale too. This may reflect a sociological understanding of their faith, however, because when asked if their worship services "stretch" them in their faith growth, less than 25 percent saw this happening in their local churches. And when we surveyed for their personal spiritual life on what we called our "piety" scale, less than half of these young people read their Bibles regularly (defined as more than once a week), and more than 60 percent never read Ellen G. White at all.

Orthodoxy is at 94 percent, higher than the 87 percent orthodoxy rate exhibited by the youth of the NAD in grades six through twelve. However, this orthodoxy scale only tells us what they say they believe, not how it impacts their spiritual growth.

In some ways Seventh-day Adventist students are much like their counterparts in public education. When we look at the activities of college students, we find they are typical of the average U.S. college student. Eighty-one percent of them play computer games one to five hours a week; 80 percent are involved in campus clubs; 80 percent watch one to five hours of television a day; and 27 percent spend more than twenty hours a week doing the homework we professors give them.

Looking at their religious participation, we have quite another picture. Only 25 percent have spent over forty hours in their lifetimes learning how to witness for Christ. At the same time, 56 percent have perceived spending over forty hours learning Seventh-day Adventist standards. Less time is spent in learning about the dangers of drug abuse in their lifetimes and even a smaller amount, only 20 percent, have spent over forty hours in their lives learning to help the poor and hungry.

2. Higher education tends to liberalize people. This is not to be taken in a pejorative way. Pluralism and liberalization do not necessarily mean less commitment or a lowering of the standards; rather, it can suggest more openness and acceptance.

Higher education exposes people to great thinkers, big worldviews, and tough questions with complex answers. If this is liberal, so be it, but it is a part of good, solid critical thinking—an important ingredient in faith maturity.

These qualities of respect and non-judgmentalism seen more often in "liberal" Christians reflect qualities of the Christian message that should be priorities for anyone's faith experience. However, if the school or church is close-minded, judgmental, critical, and unloving, young people can't identify these qualities with a Christlike life at all. Nothing closes students off to a conservative church more than one that is out of touch, unloving, out of sync with their culture, and out of clear logical arguments that aid in their critical thinking.

Higher educational experience is often seen as a "liberal education" but it must be taken in the best of understandings as reflecting Christlikeness and love. Both conservative education and liberal education should have these characteristics, and if not seen, young people who often determine the value of an experience based on the feeling tone of an experience, will reject either type of religious expression.

3. Social trends of the world impact their religious experience. The interrelatedness of these trends to their church commitment is significant. Greater and greater individual freedom and autonomy, higher levels of education, greater participation in political and social movements, greater tolerance of cultural and religious diversity, and political fervor often bring with them reduced religious orthodoxy and participation.

Our data thus far indicates that college students have pointed out some problems in our schools that they would like to change. For example, while discipline is perceived to be fair and rules are strict, students believe that there is a growing alcohol problem and drug abuse problem in our colleges. These social concerns need addressing in both curriculum and education. And while college students' attitudes toward standards indicate that they believe that standards serve a useful purpose, 77 percent suggest that overemphasis of them clouds Christ's clear message of freedom and love.

4. The relationship between spiritual or religious awareness and personal experience is important too. For example, Brenda Lealman's research shows that many young people claim to have had an experience which, in one way or another, could be described as religious. Adventist young people who have grown up in the church often claim to have had a religious experience, and while most say they have grown up religious, still some (12 percent) claim a significant, sudden experience. These realities lead us to focus on some important questions: What, in their experience, is religiously significant? What stimulates and nourishes their spiritual awareness? How can religious education contribute more effectively to the spiritual growth of young people?

Often what is "religious" is the corporate entity of religious life—churches, organizations, traditional services—while what is "spiritual" tends to be more personal, devotional, and relevant. And while these distinctions do not hold up in academic research about spirituality and religiousness, they are a helpful distinction for many young people. They like to say, I am spiritual, not religious. It is like the bumper sticker that argues, "After religion try Jesus." However, corporate involvement and participation in religious activities organized by our denomination and, as an example, involvement in service and community needs, are crucial in building a mature faith. Service involvement, while perhaps organized by the corporate church, is experienced personally and the growth that comes is experiential. These activities contribute to the blurring of what most influences the religious (corporate) or spiritual (personal) aspects of one's spiritual quest. Higher education must encourage the personalization of the religious (corporate) aspect of the denominational and let young adults know that they are not exclusive of each other, and perhaps, even show how both—the church and the religious experience—are needed if a balanced Christian experience is to be known.

There seems to be some relationship between being creative and experiencing the transcendental. Do we nurture this relationship? Higher education can encourage involvement in the arts, even though this exposure is often limited due to both budget restrictions and cultural Adventist concerns about worldliness. Although music training is given priority in our schools, replacing the energy outlet other schools channel through sports, our youth seldom learn to be creative or to openly express it. Yet experience in the arts has been shown to release, articulate, nourish, and extend awareness of the transcendental in experience, this personal aspect of experience. University educators need to ask more keenly what encourages those moments of self-transcendence that are a dynamic aid toward personal growth and transformation.[20] Research indicates that creative expression is a positive influence on the integration of faith in one's life, along with service involvement and positive climate in the classroom and the church.

The challenge

Years ago, in a class on the topic of counseling during my graduate educational experience, a professor of mine, who had written extensively about the nurture of young people, concluded his lecture with what I now recognize as a profound observation. He said, "When you finish your class lecture, or finalize the punch line in your sermon, or share an exciting insight into the Scriptures with your students, don't stop when that is said. Remember there is one more thing that must be done if learning is to begin and the teaching is to be significant in anyone's life. Ask, not what did you learn, ask not what did I say, but instead ask your students, 'So what?' " Drawing an application is crucial in any understanding of Bible study, or mastery in any discipline. What does this all mean? I would be remiss if I did not attempt to conclude with some degree of insight, explicating the implications of this chapter.

We have a clearer theory and more conclusive research now, but what will we do? I would like to conclude by posing some questions that these troubling and exciting data present to us. Questions that begin the conversation, not end it. But along with the questions, I want to propose some answers too. Beginning the conversation, and not ending it, is my goal.

1. First, what seems to be priority number one is that we do something to drastically change the way students perceive the church and school. The climate must be changed. Teachers may not continue to put students down through their comments or attitudes. People who represent the church's best values must not continue to create an unloving and uncaring environment for college youth. We must find some way to enrich the intellectual climate and, at the same time, change their feelings towards the church and school. I do not believe that this means we must get "tougher" or raise our admission requirements, nor does it mean we should drop all academic rigor. The answer has to do with personally resolving some deep religious questions. We never want to give the appearance of immediate condemnation and ultimate condemnation by God. Simply put, religious life is not currently a positive experience for many Adventist young adults. And perception *is* the reality for a large percentage of young people in academy.

The answers to this dilemma are very personal. How committed to freedom in Christ are you? Does your religion open you up to new possibilities or restrict your life? Does your faith explode with creativity and the re-creation of old traditions in responsible forms? Perhaps we must never condemn a youth again for his or her lack of conformity to the Seventh-day Adventist lifestyle, but rather challenge him or her to make life-affirming choices in light of the myriad life-denying ones possible to them. I don't know what the answer is, but something must be tried. This is a call to explore all of our rules, all of our reasons for discipline, all of our methods of approach, all of our attitudes of superiority and bigotry. Being Christlike is not easy, but it is crucial, and being Christlike may be surprising to the traditional church. Jesus was accused of being a liberal, a drunk, a blasphemer, and having questionable associates. One wonders just what He must have done to have the traditional establishment label Him thus. Just how could love, compassion, equality, fairness, and grace become so misunderstood?

2. Second, the research seems to hint that we do not understand grace and the surety that it provides. And many in the church would rather emphasize the rules of obedience rather than the responsibility Christians have, and the support God gives us, for change. When some 78 percent believe that to be saved "we must live by God's rules," and when even 31 percent of college youth believe that "they will more likely be saved if they follow Seventh-day Adventist standards," we have something to worry about. And even more specifically, when only about one half of the young collegians declare that there is "nothing they can do to earn salvation," we have a critical problem. Have we been majoring on minor things? Have we been guilty of communicating that God's love is partial if you just happen to sin? This view suggests that God's forgiveness is not really complete. Is God's acceptance demonstrated by my "Christian" exclusion? But how do you help this attitude to change? "If I be lifted up, I will draw all people to Me!" Christ says. *Drawing* is a word that implies "winning." Unless grace replaces criticism, openness replaces dogmatism, and simply being nice to students replaces authority, "drawing" and "winning" may not be possible.

3. Third, we need to begin to market Seventh-day Adventist education anew. No more feelings of inferiority, even with these problems. We have fine schools, our system is strong, and our teachers are seen as deeply committed (94 percent). On the whole, Christian education makes a positive impact on youth. We can be proud of this. We need to support our whole system; the higher educational experience is too central, too important to be critical, exclusive, and condemnatory.

When results from college and university students regarding the quality of their academic programs are positive, we have reason to boast. In our young-adult survey sample, data indicates that 85 percent of Adventist college and university youth would choose their school again. Eighty-six percent of their teachers listen to their students, and 69 percent give praise when work is done well. Ninety-one percent of students believe that teachers are interested in them, and only 22 percent feel put down. This is a marked improvement over the high school attitude where some 46 percent felt put down by their teachers, in our 1990 research.

What happens the more years that one is in Seventh-day Adventist schools? This we know: grace orientation is higher, loyalty is higher, orthodoxy is higher, and rejection of alcohol and drug use increases. This is the good news. But this joy is not totally complete because our educational system in colleges and universities seems to make youth insular, and prosocial behavior seen in care and compassion for the world and our community is not as important as it should be. We do not learn enough about or practice outreach or caring.

While our successes are significant, we can always wish and hope for more. But we must respect the fact that young adults are learning to have their own faith. We can do a better job if we continue to strive for more creative models of involvement with the community in our schools and churches. We can as well learn to appreciate the results of grace in our own lives and stretch young people in our purview to accept God's rich gift in their lives.

This research and our discussion in this chapter is a call to begin the dialogue, begin the conversation, begin to talk together about our changing church and what that means in an open, critical, intelligent, and accepting way. We are called to talk *together* about these problems and our successes, sharing our faith stories and commitments. Growing together. Being church. Finding God anew. Being forgiven. Watching God change lives. Living in the joy of that newness. Treating others as friends. Finding our faith. Re-creating our beliefs.

Psalm 73 tells the story of someone who saw wicked people prosper and almost went over to their ways. When he went to worship, he saw himself—during a moment of meditation—in relation to God, and realized that the people who built their lives on power and prestige were living in a dream world. Their feet were on a slippery place. He looked deep inside himself and recognized he needed to do some changing. After a prayer of confession for his shortcomings, he concluded, "It is good to be near God" (verse 28). He knew that nearness with the Infinite provided both power to change and creativity to solve the personal problems. He knew that a relationship with God brought openness and love. He had met a God that risked change and was not afraid to attempt new models of mission and service.

When youth graduate from an Adventist college or university, I want them to know, "How good it is to be near God!"

References

[1] Douglas Sloan, "The Higher Learning and Social Vision," *Teachers College Record* 79, no. 2 (1977): 163–169.

[2] Heath White, *Postmodernism 101: A First Course for the Curious Christian* (Grand Rapids, MI: Brazos Press, 2006), 81.

[3] http://www.reverndfun.com/?date=20070516.

[4] See James K. A. Smith, *Who's Afraid of Postmodernism?* (Grand Rapids, MI: Baker Academic, 2006), 18.

[5] Sharon Parks, "Young Adult Faith Development: Teaching is the Context of Theological Education," *Religious Education* 77, no. 6 (November–December 1982): 657.

[6] Bailey Gillespie, *The Dynamics of Change* (Birmingham, AL: Religious Education Press, 1991), 244 (manuscript edition).

[7] Erik Erikson, *Identity Youth and Crisis* (New York, NY: W. W. Norton & Company, Inc., 1968), 128–132.

[8] C. Ellis Nelson, *How Faith Matures* (Louisville, KY: Westminster John Knox Press, 1990), 146.

[9] Ibid., 148, 149.

[10] James W. Fowler, *Stages of Faith: The Psychology of Human Development and the Quest for Meaning* (San

Francisco, CA: Harper & Row, 1981), part 1. Quoted in Sharon Parks, "Young Adult Faith Development," *Religious Education,* 658.

[11] Dean R. Hoge, *Commitment on Campus: Changes in Religion and Values Over Five Decades* (Philadelphia: Westminster Press, 1974), 188.

[12] James W. Fowler, *Life Maps: Conversations on the Journey of Faith,* Jerome Berryman, ed. (Waco, TX: Word Books, 1978), 40–43.

[13] Sharon Parks, "Young Adult Faith Development," 668.

[14] Peter Benson, E. C. Roehlkepartain, S. P. Rude, "Spiritual Development in Childhood and Adolescence: Toward a Field of Inquiry," *Applied Developmental Science* 7, no. 3 (2003): 205–213.

[15] P. E. King and Peter Benson, "Spiritual Development and Adolescent Well-Being and Thriving," in E. C. Roehlkepartain, P. E. King, L. Wagner, and Peter Benson, eds., *The Handbook of Spiritual Development in Childhood and Adolescence* (Thousand Oaks, CA: Sage, 2006), 384–398.

[16] Thomas A. Trozzolo and Jay W. Brandenberg, "Religious Commitment and Prosocial Behavior: A Study of Undergraduates at the University of Notre Dame," *Research* Report 2, December 2001, 3.

[17] Brenda Lealman, "Young People, Spirituality and the Future," *Religious Education* 86, no. 2 (Spring 1991): 273.

[18] See E. C. Roehlkepartain, "Faith Communities: Untapped Allies in Service-Learning," *NYLC Generator* 21, no. 3 (2003): 20–24.

[19] See Roger L. Dudley, *Why Teenagers Leave the Church* (Hagerstown, MD: Review and Herald®, 2000), for a complete discussion of the details of his expansive ten-year study of Adventist youth and their reasons for leaving the church.

[20] Ibid., 274.

STEVE PAWLUK

Chapter 9

The Mission of Seventh-day Adventist Higher Education: Redundant or Complementary?

Introduction

Michael Scofield (public presentation at the San Diego Chapter of the Association of Adventist Forums, August 8, 2009); Richard Osborn, who presents his findings in another chapter in this book; and others have painted an arresting, and sometimes distressing, picture of the trends and future challenges of Seventh-day Adventist education, kindergarten through university. University officers and trustees of Seventh-day Adventist institutions have met often to study enrollment and financial data, to clarify institutional missions, and to consider appropriate responses to what appears to be increasing challenges presented by the simultaneously rising expenses and decreasing enrollments at most Seventh-day Adventist institutions of higher education (IHEs).

Although there is urgency to these discussions and studies, Scofield's research indicates that these problems have been building since the 1970s (see Figure 1). So, while this concern is certainly important and has, perhaps, reached a critical point, it is not a new one. It is, however, one that might best be addressed, not so much by seeking more creative methods of saving on expenses or improving market share, although those things are undoubtedly helpful, but by responding appropriately to the changed needs of the Seventh-day Adventist denomination and of the general

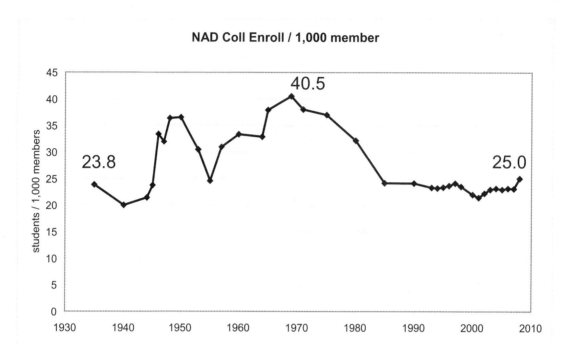

Figure 1: Michael Scofield, public presentation at the San Diego Chapter of the Association of Adventist Forums, August 8, 2009.

population that is sympathetic to Christian education.

Brand loyalty

We live in an era when Seventh-day Adventists exhibit less automatic brand loyalty than they did several decades ago (Anderson, 2009). Like others in today's society, Seventh-day Adventists, have, since the 1970s—about the time that incipient enrollment decline became evident—become more sophisticated consumers (Lipke, 2000) (dare one use the term *stewards*?), and they are increasingly more open to enrollment at other Christian institutions of higher education or at other private or public institutions.

The urban anthropologist Jennifer James suggests that when institutions experience a change that portends a perceived loss to them, leaders often experience the natural grief cycle in a way that is similar to individuals who have suffered personal loss. James refers to this as the "grief/nostalgia syndrome" (1996, 148). She suggests that administrators, faced with change that comes from outside of the organization, often respond with denial, anger, and bargaining, followed, only occasionally, by acceptance and rebuilding.

It appears that, in general, Seventh-day Adventist educational leaders may have been stuck in the denial and anger stages. Our strategic planning sessions suggest that we believe that doing things more efficiently, or doing the same thing better, will reverse declining enrollments. Task forces and *ad hoc* water cooler "committees" opine that if pastors only would preach more sermons on the importance of a Seventh-day Adventist education, as they did in the "good old days," parents might repent and increase their "brand loyalty" (Anderson, 2009, 17, 18), fortifying their commitment to "our common core" (Anderson, 2009, 30). Yet the business practice of refusing to listen to one's customers, who are expressing themselves either through complaints or by selecting another product, has rarely been an effective one.

George Knight proposes that a renewed commitment to the Adventist eschatological message would restore faith in the purpose of our educational system. He calls for a renewal of Seventh-day Adventist schools' "distinctive importance" (Knight, 2008, 11) along with "a *proper* amount of sanctified arrogance" (16). Knight reports, "The plain fact is that many, including those raised in the church, really have no grasp of why they are Adventist or even if it makes any real difference" (58). He believes that an emphasis on Seventh-day Adventism's "neoapocalyptic message" (104–106) could avoid the travesties of our past judgmental legalism while rejuvenating loyalty to the denomination's mission and ministries, presumably including its educational ministry.

However, a careful reading of Knight's book fails to reveal any teachings that are unique to the Seventh-day Adventist denomination and that are not also preached or taught by other evangelical denominations. This should be neither surprising nor dismaying. If the denomination's teachings are scriptural, such commonality is to be expected. In any event, whether renewed emphasis on Seventh-day Adventist eschatology is sufficient to revitalize brand loyalty among the denomination's members in today's climate is at least debatable.

A problem of our own making?

I would like to propose that we educators have, ourselves, helped to create or at least facilitated the problem of diminishing interest in Seventh-day Adventist education, particularly higher education. While automatic brand loyalty may still be a significant factor in the selection of soft drinks and hamburger outlets, increased consumer sophistication (Lipke, 2000), together with deficiencies in our understanding of the mission of Christian higher education, have combined to cause many Seventh-day Adventist families to conclude that something other than Seventh-day Adventist higher education may, in many cases, be what represents the best stewardship of their resources and the best option for their children.

In this chapter, I intend to develop the idea that the missions of churches, conference ministries, and educational institutions should be *complementary,* but not *redundant.* Additionally, I am proposing that educators have taught our constituents and stakeholders to measure education by a mission that is, in fact, not only redundant, but a very expensive redundancy when pursued by educational institutions; and that potential students and constituents have come to realize, without articulating it in so many words, that Seventh-day Adventist institutions of higher education are often an inefficient and excessively costly vehicle for carrying out a mission that is identical to the missions of local congregations and conference youth ministries.

Finally, I will propose, what I believe to be a more appropriate purpose for Seventh-day Adventist higher education and one which may, if rightly understood and pursued, renew the attractiveness, perhaps even belief, in the necessity of Seventh-day Adventist higher education.

Structural theory

First, some background theory. Lee Bolman and Terrence Deal (2008) identify four ways of understanding organizations and their actions. One of these perspectives is termed the Structural Frame. The term "frame" refers to a window or vantage point. "Structural" refers to one's focus on the policies, organizational charts, rules, and processes that define an organization.

Their model identifies certain assumptions that underlie each of the frames. The Structural Frame is built upon several key beliefs, including these:

1. Organizations exist to achieve established goals and objectives.
2. Organizations can increase efficiency and enhance performance through specialization and division of labor.
3. Coordination and control of specialists are essential for meeting organizational goals.

What would one think about a company that insisted that its research and development people spend more time working in sales? What if that company insisted that its frontline salespeople were more qualified, and could be better trusted, to engineer and develop the company's product? What if the company insisted that every employee, regardless of whether he or she was hired to serve in management, research and development, or the sales force, would be judged, primarily, on how much product they personally sold? Couldn't an observer rightly conclude that the organization is suffering from structural dysfunctions that will eventually lead to its demise?

One wonders if the Seventh-day Adventist denomination has inadvertently done something very much like this. We have mission statements in our churches, conferences, and educational institutions that sound quite similar. A review of a few university and college mission statements illustrates this.

> Southern Adventist University, as a learning community, nurtures Christlikeness and encourages the pursuit of truth, wholeness, and a life of service (https://www.southern.edu/about/Pages/mission.aspx, accessed September 1, 2009).

> Andrews University, a distinctive Seventh-day Adventist Christian institution, transforms its students by educating them to **seek knowledge** and **affirm faith** in order to **change the world** (http://www.andrews.edu/about/mission.html, accessed September 1, 2009; emphasis in the original).

> Walla Walla University, therefore, seeks in its mission to foster the unique gifts of every individual within this Christian community of faith and discovery (http://www.wallawalla.edu/about-wwu/an-introduction/mission/, accessed September 1, 2009).

> Inspired by faith in Jesus Christ and dedicated to a personal student-focused community, Union College empowers students for learning, service and leadership (http://www.ucollege.edu/welcome/mission-vision-values, accessed September 1, 2009).

While it is not my objective to evaluate the appropriateness of these mission statements, *per se,* or to critique the work of these fine institutions, it is difficult to miss the very broad scope of these statements or, more to the point, their similarity to statements that could have been just as easily generated by almost any local church, conference, or youth group.

Why is it that, instead of carefully engaging in a division of labor that is then coordinated to assist the organization in achieving its fundamental mission, we insist that teachers and professors, in addition to pastors, function as evangelists? Our constituents often evaluate the effectiveness and the value of an institution of higher education by the number of baptisms produced, student missionaries sent out, and service projects sponsored. Parenthetically and conversely, why is it that we rely on our evangelists and administrators to engineer our educational products, especially in our schools of theology and in various science departments? Isn't it more properly the job of academics to provide "engineering" services for our denomination?

Seventh-day Adventist Higher Education in North America

I propose that Seventh-day Adventist school administrators, kindergarten through graduate school, have sought legitimacy in the eyes of conference administrators and pastors (who, admittedly, have significant influence on subsidies and enrollment) by adopting the language of evangelists and pastors while emphasizing the metrics of soul winning in education. Similarly, school administrators have sought to appeal to parents' natural concerns about their children's eternal destinies and have overemphasized the evangelistic role of schools to them as well.

I, too, have argued in the past, along with the best of them, that Seventh-day Adventist education is a "nine month evangelistic series" and I have, in prior institutional roles, compiled statistics of the number of baptisms, church leaders, and tithe contributors that have been fostered by Seventh-day Adventist education. However, I now am convinced that this is a misleading outlook to take.

If the *primary* purpose of Seventh-day Adventist education, whether K–12 or higher education, is to convert people, then it is one of the most expensive and resource-consuming methods that the church has devised. If soul-winning or spiritual development is the only, or even the primary, mission of Seventh-day Adventist education, then I would be forced, by the requirements of responsible stewardship (Pawluk, 2006), to propose that we close all of our schools; release all of our teachers, professors, and administrators; sell the properties; and redeploy the resulting funds to fund an endowment that would pay for at least one full-time, highly trained, youth ministries specialist for each congregation in the North American Division of Seventh-day Adventists. Larger congregations could even be allocated entire youth ministries teams. There would undoubtedly be sufficient funding for all churches to provide after-school activities and outreach opportunities. Additionally, congregations, no longer having to support their constituent schools, would have more financial resources to engage in their own work. Thus, instead of serving only 30 percent of Seventh-day Adventist young adults, as some estimates indicate that we currently do, we could support the spiritual needs of virtually all of them.

Similarly, if Seventh-day Adventist education is *primarily* about providing students with guidance concerning issues relating to lifestyle, offering corporate devotional opportunities, and developing a strong community of believers (although we recognize their importance as a part of the total package, especially on residential campuses) one could persuasively argue that these kinds of objectives could be much more efficiently and, perhaps, effectively achieved by redeploying even a mere fraction of the resources that are currently used to support Seventh-day Adventist educational institutions by constructing Seventh-day Adventist residence halls near a number of high quality state and private universities and staff them with God-fearing deans, counselors, and chaplains.

Why not phase out Seventh-day Adventist IHEs?

So why don't we do this? Why shouldn't we do this? The fact that I have spent over three decades serving the Seventh-day Adventist denomination in various capacities, including two decades in education, makes it difficult for me to even pose this question. Yet, there are employees and members of the denomination who *are* asking it, and there is an increasing number who are answering it with their feet as they enroll themselves or their children in non-Seventh-day Adventist institutions of higher education.

It is tempting to blame declines in enrollment on the high cost of a Seventh-day Adventist education and to denounce the misplaced priorities of Seventh-day Adventist families with their luxury vehicles and expensive vacations. While it may be correct to question the expenditures and priorities of some, it seems that the simple question of *cost* needs to be replaced with the question of *value*. Which takes us back to Bolman and Deal's concept of organizational division of labor and specialization.

Historic changes from simplicity to complexity

Seventh-day Adventist churches and conferences were once fairly simple organizations that focused almost exclusively on traditional evangelism. Early Adventist leaders, including James White and John Loughborough, attempted to keep the organization focused on the basics by vociferously opposing, for example, the formulation of a creed, citing it as "the first step of apostasy" (Knight, 2000, 22). However, we now publish a description of twenty-eight fundamental beliefs that are sometimes used to judge fellow believers' orthodoxy and "Adventism" just as predicted by these two leaders. Whereas early Adventists lived frugal lives, preferring to divert their financial resources to the work of the gospel ministry in anticipation of the imminent coming of Jesus, Adventists now build up retirement plans and purchase life insurance (which formerly was commonly thought to be an indicator in the minds of some devout believers of a lack of faith). Similarly, Seventh-day Adventist organizations now work to grow endowments and develop long-term strategic plans. While we continue to preach the soon coming of Jesus (and some still enjoy interpreting the latest political upheaval as *the* sign of His imminent coming), we've become much more comfortable with the paradox exemplified by Reformer Martin Luther, who was once asked what he would do if he knew, with certainty, that the world would end tomorrow. His answer: "I would plant an apple tree in my garden" (http://www.arcretreat.org/, accessed September 1,

2009). Thus, our church's frame of view has become more nuanced.

A similar evolution of purpose and increased comfort with long-range thinking has occurred within Seventh-day Adventist education. Originally conceived as a way of producing ministers, teachers, and healthcare workers for the denomination, Seventh-day Adventist institutions of higher education have emerged as complex institutions of learning and research. Partly because we live in a time when our universities produce more ministers and teachers than our denomination can absorb, and partly in response to the perceived need to attract a wider market share, we've expanded our understanding of the purposes of Adventist higher education. The resulting broader array of majors and programs however, presents the new challenge of answering the question of why parents and students should pay private school tuition rates for majors and programs that can be completed with much less expense elsewhere. After all, the question is asked, what difference is there between a computer programming major at State U and one at Adventist U? Do Christian mathematicians really engage in a different kind of mathematics than do mathematicians who are not Christians? Are students paying tuition primarily for the "add-ons," such as residence hall worships and chapel, for sports activities that don't take place on Friday nights, and for a required number of credits of Bible classes?

I believe that the primary *value* of Seventh-day Adventist higher education is in the type of education that we offer.

Today's complexity requires a more productive division of labor and coordination

As is the genius of most other North American institutions of higher learning, it is the general education courses offered in our Seventh-day Adventist institutions of higher education that enable students to become broad and well-educated citizens. While the courses of a student's major generally prepares him or her for a career, general education courses, which students are sometimes advised to "get out of the way" as early as possible, represent the heart of what it means to be liberally educated. General education courses are also precisely where Seventh-day Adventist institutions of higher education can offer students an especially distinctive Christian Seventh-day Adventist education that complements the overarching mission of our denomination.

Let's return to our earlier illustration about the effective division and coordination of responsibilities within an organization. Salespeople should be expected to focus on sales, although they should relay product feedback that they receive from the field to the R&D teams. Research and development engineers should be expected to experiment and to refine and develop the organization's product, although they will certainly be influenced by the information coming from the sales team and the strategic business plans devised by the administrators. Administrators should facilitate the efficient and effective functioning of the organization so that the other departments have the resources that they need in order to fulfill their roles well.

Likewise, in this complex organization that we call the Seventh-day Adventist Church, would it not be best to expect that evangelists would evangelize, bringing people to Jesus; while pastors would nurture their developing faith and teach congregants how to live?

But what would be the role of teachers and professors in this division of labor? What are they equipped to do, by their dispositions, education, and by their opportunities, that evangelists and pastors are less able to do to promote the work of the gospel? I propose that the most important task that educators in Seventh-day Adventist institutions of higher education can do is twofold: (1) to research and add to the church's and society's understandings of our world, and (2) to engage students in research and critical analysis, guiding them as they develop Christian, and more particularly, Seventh-day Adventist worldviews. This comports not only with Bolman's and Deal's model, but with the division of labor exemplified in Saint Paul's observation that "[Paul] planted the seed, Apollos watered it, but God made it grow" (1 Corinthians 3:6).

Along these same lines, Robert Benne commends St. Olaf College as an exemplar of good Christian education, reporting that "the college aims at cultivating the minds of the students with Christian learning, not converting their hearts, which would be the proper work of the gospel in the church" (2001, 130).

The importance of worldview

Nancy Pearcey (2005) makes a compelling case in her book, *Total Truth,* of the importance of being clear about one's worldview. In essence, her argument is that "each of us carries a model of the universe inside our heads that tells us what the world is like and how we should live in it" (23). This mental model influences our interpretation of, and relationship to, everything that we see, hear, and understand.

Robert Benne, in his book *Quality With Soul* (2001), states it this way:

> [Worldview] is a comprehensive account encompassing all of life; it provides the umbrella of meaning under which all facets of life and learning are gathered and interpreted. Christianity's comprehensive account does not claim to have all the relevant data and knowledge about our life in this world, but it does claim to offer a paradigm in which those data and knowledge are organized, interpreted, and critiqued (2001, 6).

Pearcy posits that the dualistic worldview that is evidenced in public education draws a distinction between what is rational and known and what one believes and values. Rational materialistic understanding is considered, in public colleges and universities, to be valid for everyone, but one's religious beliefs and values have devolved into a private, individual preference to be enjoyed by the believer and to be tolerated by others. On the public campus, an individual's beliefs and values may be protected and even appreciated, but they do not enjoy the same level of influence as rational scientific knowledge.

The problem with this sort of dualism is that Christianity "no longer functions as a lens to interpret the whole of reality; it is no longer held as total truth" (Pearcey, 2005, 69), but rather it has become only one of many equally valid perspectives from which one may choose.

If one adopts a dualistic worldview, whether it is secular or Christian, faith becomes compartmentalized, kept in its own little container only to be brought out on the Sabbath.

If one Christianizes the dualistic worldview, one is drawn into ancient Gnostic battles that seek to constantly determine which things are holy and what things are secular. This results in synthetic distinctions that change over time. Activities that once were sinful on the Sabbath are sinful no longer, and hair or skirt lengths that were once wicked are now considered tame. Places that were once evil (bowling alleys and theaters), objects that once were the devil's tools (playing cards, jazz, and televisions) no longer are classified in the same ways. Things that were once required (beards on men and ankle length dresses on women) now seem anachronistic. What will change next? What is changing now?

One possible response to this is to presume that those living in "the good old days" had worked everything out, and then attempt to live in the prior century as much as possible. Alternatively, one can understand that the problem is intrinsic to a dualistic worldview itself and that, until one's worldview is changed, Christians will be limited to tinkering about the edges of the real issues.

Scripture teaches us that "The earth is the Lord's and the fullness thereof" (Psalm 24:1). Being spiritual does not require placing bright yellow "Do Not Cross" tape over part of God's creation and staying only in the safety zone. That is not how one functions as salt of the earth. At the risk of overapplying the metaphor, it is interesting to note that once salt has been added to food, it becomes bonded with the food, and its existence and success is recognized only by the enhanced taste of the food.

Educational mission: Thinking Christians engaging culture

This is where Seventh-day Adventist universities can offer an important and distinctive service to their students and their denomination. Seventh-day Adventist higher education should readily engage all disciplines and teach any subject, including once taboo topics such as fiction, film, evolution, human sexuality, and jazz. But it should do so from the perspective of a Seventh-day Adventist worldview.

A Christian worldview is described in Pearcey's formulation (2005, 44–46), which posits that every bit of information and reality can be best understood through lenses that recognize that:

1. God is the Creator of everything. "God's creative word is the source of the laws of *physical* nature, which we study in the natural sciences. It is also the source of the laws of *human* nature—the principles of morality (ethics), of justice (politics), of creative enterprise (economics), of aesthetics (the arts), and even of clear thinking (logic). That's why Psalm 119:91 says, 'all things are your servants.' "
2. Sin has come into the world. "The Bible teaches that all parts of creation—including our minds—are caught up in a great rebellion against the Creator" (46).

    "Of course, nonbelievers still function in God's world, bear God's image, and are upheld by God's common grace, which means they are capable of uncovering isolated segments of genuine knowledge. And Christians should welcome those insights. All truth is God's truth, as the church fathers used to say; and they urged Christians to 'plunder the Egyptians' by appropriating the best of secular scholarship, showing how it actually fits best within a biblical worldview" (47).
3. God has offered redemption and renewal "of the whole person" (47). "To talk about a Christian worldview is simply another way of saying that when we are redeemed, our entire outlook on life is re-centered on God and re-built on His revealed truth" (47).

To Pearcey's three lenses, I would add the significant contribution that Seventh-day Adventism has made to Christianity: the great controversy model. This paradigm not only harmonizes with the worldview of Christianity in general, but it also refines and clarifies certain things about the nature of God and of our reality. While other Christians may, for example, struggle with the question of whether or not God created evil, or of how a perfect God can allow bad things to happen, the great controversy model answers those questions with broad themes such as God's infinitely high value of free choice and due process.

The great controversy model, which I have explicated in an earlier chapter in greater detail, helps us understand why the evidence for God is sufficient, but not undeniable. It demonstrates God's pro-choice character and His desire for freely given, but not coerced, belief and love.

This great controversy theme enables Seventh-day Adventist scholars to understand the broad lines of history, the complex data of science, the meanings of philosophy and theology, the implications of the human story as seen through literature, film, and the social sciences, and the incomplete and sometimes conflicting data discovered by every discipline, from a truly unique perspective.

This means that the fundamental, distinctive, and unique role of the Seventh-day Adventist university is to create a community of thinking Christians who engage culture together.

Parker Palmer correctly cautions that a good Christian education is not for those who lack courage. He reminds us that

> In a sacred landscape, with its complexities and convolutions, surprise is a constant companion: it lies just around the bend or hidden in the next valley, and though it sometimes startles us, it often brings delight. But on the flatlands of a desacralized world, where we grow accustomed to seeing things approaching us long before they arrive, surprise is neither expected nor welcomed. When it suddenly arises, apparently out of nowhere, we are stricken with fear and may even respond with violence (1998, 112).

Robert Benne affirms the college that has not "retreated into pietist simplicities" (2001, 97) and encourages educators to "take on the risk of making intellectual engagement as dangerous as it actually is" (2001, 104). Arthur Holmes observes that "liberty without loyalty is not Christian, but loyalty without the liberty to think for oneself is not education" (61). Our Seventh-day Adventist universities are just the place for such courageous and clear-eyed thought.

This is not a call for an unanchored "anything goes" multiversity educational experience for our students. However, it does seem valuable for students to explore the edge of their intellectual envelope while the assistance of critically thinking Seventh-day Adventist professors is conveniently available to them.

A highly effective Seventh-day Adventist institution of higher education should offer an education that is akin to that experienced by the aviation student who is expected to "push the envelope" of his or her abilities, sometimes with simulated emergencies initiated by the flight instructor, so that the student can develop appropriate diagnoses and habitual response patterns while the instructor is still available to prevent any fatal errors. The flight student learns to think like a pilot from the complex array of promptings, questions, problems, simulated emergencies, and assistance of an experienced instructor. Later, when the student is flying solo and an unplanned, but not unexpected, problem arises, he has experienced something like it before and can proficiently handle the crisis.

This model seems to offer a more responsible educational experience than the one that engages in only "safe" learning, subsequently finding the student unprepared when, after graduation, he or she reads a thought-provoking book or engages in discussion with an individual who has been well-versed in a non-Christian worldview.

Some parents, students, pastors, and educators express concern that students graduating from a Seventh-day Adventist college or university are not sufficiently indoctrinated in the denomination's fundamental beliefs and lifestyle. However, that fundamental training of students should be the foundation provided by the parents in the home, the local church, and Christian elementary schools. The function of higher education is to build upon that information, teaching believers to develop their worldview, especially in the crucible of difficult ideas, so that they will be facile critical thinkers when faced with new information or problems. Parker Palmer posits that

> good education may leave students deeply dissatisfied, at least for a while.... Students who have been well served by good teachers may walk away angry—angry that their prejudices have been challenged and their sense of self shaken. That sort of dissatisfaction may be a sign that real education has happened.

It can take many years for a student to feel grateful to a teacher who introduces a dissatisfying truth. A marketing model of educational community, however apt its ethic of accountability, serves the cause poorly when it assumes that the customer is always right (1998, 94).

So, the Seventh-day Adventist university holds a special, and even sacred, position among institutions of higher education. The university's educational and organizational climate should produce a community where *thinking Christians engage culture together.*

Of course, all universities purport to engage in thinking. But ours are *Christian* universities, and to sharpen the pencil a bit, *Seventh-day Adventist* universities. This means that we begin with certain assumptions and with a particular worldview as described earlier in this chapter. Our worldview affects how we approach literature, interpret scientific data, understand history, interpret and apply Scripture, and relate to each other, as well as influencing the content, pedagogy, and research that we employ to foster student learning.

And while we are Christians, we are *thinking* Christians. There are blind-faith Christians. There are Uncle Arthur-sanitized-Bible-story Christians. There are seed-on-the-shallow-ground Christians. But we aspire, together, to use the minds that God has given each of us to seek God and God's truth. We affirm that all truth is God's truth (White, 2000, 9) and so we aim to challenge each other respectfully. We agree to provoke each other to do good work (Hebrews 10:24) through disciplined critical thinking, which aims for (Paul and Elder, 2008):

- Accuracy, precision, and clarity
- Relevance and sufficiency
- Logic
- Depth, breadth, and significance
- Fairness

We agree to study the Scriptures with informed inquiry, seeking eternal principles that are derived from careful investigation of the style and context in which the text was written (White, 2000, 102, 103).

Although our worldview is Seventh-day Adventist, our universities and colleges (and our students) must function in this world. Remember that Jesus prayed that God would be with His disciples in the world (John 17:11, 15), not to take them out of the world as a fearful and anachronistic cult. So we research and study, not in order to escape culture, but to *engage* in it.

Now, "engage" does not mean to automatically adopt. It means *engage*. This can include the following:

- Benefitting from culture
- Decrying culture
- Transforming culture
- Adapting culture
- Enjoying culture

And, finally, we do this *together*. Although each institution of higher education offers its own community, we are, also, all part of the one body of Christ (1 Corinthians 12:27). There are, it seems, strident voices calling for amputation of some parts of the body. But we must resist fighting against ourselves and among ourselves. Now, isometric exercise can be beneficial, and some honest and respectful push and pull will improve our denomination, but we must stop our self-mutilation of the body of Christ and seek to be a healthy, growing, and serving body.

Holmes affirms that, "To the Christian in the Christian college, then, the development of an inquiring mind becomes an expression of faith and hope and love addressed to God. It is part of our response to God's self-revelation" (31). Richard Hughes adds,

> But I embrace [students' critical questions and their freedom to formulate their own answers] because I serve a God whose majesty defies description, whose sovereignty shatters human orthodoxies of every kind, and who finally forces me to respond, not with answers, but with wonder, creativity, and imagination (2001, 106).

Toward praxis

How would this work in practical terms? The Seventh-day Adventist institution of higher education should expect its students to become fluent in their use of the "rules of engagement," which the various disciplines have developed over the centuries in their search for truth. Seventh-day Adventist institutions of higher education must value, and even enhance, their general education requirements for all students. We must teach students how to think in disciplined ways, and to evaluate their conclusions through the lens of the Seventh-day Adventist worldview that is informed by Scripture. For example,

- Students should become adept in the methods of literary or film analysis and become skillful at discerning the assumptions, attitudes, concerns, and beliefs of classical and contemporary authors and producers. They need to deeply understand what Shakespeare, Maya Angelou, and Steven Spielberg propose about the human condition. And they should learn to respond to these assumptions from the Christian Seventh-day Adventist worldview.
- Students should learn to skillfully and honestly apply the tools of historical investigation to documents and events. They should learn to appraise the uses of power, the clash and rise and fall of nations, issues of justice and human rights, and the needs of nations and states, and do so from the Christian Seventh-day Adventist worldview.
- Students must learn to reverse-engineer creation by applying the scientific method with skill, honesty, and fluency. They should, without fear, consider the evidence of ice cores, cell functions, cosmic background radiation, and DNA. And they should learn to interpret the

- Students should learn to mine Scripture for its meaning by carefully using the tools developed by theologians—the historical critical method, textual criticism, and others. They should competently deduce the historical meanings of texts, the cultural assumptions of the writers, the multiple versions of the Creation story and of the fourth commandment, and the "jazz-like harmony of the four gospels" (devotional talk presented at the Adventist Association of Academic Administrators by Warren Trenchard, 2003). And they should learn to interpret these data from the perspective of our Seventh-day Adventist worldview.

This educational pattern can be replicated for each discipline. Students must be taught to discover truths that emerge as a result of the skillful and honest application of the tools of investigation and interpretation developed by the various disciplines, and, simultaneously, they should be taught to contextualize and understand them from the perspective of the Seventh-day Adventist who recognizes humans as creations of God, damaged by sin against God's will, and restored through the grace of Jesus Christ who continues to see value in each person. This does not mean that every idea or question will be neatly wrapped and tied with a Seventh-day Adventist bow by Friday noon of each week. It does mean that honest professors will help students to think critically and, in developmentally appropriate ways, to

- know how to engage ideas and investigate questions using the tools of each discipline;
- understand that there are ideas and beliefs within each discipline that comport with the Christian Seventh-day Adventist worldview;
- recognize that there are incomplete or contradicting data and that there are some facts and understandings that do not seem to fit easily into the Seventh-day Adventist worldview, and for which Seventh-day Adventists do not yet have a clear response;
- discern the difference between what one knows and what one believes; and
- know why the Christian Seventh-day Adventist worldview remains a robust model in the life and work of each professor who con-

tinues to investigate in his or her discipline without fear.

Thinking Christians, steeped in a Christian Seventh-day Adventist worldview, can confidently participate in contemporary culture, genuinely serving as the salt of the earth rather than seeking to avoid contamination by the ideas, concerns, conflicts, interests, and questions of all of God's children.

It is the joy of believers to be saved by the grace of Jesus Christ. It is the opportunity of every believer to grow in grace and to serve others. But it is the responsibility of university-educated believers to courageously engage the assumptions, beliefs, and truths of contemporary culture through a well-developed Christian Seventh-day Adventist worldview, and to stimulate our church to become increasingly clear about the positives which merit our appreciation, the injustices which require our criticism, and the circumstances which would benefit from our correction. Ellen White asserted, years ago, that

> A cultivated intellect is now needed in the cause of God, for novices cannot do the work acceptably. God has devised our college as an instrumentality for developing workers of whom He will not be ashamed (*Testimonies for the Church*, vol. 4, 1948, 426).

She believed that

> Ignorance will not increase the humility or spirituality of any professed follower of Christ. The truths of the Divine Word can be best appreciated by an intellectual Christian. Christ can be best glorified by those who serve Him intelligently. The great object of education is to enable us to use the powers which God has given us in such a manner as will best represent the religion of the Bible and promote the glory of God (Ibid., vol. 3, 1948, 160).

We would do well to remember that the Hebrew prophet Daniel was not tested by the Babylonian emperor in the finer points of Hebrew theology. Daniel and his companions were tested in the arts, sciences, and magic of Babylon and found, with God's assistance, to be ten times better equipped than "all the magicians and astrologers" (Daniel 1:17–20). It was Daniel's ability to use the knowledge of Babylon in the context of his Hebrew worldview that allowed him to serve with distinction in successive pagan kingdoms and to promote the kingdom of God.

The apostle Paul, the most prolific writer of the Christian Scriptures, was able to quote pagan authors and to use the language of both the educated Greeks as well as the most pious

Hebrews. Yet his well-developed worldview allowed him to apply those sources in unique ways that promote the gospel and continue to be challenging and relevant to readers almost two millennia later.

Conclusion

Although employees in our Seventh-day Adventist institutions may be cross-trained to some degree, generally, it is the case that local church pastors and evangelists are not well-equipped, either by education, role, or by access, to help individuals build, refine, and apply complex worldviews. That is, after all, not their primary function. Most have not found it necessary to become fluent in the various academic subjects or to obtain a nuanced understanding of young adults' developmental learning readiness. Furthermore, their professions generally do not offer the resources for conducting academic research, as is more common among teachers and professors. But, Seventh-day Adventist higher education can offer a crucial and complementary service to the overarching gospel commission of the church. Academics have the disciplinary preparation, the resources, and the time for research; as well as sustained interaction with students; which enable them to address complex and critical issues and to seek honest answers and solutions shoulder to shoulder with their students. And in doing so, educators assist students as they develop worldviews that are faithful, robust, and productive.

I propose that, if Seventh-day Adventist students and their parents clearly understood the importance and lifelong impact of one's worldview, recognizing how one's worldview shapes all of one's understandings, beliefs, and choices presented by contemporary science and culture, they would seriously question whether public, or even other Christian, institutions of higher education are able to provide a satisfactory education for them. It may be that this more precise division of labor, aligned more closely with the differing dispositions and skills of pastors, evangelists, and professors, would revitalize appreciation of, and a felt need for, Seventh-day Adventist higher education.

Bibliography

Benne, Robert. *Quality With Soul: How Six Premier Colleges and Universities Keep Faith With Their Religious Traditions.* Grand Rapids, MI: William B. Eerdmans Publishing Company, 2001.

Bolman, Lee G. and Terrence E. Deal. *Reframing Organizations: Artistry, Choice, and Leadership.* San Francisco, CA: Jossey-Bass, 2008.

Holmes, Arthur F. *The Idea of a Christian College.* Grand Rapids, MI: William B. Eerdmans Publishing Company, 1975.

Hughes, Richard T. *How Christian Faith Can Sustain the Life of the Mind.* Grand Rapids, MI: Wm. B. Eerdmans Publishing Co., 2001.

James, Jennifer. *Thinking in the Future Tense: A Workout for the Mind.* New York, NY: Touchstone, 1996.

Knight, George R. *A Search for Identity: The Development of Seventh-day Adventist Beliefs.* Hagerstown, MD: Review and Herald®, 2000.

———. *The Apocalyptic Vision and the Neutering of Adventism: Are We Erasing our Relevancy?* Hagerstown, MD: Review and Herald®, 2008.

Lipke, David J. "Pledge of Allegiance." *American Demographics* 22, no. 11 (November 2000): 40–42.

Palmer, Parker J. *The Courage to Teach: Exploring the Inner Landscape of a Teacher's Life*. San Francisco, CA: Jossey-Bass, 1998.

Pawluk, Steve. "Stewarding Our Resources." *CASE Currents*, February 2006.

Pearcey, Nancy. *Total Truth: Liberating Christianity From Its Cultural Captivity*. Wheaton, IL: Crossway Books, 2005.

Trenchard, Warren. Unpublished devotional presented at the Adventist Association of Academic Administrators, 2003.

White, Ellen G. *Education*. Nampa, ID: Pacific Press®, 1952.

_____. *Testimonies for the Church*. 9 vols. Mountain View, CA: Pacific Press®, 1948.

DOUGLAS HERRMANN

Chapter 10

The Caring Questioner: A Model for Educators

Give me a child until he stops thinking and I will show you the man.
—Doug Herrmann

During a research project that lasted a period of several months, I had the opportunity of working with thirty individuals in their thirties, all of whom had experienced Seventh-day Adventist education from grades one through eighteen. I was interested in discovering what affect their home, church, and school experience had on their current status in regards to Seventh-day Adventism. The interviews provided many insights, but most surprising to me was the number of interviewees who spoke of their college and young adult years as a time of significant growth and critical decisions. Many specifically mentioned individuals from these years who had a profound impact on their lives. Perhaps this comes as no surprise to many others.

Let me provide a bit of personal background. I recall what was possibly a passing comment by an elementary teacher when I was a child. It was a variation on the theme of "give me a child for the first seven years, and I will show you the man." This has bounced around in my thinking ever since. One might conclude that were this to be true, the role of Christian education is minimized. I have spent most of my professional experience with high school students and I am aware of the profound changes that occur during those very impressionable years. My thirty interviews illustrate that much growth occurs at later stages as well.

But what of the statement? Not surprisingly, its origin is uncertain. Most often it is attributed to Saint Ignatius of Loyola, the founder of the Society of Jesus. Is the maxim true? Is the person's character determined by his or her first seven years of life?

I propose that, while it may be true for the eight-year-old, there will remain many critical periods of growth and decision making. While no one would doubt the importance of the first years of life, we all face significant turning points in our lives at any age.

Attachment theory provides us with insights into this issue. While the word *attachment* could be misunderstood as a casual connection, psychologist John Bowlby had no such intention as he developed the theory. He described attachment as a "lasting psychological connectedness between human beings" (1982, 194). "Bowlby's landmark theory (1969, 1973, 1980) argues that childhood attachment forms the working model for a system of later attachment behavior that is active and influential throughout the lifespan" (TenElshof and Furrow, 2000, 100). Early bonding with the caregiver becomes the foundation for future development. Pehr Granqvist (2005) has applied this theory in the psychology of religion. It is a bit simplistic to reduce the large volume of work in this area to one idea. However, in respect to this present issue, an individual's view of God is greatly affected by his or her earliest social connections. "Some believers' relationships with God bear striking resemblances to the child's attachment to caregivers, and seem to meet important criteria for defining attachment relationships" (36).

To what degree will a child's attachment to the caregiver dictate the adult's relationships, especially the relationship with God? The findings of Granqvist (2005) certainly have implications for educators as they consider the process of spiritual growth and developing maturity. However, the influences of the caregiver during childhood need not dictate adult attachment patterns. Judith TenElshof and James Furrow (2000), in a study of the spiritual maturity of seminary students as it relates to secure attachment theory, draw this very important conclusion:

> The faith maturity of seminary students is explained in part by their current relational attachments, even over and above their childhood attachments. This means that God's incarnational ministry impacts development in a nonlinear manner, and students are not doomed by their childhood experiences. Adult relationships can impact students' spiritual lives (106).

They conclude that, even at the seminary level, teachers must intentionally create a nurturing Christian community where students are mentored by adults. "[A]s a professor and student develop a secure style of relating, including the imparting of wisdom, virtue, and security to explore new ministry to others, the student will find it easier to trust and get close to others including God" (2000, 106).

While one cannot discount the foundation of home and early schooling, a majority of interviewees, in my study, pointed to an individual from their young adult years as a key influence in their life. It is during the college years that they experienced freedom more than they have probably ever had before. Not surprisingly, the adults, the professors, they encountered represented a change from the home and the high school, and there was a natural openness to the influence of these people.

For Jocelyn, one of my interviewees, this period included a significant clash with her church. She found that her college-campus church had an energetic worship style that appealed to her. She became involved and her enthusiasm for church increased. However, some of the older members of the college church were not as pleased with the direction the church was going and spoke against the students and the style. She described her reactions in these words:

I just remember being so frustrated with the hypocrisy that was taking place in the church at that time. I was sick and tired of watching them judge us and then turn around and do their own thing that maybe was just as bad. You know, it's like they're sitting there criticizing me for something yet they're doing the same thing or something worse and I was so frustrated. I thought if this is the kind of church, if this is what Adventists are about, I don't want any part of it. I don't [want] to raise my kid this way. I don't want to be a part of it.

It was at this low point that she received an annual survey to fill out. She was part of the ten-year study being carried out by Roger Dudley of Andrews University (2000). Every year for ten years she responded to questions about spiritual development. The survey for that year arrived while she was experiencing this frustration with her church. When asked if she would send her children to Seventh-day Adventist schools, she took the occasion to unload her thoughts and feelings. If what she was experiencing was typical of how young people were going to be treated, she did not want any child of hers to grow up in such an environment. A short time later, she received a personal reply from Dudley encouraging her to keep her eyes focused on Jesus. There will always be people like that, he explained, but she would have to learn to let it go. Her relationship with God was most important. Jocelyn continued,

> It was a lightbulb moment for me. And once that really clicked, that it was all about my relationship with God and not what anybody else was doing, not what anyone else in the church was saying or doing or thinking of me, I thought, who cares? They don't have anything to do with my salvation. And once I got that, it made Christianity so much more alive for me and made God much more alive.

Jocelyn's experience is a simple example of the influence that one person can have when he or she takes time out to encourage and to help. She was between her junior and senior years in college. One might have thought that the time for influencing was past, that now it was up to her to work it out. But a researcher read the struggle that came through the written response and stepped out of his role, taking the time to interact with one of his subjects. That experience became a turning point for her.

Kelly faced a crisis as well. She grew up as a missionary child, steeped in Adventism. Her personality and environment led her to almost extreme levels of activity and involvement. After several years of studying in self-supporting Adventist institutions, she had grown weary of an emphasis on behavior and works. To her, it seemed that the focus was more on rules than on people, and that just didn't make sense to her. Such an emphasis did not fit with the picture of God that she had learned from her family and her study of the Bible. The doctrines of the church, she felt, were right, but she just never believed that she could ever be good enough. She heard a sermon at camp meeting on the assurance we can have of salvation and was enthralled. She made a point to talk with the speaker and over the next six months that very busy man exchanged letters with her about twice a week, helping her sort out her thinking. This relationship was her turning point. She has, in turn, been able to work with many young people coming from similar backgrounds, helping them to grasp a richer perspective of salvation.

Walter experienced a conversion from nominal, cultural-only Adventism to a Christ-centered relationship. He places the credit for this, besides the obvious promptings and conviction of the Holy Spirit, to a pastor who opened his eyes to the life of Jesus. This happened after he had graduated and been married. That pastor was able to mentor this young adult in his spiritual development.

These examples are of adult mentors working with young adults. Though two were in school, the association had nothing to do with the schools they were attending. In each case, the teachable moment was addressed by people willing to become involved. But make no mistake; teachers and professors in colleges and universities have the potential of having a profound effect on individuals on a daily basis.

As TenElshof and Furrow (2000) point out, adult mentors can have an effect on the college or seminary student that exceeds even that of the parents. How one is raised is not the final determining factor. Decisions are being made in the university years that can be meaningfully influenced by the relationships formed with professors and other adults in the school.

"Here, read this." This is a most basic type of an assignment. It is done thousands of times a day in schools around the world. Individuals do the same thing less formally among friends. "You've just got to read this book!" or "I want you to read this article. It's what we were talking about." The written word provides one with an opportunity to share an idea that he or she agrees with, struggles with, or has questions about. An individual can encourage someone, inspire someone, instruct someone, or even disturb someone, depending on what he or she chooses to share.

The power of the shared document is affected by the person sharing it. If a random person in the street gives a piece of literature to a stranger, he or she is as likely to throw it away as to read it. That reading assignment does not carry much weight. However, if a teacher, in a class in which the individual wants to do well, tells him or her to read a certain article for a discussion and a quiz, the person will more likely study it very carefully. And if that teacher is also someone admired, perhaps even seen as a mentor, the assignment becomes an endorsement of the writing. Not only will it be read, but it will more likely have a significant effect on the individual. In this way and others, college and university professors are in a position of great influence.

Consistently, as the participants in my study looked back over their lives through the course of the interviews—having occasion to consider their homes growing up, their local church experiences, as well as school, including the elementary years, the tumultuous and impressionable high school years, college and beyond—many of them pointed out a college event or person that made the difference.

Don's experience in college provides a good example. He chose a college in part due to its geographically being the farthest from both parents. Home had provided no security for him, nor had his education offered any inspiration. He recalls his Bible teacher in academy refusing to allow discussion because, if the class did take time for the exchange of students' ideas, there would not be enough time to cover all of the material. So perhaps he was more open than most for a professor to take him under his wing. Don found such a man in the anthropology professor on campus.

The professor handed Don a book and said, "Here, read this." Don did so and his questions started flowing. He went to his professor with several questions about religion and God. The professor agreed that they were good questions and responded by giving him another book. After reading that book, Don had more questions. He was not able to reconcile the issues raised with the teachings of Christianity, and he found no one who could help. As he put it,

> I never really had anyone who took me under their arms and said, "Let's work through this together. Let's go to the Bible. Let's see what the Bible has to say. Let's study it. What does God's Word really mean?" And I think really, the reason why was because none of them had really been given the gospel. None of them understood grace. None of them could go to the Bible and say, "Well, this is what it says, here's what it means, this is where we're going, this is how it all fits together, and these are the issues you have that you shouldn't be worried about."

Now, undoubtedly, he did not go to all the professors to which he possibly could. But clearly, that one professor had a significant influence. While Don does not call it a mentor–mentee relationship, he has this to say about it:

> We never had the chance to sit down and actually explore in a true mentor style relationship what that meant. I moved on by then. But, I mean, he at least planted the seed that caused the roots which caused the walls to crack.

He goes on to summarize this man's influence in these words:

> [H]e's responsible for driving me out of the church because he gave me the intellectual—it's a question I was handed and the bad thing was, well, how can God give you the gift of intellectual freedom and then tell you not to ask those questions because it's not appropriate. I said that's not the kind of God I want to serve.

In Don's view, the professor rendered him a great service. In light of the mission of the Seventh-day Adventist institution in which he was enrolled, many would say he was rendered a great disservice. Clearly, the incident illustrates the great influence of the teacher.

Admittedly, there exist very difficult theological questions. A student encountering these challenges either embraces the doubt and chooses against religion, or he or she faces the doubts and discovers a solution. How a teacher or a parent reacts to the student who is experiencing this struggle is a fundamental issue in education. The evidence of my interviews reveals that mentors and teachers, either in the school, home, or church, who help students navigate through the hard questions, play a major role in those students remaining Christians and Adventists.

Like Don, Judy was significantly influenced by a university professor. She became an atheist during her college years after taking a philosophy class at a state university. She has more recently adopted Buddhist philosophy but still does not believe in a God. Judy is quick to identify that particular philosophy professor as the primary influence in her eventual decision to not be an Adventist or a Christian. She insists that it was not the church, home, or school that drove her away.

I am inclined to propose a variation on the adage mentioned above: "Give me a child until he or she stops thinking and I will show you the person." It is the responsibility of educators in the home, the church, and the school to nurture the skill of thinking and reasoning. Several of the interviewees with whom I worked spoke of having that environment as they matured.

Erin grew up in a very conservative Adventist home. Though her parents were clear in their desires that their daughter attend an Adventist college, which she in fact did choose to do, throughout her life they also recognized that she was a particularly inquisitive child and would not be satisfied with pat answers. So whenever she expressed interest in a different religion, they would take her to that church. Erin put it this way:

> When I wanted to be Buddhist, they took me to the Buddhist temple, or I wanted to be Catholic they took me to a Catholic church, and a Baptist, to a Baptist church. But they were there and they guided me. And now I know the difference between half-truth and truth and I know where to go and look and find the source. When other people say, "Oh you know, this prophet said this," I can say, "Well, you also believe in the Bible, right? Yes? Well this is what the Bible says."

Lori appreciated having a similar experience in her academy years. Her junior religion class was a study of Seventh-day Adventist beliefs and doctrines. The teacher would bring in representatives of other religions to present a firsthand account of their teachings. So rather than just hearing about Jehovah's Witnesses, for example, they were able to hear from someone, ask questions, and then compare and discuss.

Ted appreciated the opportunity to visit

other churches. He recalls specifically going to a Jewish synagogue, but also refers to his experience in Bible class of comparing religions. His affirmation of the Seventh-day Adventist Church is expressed in terms of that process.

> When I looked at [the beliefs of the Seventh-day Adventist Church], I didn't see anything that wasn't from the Bible. Well, when I would look at any other religion, I would see that they were doing something that seemed to me that wasn't straight from the Bible. Now that I've been around for a while, the only other church besides Adventism that seems to go straight from the Bible is the Calvary Chapel Church. And I really like what they have to say. But I hear their beliefs on Sabbath and I don't agree with it. So Adventism is the only way for me.

In the office where I worked as an associate superintendent of schools for a district of Seventh-day Adventist schools, we received letters from students as part of an application process for scholarship money. The letters addressed one reason why the applicants wish to attend a Seventh-day Adventist school. One student wrote the following:

> The most important reason why I wish to continue my education at the academy is the Christian atmosphere. Knowing that the school is based on Seventh-day Adventist principles helps me feel more relaxed and confident. We are taught about other religions and cultures so that we can understand why other people believe what they believe. This also helps me understand why being a Seventh-day Adventist is the best choice for me. Sometimes I feel myself starting to doubt my religion and God, but the teachers at my school have never failed to answer any questions that I might have. The best thing about this is that they never judge me or make me feel uncomfortable about asking questions.

This young lady has had the good fortune of having teachers who allowed exploration. Her teachers also were aware of the importance of remaining with the student throughout the process.

Marvin is representative of a significant group of people in the church as well as the general population. Like Erin, the Marvins of the church question things. A traditional answer given without reasons does not suffice. "Because Mrs. White says so," is a particularly troublesome answer to these people. They are comfortable with arguing and find it to be an important part of learning and exploration. Not surprisingly, Marvin had many conflicts with his father, who was, for much of his early education, his principal as well as his teacher. A major point of contention was Sabbath keeping. Many arguments began with, "What's wrong with . . ." Standard answers were provided, but were not accepted. He also observed that in many families, what was once not OK on Sabbath eventually was accepted. These observations were part of his ultimate conclusion that religion is a man-made construct and, eventually, he questioned the very existence of God.

When Marvin reached high school age and began to have his father as a teacher, the conflict came to a head. His father decided that a junior academy was too small for both of them and, in the middle of his sophomore year, sent him to boarding school.

Marvin loved the new school. He found a creative outlet in drama. His science teacher encouraged his inquisitiveness and accompanied him on treks through the desert. His religion teacher asked probing questions and encouraged questions and discussion. Still, he never really got out of the Adventist bubble, as he called it.

Unfortunately, he found college to be pretty much a continuation of academy except that, ironically, the religion teachers were not at all open to questions or doubts. Only the pastor of the college church provided some relief, as he was willing to present controversial topics that stirred up the congregation. This was, to Marvin, how church should be.

It was during those years in college that he, for the first time, ventured outside of the bubble. He took some classes at the local university and discovered a new world filled with people who were of other denominations and beliefs. Because they were all correct, at least in their own eyes, he concluded that they might just as easily all be wrong. Thus, his conclusion about religion being a human construct was nearly complete.

The final step in the process of leaving the church involved his father's illness and death. When people said they were praying for his father's healing, he decided that prayer made no sense. If there was a God, he would know what was best and would do it anyway. Answered prayer was not a miracle, but rather chance, because unanswered prayers were simply explained as God saying, "No."

While it is difficult to determine what should have been done differently, analysis of my research data suggests that Marvin, and other students like him, are best served by supportive exploration with teachers that allows for discussion and even argument. Had a teacher or mentor joined Marvin in exploring his ideas and questions, much like his science teacher had done with him on their treks in the desert, he would likely have been better prepared for the issues he ultimately faced.

In summary, two points emerged from my analysis of the interviews on this point. First, providing an environment that allows for the natural questioning of young people is a critical element in faith development and denominational loyalty. This element would include the age-appropriate posing of questions, challenging individuals to think in new directions. Second, the individual creating the environment or posing the questions, be it parent, or pastor, or professor, needs to remain as an active participant in the process. That person need not, ought not, always provide answers; rather, he or she supports, guides, and encourages along side.

In my interviews, I used the term *mentor* without defining it and the candidates responded with their own filter. My intent was to suggest someone who was more than "just a teacher." I found it interesting that when any of my thirty interviewees described a favorite teacher, there was no essential difference whether speaking of an elementary, high school, or college teacher. The key word was that the individual cared for the students.

Jocelyn spoke very highly of her college experience primarily because she recalls the professors at the school knew her and called her by name whenever she encountered them on campus. Gina tells about one of her nursing instructors seeing that she got a special coupon to buy an extra required scrub top because she knew that Gina was a single mom and needed the help. Shirley was very impressed with her history professor, who made a point of attending her football games. In short, good teaching, call it mentoring or not, is a function of relationship whether one is in kindergarten or graduate school. Tom put it this way:

> I think education so much boils down to the teacher that's giving it. I think that's huge, the take that they have on things, you know, they're just not offering information, they're offering who they are in the material that they give, and that's huge, that's huge.

Young people are best served by an open approach to their questioning. Not allowing for their curiosity does not make it go away, as Don will attest. The Bible teacher that had no time for open discussion in his religion class did not serve his students well. The parents that allowed their daughter to ask questions about other religions, even taking her to experience and explore those faith traditions, provided a safe and authentic environment for investigation. Encouraging academic curiosity and exploration may not always be neat or easy. Doing so can even destroy a lesson plan. But a primary goal of Adventist education, as stated by Ellen White, is helping students become thinkers and not mere reflectors of others' thoughts (1903, 17).

So allow the questions, encourage the struggle, and stay around for the whole process of helping students to navigate the difficult areas. The questions, topics, and depth of discussions will change as the student grows, but the process is always important. Mentoring is not a matter of simply dispensing information and asking questions; it is a matter of caring. It involves leading and prodding another individual, opening him or her up to new ideas and understandings within a context of a relationship that has developed between the student and the teacher. The kindergarten teacher knows this; the university teacher must never forget it.

Bibliography:

Bowlby, J. *Attachment* [vol. 1 of *Attachment and Loss*]. 2nd ed. New York: Basic Books, 1982.

Dudley, R. L. *Why Our Teenagers Leave the Church: Personal Stories From a 10 Year Study.* Hagerstown, MD: Review and Herald®, 2000.

Granqvist, P. "Building a Bridge Between Attachment and Religious Coping: Tests of Moderators and Mediators." *Mental Health, Religion and Culture* 8 (2005): 35–47.

TenElshof, J. K., and J. L. Furrow. "The Role of Secure Attachment in Predicting Spiritual Maturity of Students at a Conservative Seminary." *Journal of Psychology and Theology* 28, no. 2 (2002): 99–109, 13p.

White, Ellen G. *Education.* Mountain View, CA: Pacific Press®, 1903.

Section 3

External Perspectives

E. GRADY BOGUE

Chapter 11

A Place for "Dreamers of Day": The Heritage Distinctions of Higher Education in America

And ye shall know the truth, and the truth shall make you free.
—John 8:32

And the gift which the University has to offer is the old one of imagination. . . . It is a dangerous gift, which has started many a conflagration. If we are timid as that danger, then the proper course is to shut down our universities.
—Alfred North Whitehead, *The Aims of Education*

In the early years of the twenty-first century, American higher education is challenged by multiple issues: increasing access and enhancing diversity, insuring quality and demonstrating accountability, managing under-revenue constraints and seeking new revenue sources, improving productivity and making proper response to marketplace management pressures, increasing retention and graduation rates, and putting technology to work. For many colleges, we may add the tension between institutional and intercollegiate athletic missions. Finally, some religiously affiliated institutions have been navigating turbulent doctrinal and governance waters with their sponsoring religious fellowships.

In this essay, our first intent is to celebrate the distinctive and complex mission of both secular and faith-based colleges in America. Secondly, we plan to canvass the changing demographic, economic, socio-cultural, and technological context in which colleges serve. Thirdly, we explore the special challenges in pursuing and communicating truth in faith-based colleges, balancing reason and revelation. Finally, we offer personal reflections on Adventist higher education, perceptions from one with secular higher education experience, but having enjoyed extended association with Adventist higher education.

Mission complexity in American higher education

How are colleges distinguished from other organizations, especially corporate enterprises? As earlier noted, at a time when there are important pressures to "corporatize" the university—to accent efficiency, to view the student as customer, to offer accountability evidence, to maximize revenue sources, to employ marketplace principles in collegiate leadership and management—we will want to understand how a college community is distinctive from a corporate enterprise, and more especially for a college with religious affiliation.

There are distinctions in mission, in governance, and in outcome that mark the collegiate organization (Bogue and Aper, 2000). On the theme of mission and motive, American higher education is expected to be both cultural curator and cultural critic, to honor heritage and to assault the limitations of common sense. Universities are expected to teach their students a reverence for democratic and cultural heritage and at the same time teach them to frame probing questions that challenge conventional wisdom. This is an expectation destined to keep our colleges and universities in the spotlight of public scrutiny and in the crucible of criticism. Mission complexity is further exemplified in multiple mission expectations, as follows:

- **Transmission**—the teaching and learning mission
- **Discovery**—the research mission
- **Application**—the public service mission
- **Conservation**—the library and information services mission
- **Renewal**—the continuing education mission
- **Evaluation**—the public forum and policy analysis mission

None of these six mission expectations have outcomes that yield to a single data point expression.

American colleges and universities constitute a system of both privilege and opportunity in which elitist and egalitarian impulses contend. It is a system in which the principle of autonomy, so essential in the pursuit of truth and in the nurture of democracy, is in dynamic tension with the principle of accountability, which is an antidote to professional arrogance and intellectual narrowness.

Colleges and universities constitute an organized assault on the perimeters of common sense and the bondage of superstition. The birth of new truth may contradict conventional wisdom and discomfort majority belief.

Adding to this complexity of mission are nuances of governance and culture. There are many stakeholders who could claim a legitimate voice in addressing questions of higher education purpose and performance: students, faculty, administrators, parents, civic friends and political officers, board members, leaders of closely affiliated organizations (e.g., religious leaders), and alumni. Thus, the ambiguous governance processes, the concept of shared authority among this extensive range of stakeholders, and the tedious processes of consensus decision making add to the challenge of understanding the nature of a college or university.

If the complexity of mission and governance were not sufficient challenges to understanding collegiate community, let us consider method. Conflict and argument are integral to the work of our colleges and universities. An organization whose mission embraces the unswerving search for truth, whose methods include the adversarial testing of ideas in public forum, whose spirit embraces a certain irreverence—such an organization will not find the search for community an easy one.

If we may borrow a thought agenda from Neal Postman (1996), American educational institutions are asked to serve many gods: the god of economic utility (get a job and be a competent worker), the god of consumership (spend money and acquire material possessions), the god of technology (use tools and be efficient), and the god of multiculturalism (accent and respect differences).

Postman (1996) goes on to suggest that America "is a story of continuing experiment, a perpetual and fascinating question mark" (71). In this view, America is a narrative of questions and arguments. American higher education, then, is a guarantor of democracy and a guardian of liberty, because in some ways higher education is an organized and continuous argument. Thus colleges and universities serve a critical and civilizing purpose in our society via the maintenance of argument, in serving as a forum in which contending ideas may be engaged in a public forum.

Here also is an enterprise often criticized for its ponderous processes, its momentum and culture making change difficult. There is something to be said, however, for the andante majesty of higher education in its pace of change. Nurturing truth and talent is an eminently personal occupation, a work of the long term whose success is not to be found in a neat balance sheet for the current quarter or year. It is a work largely of faith and optimism.

In the corporate sector, accents of policy and principle center on the motive of self-interest, the culture of competition, and the outcome of profit. In the collegiate sector, the accent is on seeking truth, on the culture of dissent and argument, and on the outcome of meaning and understanding.

Understanding the sometimes contradictory culture of higher education is not made any easier when we think about its outcomes. What test, what metric will serve to describe an "educated" man or woman? What value may we place on new truths and discoveries emerging from research laboratories? Where is the number to circumscribe the economic and social impact of agricultural and industrial extension services? Will we use *U.S. News and World Report* college rankings as an outcome proxy for profit?

Higher education would appear to be the only enterprise in which one of its "products," an educated person, is also described as a "customer." Will market pressures distort the search for truth in colleges and universities? Will faculty become hired hands and entrepreneurs rather than discoverers of truth? Will college presidents become captains of enterprise, the new CEOs, rather than captains of erudition? Will the house of intellect become a house of merchandise where faculty are salespeople hawking their wares to credential hungry students? Will learning become just another consumer good?

The American college and university is a guarantor of an open society—a place where each citizen is equipped and encouraged to think for him- or herself, to challenge conventional wisdom, to ask obnoxious questions, to be a dangerous person. Where is the metric that will furnish evidence of higher education as a guarantor of an open society? It is a place where we are invited to think about what brings meaning to our lives, what makes us glad to be alive. It is a place of both faith and fact where the humanizing and elevating forces of curiosity and wonder are celebrated.

It is a place for what T. E. Lawrence described as "dreamers of day":

> All men dream, but not equally
> Those who dream by night in
>   the dusty
> Recesses of their minds
> Awake to find that it was vanity,
> But the dreamers of day are
>   dangerous men,
> That they may act their dreams
>   with open
> Eyes to make it possible.

"My Father's world": A changing context

These opening comments strike a celebratory, optimistic, and constructive tone. In this discussion, we turn to more cautionary matters. There's a classic old hymn that opens with the phrase "This is my Father's world . . ." Over the past century, that world has been changing dramatically and exponentially—shifting the social, cultural, economic, and political context in which our colleges and universities do their work

In the technological realm, we've seen the emergence of air and space travel, from a max of one hundred miles per hour in the late nineteenth century to twenty-five thousand miles per hour in late twentieth century. Will Einstein's assertion that we cannot travel faster than the speed of light be moved to the museum of discarded ideas in the years to come? We have changed perspectives on our world, from looking up via telescopes to looking down via satellites. We've seen the birth of computers from massive machines requiring immense spaces and air conditioning to the same computation power carried in a palm-held instrument, from the old ring-you-up, multiparty telephone to everyone with a cell phone connected anywhere in the world. The discovery and development of nuclear power has influenced the nature of war, medical and materials diagnostics, and power generation. Perhaps the most impressive and powerful conceptual birthing may lie in the discovery of DNA and the development of genetic engineering. Formidable ethical dilemmas are associated with all of these technologies.

Politically we saw the birth and death of Communism as a contending political philosophy. We experienced the transformation of apartheid in South Africa. We are experiencing a new globalization represented in the flow of money, energy, information, and influence across national borders (Wolf, 2004). And sadly, in what might be argued as the most educated moment in civilization, we experienced over the last century successive, barbaric acts of genocide—the killing of Armenians, the killing of millions of Russians between the two world wars, the Holocaust of World War II, the killing fields of Cambodia, the killing of thousands in Rwanda, and in the Sudan and in Bosnia and Kosovo (Power, 2003).

Our nation has become more diverse, with rapidly growing Hispanic and Asian minority populations. We are an older society. There are more single-parent families. In the last century, we took contentious personal and policy journeys in the elimination of the prejudicial treatment of women, of blacks, and of handicapped citizens.

A recent report from the National Center for Management Systems (2005) reveals that "By the year 2020, the U. S. Census Bureau projects a 77% increase in Hispanics, a 32% increase in African Americans, a 69% increase in Asians, a 26% increase in Native Americans, and less than a one percentage point increase in the White population" (Kelly, 2005, 1). These demographic shifts are important challenges for American higher education.

The differential earning power between college graduates and those with only high school or less than high school is well known, and the gap in earnings appears to be widening slightly—now an average of about twenty thousand dollars per year for one with less than a high school diploma to over seventy thousand dollars per year for someone with a graduate degree. Another economic indicator of incendiary potential is the escalating distance between the pay of those on the firing line and those in the executive suite. What was a 40 to 1 ratio in the early 1980s is now 500 to 1 (Tobias, 2003). The salary gap between college administrators and college faculty and staff is also growing, a point to which we will return in a moment.

While the percentage of U.S. citizens holding bachelor's degrees increased in the twenty years from 1980 to 2000, we have fallen behind several other countries such as Sweden, Canada, Norway, and South Korea. This latter matter speaks directly to the ascendant role that U.S. higher education has historically played in international education. Whether we will remain as attracting amidst a growing competition from other nations is an open question.

The "pipeline" problem on the loss of students as they move from ninth grade to high school graduation and then to college and graduation remains a challenge. While this challenge may be fairly assigned to educational leadership at every level, as I earlier noted, it helps to remember that college students are the only customers simultaneously referred to as products. They participate in an enterprise in which the quality of the outcome—an educated person—is codependent: that is, not totally dependent on the quality, the discipline, and the effort of faculty and staff. Students make contributions to the quality of their own outcome—deciding what investment of time and thought they will make in their educational efforts. Moreover, students are not isolated from the aspirations, and influence, of parents and peers and other models and mentors in their lives.

On this last matter, American higher education scholar George Keller has noted that, "It is popular sport in the United States to castigate schools and colleges; critics seem to imagine that students and classes are immune to powerful new forces such as broken and fatherless families, television, urban crime and violence, drugs, computers and rock music" (2009, xi).

On the other end of this traditional age pipeline is the growing number of older Americans, who are referred to as "woopies" (well-off older people). Their age does not dull their curiosity, and this is a new client base that higher education has begun to recognize more fully.

Keller speaks with fact and force about this contextual transformation in his book *Higher Education and the New Society* (2009), published posthumously. In exploring demographic shifts, Keller remarks that between 1960 and 2000 the divorce rate in this country more than doubled. The percentage of children born to unwed mothers moved from 6 percent to 35 percent. Among black Americans, the illegitimacy rate is approaching 65 percent. Some 63 percent of out-of-wedlock births are now to white and Hispanic women. About 39 percent of the poor today in our society are children.

We have been concerned, and rightly so, about improving programs of financial aid as an instrument to promote college access. Perhaps we should frame a federal policy requiring good parenting.

On the technology transformation front, Keller recounts the invention of writing and movable print as two historical technical/communication breakpoints. The new digital revolution now means that most of us are trying to do two things at the same time—whatever we are doing and talking on the cell phone. Cell phone technology and laptop computers have also ushered in a new form of incivility: the euphemism for this incivility is multitasking—pretending that we are listening to a speaker or teacher while we text, tweet, e-mail, or launch an Internet search on our Blackberry or iPod. One wonders whether the future will bring a time when we send and receive but no longer think.

If we read chaos theory, we learn that the flap of a butterfly wing in China may eventually affect the weather in North America. Clearly, we experience such far-flung ripples and interdependencies in our new globalized economics. We have already cited Wolf as premier commentator. Others include Thomas Friedman (2005) in *The World Is Flat* and Pat Choate (2008) *in Dangerous Business: The Risks of Globalization for America*—detailing the evidence and the dangers of globalization.

Countries such as China offer low-wage rates, and the tendency for American manufacturers to "move off shore" is great, often leaving behind devastated local economies and out-of-work folks. Some claim that we have moved to the information economy. If, however, America does not make anything, what will we have to talk about? What others are making?

Keller makes passing reference to the effect of terrorism on our economic system; that development is a dramatic new challenge to civilization. War has a new face. In the past, uniformed armies representing one nation faced off against a uniformed and well-recognized enemy from another nation. The events of 9/11 changed all this. Any small group with a cell phone and a bomb (conventional or nuclear) can wage asymmetric war—striking at weak points in our transportation, electrical, communications, and infrastructure (water and highways) systems. For Americans, war has historically been "over there"—but not anymore. A small dollar investment can produce a multibillion dollar cleanup. More critical to any society, but especially to a democratic society, such acts bring disorder. Order is both a fragile and essential condition of an open and free society.

Not extensively explored in Keller's informing little book are major stories of the seduction of leadership conscience in every field of endeavor in our society. Wealthy executives, such as Ken Lay of Enron Corporation (who held a PhD), kill off their own companies and send employees and retirees into economic depression, with loss of personal savings and retirement benefits.

CEOs take multimillion-dollar bonus packages and retirement benefits, while they are asking employees to take pay cuts to keep the corporation out of bankruptcy (Bogue, 2007). Wall Street banking and corporation executives accept multimillion-dollar bonuses, while they are asking the American taxpayer and government for bail out money to keep their banks and manufacturing enterprises from bankruptcy and insolvency. In addition, the steep decline in the stock market associated with this mess lowered the value of both personal and institutional investment accounts. College CEOs (formerly known as presidents) take big dollar salary increases while their faculties labor in the salary doldrums and their staff in below-poverty wage zones. What has happened to sear the consciences of our corporate and collegiate leaders?

From what college or university did these "Conscience Empty Officers" (a new way to think about the acronym CEO) graduate? Can you remember reading about their higher education heritage in *USA Today* or the *Wall Street Journal*? Colleges have to make a public report on campus crime rates. Perhaps we should require a new accountability report on alumni crime rates. Are American colleges educating for competence but failing to touch the conscience and the heart?

This seems like a useful segue to our final theme—the special challenges of the religiously affiliated college and, more specifically, the future of Adventist higher education.

Heritage and challenge in faith-based colleges and universities

Faith once required a belief that the earth was the center of the universe and that the earth was flat. It took the dissent of Galileo and the evidence of seafaring explorers who did not fall off the end of the earth to dislodge these "truths." We are years past the accepted theory that disease and illness were carried by "humors" in the blood and that what was needed for an ill patient was to have leeches placed on him or her to bleed out these ill humors. Is truth a platform that we stand on to discover our error and to move forward in our understanding of self and universe? Are our colleges and universities not a premier instrument for challenging conventional wisdom in every field and advancing to new understandings and truth?

Nothing is clearer in the history of American higher education than the religious foundations, primarily Christian, that served as the motivating aspiration behind the founding of early American colleges and that continue to birth many religiously affiliated colleges in our nation. The current mission of Harvard University does not read like its original mission charter in which the second article read that "Every one shall consider the main End of his life and studies, to know God and Jesus Christ which is Eternal Life" (Hofstader and Smith, 1961, 8). This evolution in mission points to a difficult journey that many faith-based and religiously affiliated institutions have taken and continue to take as they struggle to serve their sponsoring religious fellowships and to serve the call of truth. Benne has nicely described that journey from soul to secular in his informing book *Quality and Soul* (2001).

Doctrinal and governance ferments abound as the governing bodies of religious fellowships understandably look to their colleges to affirm and perpetuate the religious principles and heritage of the fellowship, and the colleges struggle to avoid the smothering effect of doctrinal rigidity that brooks no dissent or discussion on the unfolding of religious understanding.

A premier issue faced by the faith-based college is how to honor religious heritage while cultivating curiosity in every form of human endeavor—and whether that light of curiosity will be focused on its own religious heritage. Arthur Holmes writes in *The Idea of a Christian College* that "While Scripture is our final rule of faith and practice, not all the truth about everything is fully revealed therein" (1975, 63).

Clearly, we take journeys of understanding. The wording of the Bible remains steadfast, though several translations attempt to bring clarity to the King James Version. Even so, the basic verses remain the same. When there are contested ideas between the Christian worldview and secular understanding, will we assume, as many religious scholars would insist, that the secular worldview must be flawed or in error? Clearly, however, the Christian worldview of the universe in the time of Galileo was the flawed view.

We no longer use the Bible to justify slavery or to confine women to making biscuits. So what has changed? Our understanding and our interpretation! Will the truth of the Good Book leap automatically to mind without having passed through an interpretation? Many religious fellowships are born from a new and fresh understanding of the Word, but then make the strange assumption that no other conceptual awakenings will occur on the meaning of the Word.

Here I wander into dangerous theological and philosophic territory, where minds much larger in capacity and preparation than mine have engaged the nature and source of truth and grappled with the friction between religiously affiliated campuses and their sponsoring religious fellowship.

Might the history of religious thought suggest, however, that while the Word remains constant our understanding and interpretation continue to unfold? How else to explain the proliferation of fellowships just within the Christian religion? Religious thought was revolutionized by the Reformation—and the Inquisition accompanying. Great cruelty was visited upon dissenters by those who would claim a heritage of love. There followed a birthing of understandings brokered by the many different contemporary religious fellowships, each offering a "new truth" about the meaning of the Scriptures. Too often these new births were marked by a bloody and prejudicial history and by cruel treatment of dissenters. We seem incapable of learning that matters of faith and love cannot be forced.

It is a wrenching matter to be caught between obedience and curiosity. As a person of faith who has spent his career in public higher education, with a sabbatical tour in a religiously affiliated university, this has been a "Gordian knot" issue in my own thinking and in my own religious journey. My resolution of this dilemma looks something like this. Clearly, there are multiple scriptural passages that depict and teach the costs of disobedience. However, if we are created in the image of God, might that include and affirm our inclination to curiosity, which some scholars suggest is the one thing that distinguishes our humanity from the other animals? Surely, then, believers are not expected to park their brains, to pose no questions. Does faith require the absence of thought or reflection? Are reason and revelation enemies? The question for faith-based colleges is how they can have their students live in the sanctuary of doctrinal teaching and in the arena of ideological contest at the same time.

How can I lay claim to a religious conviction if it has never been tested? Years ago, leaders in my church were furious that I invited friends from several other religious fellowships to visit a Sunday School class where we were studying religions of the world. Why just read about these, I reasoned, when we can experience the faith and belief in action via the testimony of those living in that belief? Into our study fellowship came the Methodists, the Baptists, the Seventh-day Adventists, the Mormons, the Catholics, the Presbyterians, the Episcopalians, the Church of Christ, the Jews, and others. Had we been more international in those earlier years, I might have had a Muslim there as well.

There is a story told that the ancient monks were engaged in a furious and intensive debate about the number of teeth in the mouth of a horse. A young, naive monk—unmoved by the tradition of syllogistic reasoning—suggested that a horse be brought into the fellowship and the teeth counted. He was, the account reported, "smote hip and thigh" and thrown from the fellowship. Well, I was not exactly smote hip and thigh and ejected from my own fellowship, but I got a good "talking to."

My reconciliation of this mission tension for religious colleges comes in an anchor verse from John 8:32, quoted in the opening of this essay. If Jesus says we are to know the truth and the truth will make us free, shall we fear the search for truth—especially in our colleges and universities?

This, of course, leads to the question of who is "under the tent" of religious fellowship?

I am a member of a fellowship where if fifty years ago you even thought about attending a Billy Graham revival or crusade, you would be subject to disfellowship. Our view on who might be under the tent of fellowship and entitled to enter heaven's gate has been transformed over the years—even though the wording of the Bible remains the same. How to account for the transformation of that understanding?

How do we balance the call of conviction and openness? My answer is that one cannot claim a conviction until it has been tested against a contending idea. And that is the heart of higher education culture and method. Was Jesus a dissenter, a radical, a heretic to conventional religious wisdom? He surely brought powerful and radically new ideas to the table of culture and religious belief in His teachings, and surely we must see those teachings as a challenge to the conventions and common sense of that time.

Colleges and universities are sanctuaries for scholars seeking truth on many fronts, using diverse methods, and honoring a wide variety of philosophic assumptions about the nature of truth. Scientists want an experiment and lawyers an adversarial hearing. Mathematicians want a logical argument and theologians a search of sacred literature. Sociologists want a compilation of opinion via interview or survey and historians an analysis of prime sources. Novelists, musicians, and visual artists bring an interpretative spirit to the enterprise. Scholars in the professions look to the practical application of ideas.

Is truth revealed, discovered, or constructed? The answer may be "Yes" to all three questions in the halls of the academy. Does truth exist independent of the observer, or is the observer a part of the truth event? Again the answer may be "Yes" on both counts. Is truth relative or absolute? "Yes!" As we noted, colleges and universities are companies of fact and faith—enterprises in which ideological conflict and argument are woven into their very fabric.

The soul of a university is a complex soul. I have several books in my library with the word *soul* in the title. One book is by Nobel Laureate Francis Crick and entitled

The Astonishing Hypothesis: The Scientific Search for Soul (1994).

Not surprisingly for a world-renowned scientist who, with James Watson, discovered the molecular structure of DNA, Crick's work centers on the scientific study of consciousness—a conceptual counterpoint to what he describes as "the hypothetical immortal soul." His "astonishing hypothesis is that 'You,' your joys and your sorrows, your memories and your ambitions, your sense of personal identity and free will, are in fact no more than the behavior of a vast assembly of nerve cells and their associated molecules" (Crick, 1994, 3). Such a view constitutes a jarring counterpoint to the spiritual nature of soul.

It is this idea of established disbelief that Marsden probes so well in *The Soul of the American University* (1994). He profiles the transformation in higher education's mission from instruction in religion, the study of moral philosophy, and belief in God to the ascendancy of science, pragmatism, and relativism. He poses this question on science and religion: "In a world where there were no longer self evident first principles based on God-created natural laws, what happened when allegedly scientific definitions of the 'good' conflicted? How could one argue, for instance, that all humans are 'created equal' if one denied that humans were created?" (375).

Now what do these ruminations on soul in general and on the soul of the university have to do with the nature of community in colleges and universities? First, scientific and religious inquiries coexist in the collegiate community. That scientific and religious inquiry can coexist—that these two wildly different assumptions about the nature of reality and the human experience can both guide inquiry within the community of higher education—is a matter of some marvel.

I cannot think of two volumes that speak more clearly to the contrasting but essential duty of the university to put forward cultures of reason and cultures of faith than Carl Sagan's *The Demon Haunted World* and Bishop Desmond Tutu's *No Future Without Forgiveness*. In *The Demon Haunted World*, Sagan presents science as a way of knowing that celebrates openness, that invites critical scrutiny of method and outcome. The science way of knowing, open to criticism and questioning, Sagan sees as a serious departure from the religious way of knowing that treats dissent as wickedness and waywardness of heart and questions as an act of disloyalty and disobedience.

However, it was not science—not physics, chemistry, or biology—that moved Nelson Mandela and others in South Africa to create The Truth and Reconciliation Commission once he was released from his apartheid-driven, twenty-seven-year confinement in a South African prison to become prime minister of South Africa. Writing in *No Future Without Forgiveness*

(1999), Bishop Tutu describes the extraordinary foundation of this commission in works of public forgiveness for wrongful and mean acts committed under apartheid. Replacing "eye for eye" justice with forgiveness in the new nation has to be one of the most extraordinary political acts of history.

However, when physicists began to talk about alternative realities, parallel universes, and dark matter, we are led to the surprising idea that the hallway between science and religion may be shorter than we thought. When astronomers think about the big bang theory of the universe's origins, the theologians are anxious to solve the scientific dilemma of an effect without a cause by reference to the Genesis scripture, "In the beginning, God created the heaven and the earth." To talk about the soul of higher education, therefore, is paradoxical, because we must acknowledge that for some colleagues the concept of soul has no meaning. And how paradoxical can it be to acknowledge that the argument over the existence or nonexistence of soul is a part of the soul or essence of collegiate community?! (The rarely employed interrobang is certainly an appropriate punctuation here.)

The Adventist promise

As a part of my assignment for this essay, I was invited to bring an external perspective on the form and function of Adventist higher education. I should like to say immediately that my extended but periodic association with Adventist higher education has been of the most pleasant texture. As with most of our associations, my reflections are fashioned heavily by the hearts and minds I encountered in a single Adventist University, Southern Adventist University (SAU).

I had Adventist students in my doctoral classes at the University of Tennessee. One student was Dr. Ruth Liu, and she introduced me to incoming SAU president Dr. Gordon Bietz over a decade ago. I spent a year in a consulting relationship with Dr. Bietz and the university. I found him to be a leader of splendid values and effective instincts, a man in whom faith and behavior were lovingly linked. I met other men and women of the faculty and staff of SAU over those years in workshops and other settings and came to appreciate the loving care and conviction that their faith brought to the students and the community of the university. I was struck with the service spirit exemplified in the framing and pursuit of academic programs to serve the Adventist fellowship regionally and worldwide—in educational, healthcare, business, and religious settings.

I will not tell you that there were not occasional surprising moments. One such moment was as follows. A senior academic administrator relieved a subordinate academic administrator from his position. Now, being relieved from duty is not surprising but the mechanism was surprising. The subordinate administrator relieved of duty learned about his departure for the coming year not from a personal, eyeball-to-eyeball conference but from an impersonal action memorandum that simply informed him of what his salary for the new year would be (a notably lower salary). Religiously affiliated colleges are not free from the imperfections of conscience and flawed ethical thought.

This modest departure in effective leadership style notwithstanding, I was amazed at the devoted mission spirit associated with work at the university and the financial implications of that spirit. Striving to meet that mission spirit and to attract and hold men and women who might realize much larger financial recognition at competing secular institutions, is not a small leadership challenge. My conclusion is that Adventist higher education is not only a beacon of faith to those within the fellowship but to those without who are touched by the competence, conviction, and caring of Adventist exemplars.

Several collegiate beacons of faith are identified by Benne is his book *Quality and Soul* (2001), exemplars of colleges that have managed to avoid the secularization shift and remain steadfast to their religious heritage. Calvin College, Wheaton College, Baylor University, Notre Dame University, St. Olaf College, and Valparaiso University are cited as examples of institutions whose governing board members, faculty, and students come from the sponsoring tradition; whose academic and student life cultures reflect deep commitment to Christian worldviews. In my judgment, Southern Adventist University might qualify for Benne's list of exemplar religiously affiliated colleges.

Institutional beacons of faith, such as found in Adventist colleges, have been instrumental in our democracy and remain so. They keep alive the flame of faith and ensure that the moral and mental are linked. They encourage engagement of questions of meaning that may not be found in the numbers alone. They instill a commitment to character and service, to love and nobility. They are not morally neutral but stand to duty on calls of right and wrong.

Religiously affiliated colleges, such as Southern Adventist University, are an investment in both public and private conscience and are an instrument for the prevention of soul erosion in our society.

Is there a distinctive place for Adventist higher education in the overall fabric of higher education? The answer will be "Yes," so long as the adherents of the fellowship continue to entrust their sons and daughters to the loving and developmental care of Adventist colleges.

The uniting force of curiosity and wonder

Colleges and universities exist for purposes beyond developing knowledge, skill, and belief in our students. They must be more than a collection of buildings connected only by steam lines and fiber optic cables.

With all the complexity in mission and motive cited in these reflections, what provides the uniting force for the special and distinguishing character of American higher education? American higher education is a forum of fact and faith, where some truths reside in the numbers and some in the mist, but the search for truth is a uniting aspiration. It is a lively and often contentious argument over the nature of truth. It is a museum of ideas once fresh and energizing but now quaint and outmoded.

It is the home of our hope, where scholars labor to solve those problems that rob men and women of their dignity, their promise, and their joy. It is conservator of the record of our nobility and our barbarism. It is the theater of our artistic impulses. It is a forum where dissent over purpose and performance may be seen as evidence that higher education is meeting its responsibility for asking what is true, what is good, and what is beautiful. It is a place where all—students, faculty, and staff—are called to ask what brings meaning to their lives and makes them glad to be alive. It is, above all, a place where we celebrate the humanizing force of our curiosity and wonder.

A place for dreamers of day.

Bibliography

Benne, R. *Quality With Soul*. Grand Rapids, MI: William B. Eerdmans Publishing Company, 2001.

Bogue, E. *Leadership Legacy Moments*. Westport, CT: ACE/Praeger, 2007.

Bogue, E. and J. Aper. *Exploring the Heritage of American Higher Education*. Phoenix, AZ: Oryx Publishers, 2003.

Choate, Pat. *Dangerous Business: The Risks of Globalization for America.* New York, NY: Alfred A. Knopf, 2008.

Crick, F. *The Astonishing Hypothesis: The Scientific Search for the Soul.* New York, NY: Scribner, 1994.

Friedman. T. *The World Is Flat*. New York, NY: Farrar, Strauss, and Giroux, 2005.

Hofstader, R. and W. Smith. *American Higher Education: A Documentary History*. Chicago, IL: The University of Chicago Press, 1961.

Holmes, A. *The Idea of a Christian College*. Grand Rapids, MI: William B. Eerdmans Publishing Company, 1975.

Kelly, P. *As America Becomes More Diverse: The Impact of State Higher Education Inequality*. Boulder, CO: NCHEMS, 2005.

Marsden, G. *The Soul of the American University*. New York, NY: Oxford University Press, 1994.

Postman, N. *The End of Education*. New York, NY: Vintage Books, 1996.

Power. S. *"A Problem From Hell": America and Genocide.* New York, NY: Basic Books, 2003.

Sagan, C. *The Demon Haunted World*. NY: Ballentine, 1996.

Tobias, W. "How Much Is Fair?" *Parade Magazine,* March 3, 2003, 10, 11.

Tompkins, J. "The Way We Live Now." *Change*, November-December 1992, 13–19.

Tutu, D. *No Future Without Forgiveness.* NY: Doubleday, 1999.

Wolf, M. *Why Globalization Works*. New Haven, CT: Yale University Press, 2004.

JAMES A. TUCKER AND PRISCILLA TUCKER

Chapter 12

We Are Higher Education, and We Change Not

A 1980 Carnegie report contained a remarkable statement pertaining to the stability of universities:

> Taking, as a starting point, 1530, when the Lutheran Church was founded, some 66 institutions that existed then still exist today in the Western world in recognizable forms: the Catholic Church, the Lutheran Church, the parliaments of Iceland and the Isle of Man, and 62 universities. . . . They have experienced wars, revolutions, depressions, and industrial transformations, and have come out less changed than almost any other segment of their societies (Kerr, 1980, 9).

Our experience in studying leadership and learning over the past fifteen years has led us to an ongoing interest in the reasons for such stability. Is that stability unique to higher education? Or is it more likely a function of higher education's dependence on its organizational structure? That interest further led us to the emerging literature on learning organizations in general—as opposed to institutions, such as universities, whose primary function traditionally has been dedicated to learning.

Since the 1970s, when it became clear that the future of business and industry was at best changeable and at worst unpredictable, corporations have regarded learning as contributing to their competitive edge (Argyris and Schön, 1996, 1978; Senge, 1990). In order to support the learning necessary to maintain that edge, organizations began to implement ways in which to become *learning organizations*, including hiring *chief learning officers* (CLOs) to oversee the process. Even more recently, in 2002, the *CLO Journal* has emerged, a periodical that addresses the learning issues involved in operating a corporation.

What *is* a learning organization? According to most learning theorists, learning is represented by change—either change in behavior, change in knowledge, or both (Schunk, 2008). Is a learning organization, then, a random collection of learners in an organization, or is it something more than that—a more holistic concept within which the result is greater than the sum of its parts? Is a learning organization simply one that promotes learning by policy and by practice? Or is it all of the above or some subset of these and other elements? By extension, then, is a university a learning organization; is it just a collection of learners, or is it simply an organization dedicated to learning? Or is it both?

Several key authors have attempted to describe the learning organization. Among them are Nancy M. Dixon, M. Pedler, J. Burgoyne, Tom Boydell, and Peter Senge.

The essence of organizational learning is the organization's ability to use the amazing mental capacity of all its members to create the kind of processes that will improve its own (Dixon, 1994, 122).

A learning company is an organization that facilitates the learning of all its members and continually transforms itself (Pedler, Burgoyne, and Boydell, 1991, 1).

[Learning organizations are] organizations where people continually expand their capacity to create the results they truly desire, where new and expansive patterns of thinking are nurtured, where collective aspiration is set free, and where people are continually learning to learn together (Senge, 1990, 3).

Senge (1990) further supported his definition by describing five "disciplines" that characterize learning organizations:

1. *Systems thinking:* The actions, knowledge, and tools that, over time, comprise the framework of an organization.
2. *Personal mastery:* The ongoing process by which an individual realizes his or her highest level of proficiency.
3. *Mental models:* The internalized

assumptions that influence how we relate to the world.
4. *Building shared vision:* The process through which we become committed to a corporate goal (rather than simply acquiescing to it).
5. *Team learning:* The interaction that produces "extraordinary results" while individual members grow "more rapidly than could have occurred otherwise" (6–10).

In an interview with Alan Webber (1999), Senge further reflected on the landscape of organizational development by suggesting the adoption of the following biological metaphor: "At the deepest level, I think that we're witnessing the shift from one age to another. The most universal challenge that we face is the transition from seeing our human institutions as machines to seeing them as embodiments of nature" (180). Later in the interview, Senge advanced that "we need to think less like managers and more like biologists. We keep bringing in mechanics when what we need are gardeners" (184). An organization, including a university, then, can be thought of as a living entity—and, as such, it should be kept vital in order to grow and function effectively.

In this chapter, we will build on Senge's biological premise. The semantic relationship between *organism* and *organization* is an obvious one. Both are entities comprised of interrelated parts. Our purpose is not, however, to discuss the semantic meanings of the terms but to develop the idea that the nature of higher education is a function of the organization or organizations that provide it. To do so, we first will explore the concept of *organization* in terms of its similarity to the concept of *organism* by discussing the DNA of each and the effects of their DNA on change. We then will discuss the effects of biological and institutional DNA on organisms and on organizations. Finally, we will briefly explore the implementation of Seventh-day Adventist higher education in terms of how its philosophy and traditions affect its DNA-type structural and procedural elements and how that structure affects its ability to change.

Note: Metaphors have limitations, so comparisons between biological DNA and organizational DNA will be broad and should be interpreted with care.

Organic and organizational DNA

To begin the discussion, we have adopted two biological terms, *phenotype* and *genotype,* to introduce the DNA-based metaphor. Although the two terms typically describe living organisms, they are used here to facilitate a discussion of organizations as well. The *phenotype* of an organism is its appearance. The phenotype is superficial and can, as a result, reflect superficial change. Bleached or colored hair. Tanned skin. Weight loss or weight gain. All are phenotypical alterations. Other people may fail to recognize you as a result of such changes, but such changes do not alter your DNA. Losing a limb. Reshaping a nose. Even dramatic changes such as these do not change who you are fundamentally.

The *genotype* of an organism is its genetic makeup. The genotype is unseen and represents the essence of the organism. Changing oneself at the DNA level is a concept that can be discussed only in theory. You may want to be someone else, but genetically you cannot be anyone other than who you are. Organ transplants from one organism to another are possible only by suppression of the host's immune system, because the DNA of the host organism will not readily tolerate the alien DNA. The replacement organ is seen as an invading force to be rejected and deleted.

Using DNA metaphor, we propose that the workings of living organisms and organizations are analogous. Indeed, the proposition that biological DNA is at least metaphorically analogous to organizational DNA is a concept that has been widely suggested (Kransdorff, 2006; Senge et al., 1999; Baskin, 1998). In both types of DNA, the phenotype—or physical appearance—may change. Also in both, the genotype—or essence—remains constant. Just as biological DNA governs an organism's conception, growth, and ongoing survival, organizational DNA governs an institution's establishment, development, and ongoing operation.

What is organizational DNA? An organization is founded in accordance with the vision and mission of the individual or individuals who imbue it with certain values. It may take some time for these values to be clearly articulated, but when they are, they define the culture. They become traditions—and, as such, they become fixed. The organization remains true to its basic values throughout its existence. Administrators and employees may attempt to make changes within and to the organization, but they can make only superficial changes in the way the organization appears. Even as individuals come and go, the essence—the DNA—of the organization continues to emerge in the form of established traditions, and any attempts to make fundamental changes are at best temporary, lasting only as long as the presence of the individuals who champion them are present to suppress the organization's innate immune system. When an organization's fundamental traditions become concretized, they often lose the impact of their original meaning or purpose. They become little more than the bureaucratic ritual with which we are all so familiar. Hindered by tradition, significant, permanent organizational change is not just difficult; it is impossible to make. In short, owing to its organizational DNA, a mature organization not only *does not* change; it *cannot* change.

In a living being, transplanting within

the organism is simple; pelvic bone used as a graft to repair a shattered elbow, for example, is readily accepted. The organism accepts any part of itself moved to another part. But in the case of an organ transplant, the recipient's immune system must be suppressed in order for a foreign organ to be tolerated. As Mitch Leslie (1999) observes, what has to be overcome is the organism's natural rejection of alien organs:

> Organ rejection stems from the body's uncompromising xenophobia. The immune system tries to attack anything it identifies as foreign, making no distinction between harmful microbes and a potentially lifesaving organ transplant. Over the last 30 years, prospects for organ recipients have grown much brighter with the discovery of cyclosporine and other immune-suppressant drugs that stifle "acute" rejection, the body's immediate assault on a transplant. Without these drugs, immune attacks would destroy the transplanted organ within a few weeks.

Similarly, personnel may be replaced, procedures may be adapted to technology, and entire departments may be reorganized, but only as long as the actions are in keeping with the genotype of the organization. However, in order for a change in the genotype to take place and endure—a change in the mission, for example—established traditions must be suppressed in order for significant change to take place and for that change to endure. Unfortunately, organizational cyclosporine is nonexistent. Permanent fundamental change can occur only through the total demise of the old system.

Every organization has a life cycle. Every organization is conceived (e.g., by having the big idea), developed (e.g., by producing the business plan and being launched accordingly), and brought to maturity (e.g., by hiring staff and purchasing equipment). Every organization carries out its distinctive purpose. Its founding documents, artifacts, and fundamental values reflect its unique mission. And, of course, each organization also has a lifespan; it eventually declines (e.g., through product obsolescence, loss of investors, or the death of the principal partners) and dies (e.g., through cessation of production or services or through a buy-out that results in major changes). Partnerships dissolve and nations collapse. Whenever one organization dies, another is likely to take its place in one form or another. That new organization is likely to repeat the cycle, with founding documents, artifacts, and fundamental values that reflect its mission.

The futility of attempting institutional change

As already stated, every organization

is built on a set of fundamental values that dictate its practices. Individuals who do not adhere to the philosophy of the organization and who do not conform to its practices tend to be disgruntled. Because taking action against the organization only results in conflict, such individuals are likely to leave by one means or another. The organization always prevails in such situations, and people who remain do so either because they see no alternative or because they have found their comfort zone. If enough people call for a change in the fundamental values of an organization, however, a revolution occurs. As a result, the uprising either will be quelled or a new organization will be born. These conditions apply to an organization as small as a partnership and as large as a nation—even to a "league" of nations.

A nation might be considered as the ultimate learning organization, because a nation is a macro-organism. Government is the mechanism that a nation uses to organize and maintain its role and function, so even an institution as large as a national government can be thought of in terms that allow for growth and development. Consider the United States and the apparent astuteness that influenced its establishment. In setting up the new nation, the founding fathers made accommodations that they thought would allow the government to continue to evolve. The Bill of Rights and the U.S. Constitution allowed for changes to be made. Every four years, for example, a major turnover in government officials has the potential to take place. A problem exists with the fundamental premise, however. The accommodation for a periodic change in elected officials has little effect on change in nonelected personnel, who now represent a much larger portion of the government machine. Slowly but surely, the federal government is becoming concretized into an organization that cannot—and therefore will not—change. The current bureaucracy disallows the actions that could—and once did—bring about the periodic reformations, if not revolutions, that were intended to keep the government in line with voters' wishes. As with an immune system that attacks the body, the DNA of the original establishment now actually interferes with the intended purpose of the system.

The same holds true for universities. Consider an attempt to introduce a new academic program, say, a nontraditional master's degree that is significantly different from the traditional programs already in place. The introduced program does not derive from the same DNA as that of existing programs or of the parent organization; rather, it represents a foreign organ transplanted into the host organism. If the developers of such a program are to be successful, they must suppress the institutional immune system, and they can accomplish that goal only through the intervention of sympathetic or supporting administrative policy functions. With each change in personnel in the new program, however, it is highly likely that *tradition creep* will occur in the form of a systematic reversion to the stable condition supported by the institution's DNA. In statistics, we refer to this tendency as *regression toward the mean*. In the institutional case, we are using *mean* in the Aristotelian sense of the golden mean—an ideal state of equilibrium.

Institutional DNA may accommodate some variance, and the degree to which a proposed or attempted change deviates from the mean is correlated with the amount of resistance that the organism exerts against the change. That resistance must be suppressed in order for the change to take place, and then the change must be supported in order to flourish. If the change deviates too far from the institutional DNA, the DNA will either eliminate the change or compromise it until it is within tolerable limits. In other words, the change will either be rejected outright or it will systematically be altered until its essence is in line with the norm. Paradoxically, an organization often welcomes change-agents but then rejects the actual implementation of new ideas that deviate from its fundamental values—even if the ideas are current and dynamic.

In his book *Organizational Culture and Leadership,* Edgar Schein (1992) calls organizational resistance to change *structural stability* (10). Schein acknowledges that an individual in a position of hierarchical leadership can change the organization, thereby affecting that structural stability. We are prepared to argue, though, that the belief that a new leader or even a new regime can effect a significant change is a myth. We contend that reform happens only if the old system, including its supporters, is completely and permanently suppressed—in a word, annihilated. If a critical portion of the previous organization remains, the tendency toward structural stability will lead back to the re-institution of the original standards and practices. In other words, the phenotype may be manipulated, but the genotype remains constant.

Several years ago, we asked Dr. Mark de Rond, formerly of the Wharton School of Business and now on the faculty of the University of Cambridge, to identify an established business that may have changed fundamentally without experiencing a revolution in the form of the death of the old organization. Dr. de Rond, while not disagreeing with our premise, suggested that we consider Nokia, the Finnish company that currently leads the world market in cell-phone production and sales. In 1865, Nokia was founded as a lumber company. Subsequently, Nokia evolved into a paper company, then a rubber company, then a cable company, and then an electronics company. Finally, Nokia became the world's leading cell-phone manufacturer.

If our premise that organizations do not and cannot change is valid, then how can Nokia's dramatic metamorphoses be explained? Steinbock (2001) answers that question in *The Nokia Revolution: The Story of an Extraordinary Company that Transformed an Industry*. In 1865, Fredrik Idestam and Leo Mechelin established the Nokia company as "the most innovative company in Finland" (Steinbock, 2001, 10). In 1916 when Idestam died, the fundamental value endured and the company continued to adapt to the changing demands of the market. "This strategic objective remains strong even today," Steinbock asserts, "although little tangible evidence of Idestam's Nokia remains" (10).

Because of its adherence to its genotype, the company survived. Phenotypical changes, however, kept the company vital and viable. Steinbock (2001) observes, "as the saying goes, the first generation creates, the second inherits, and the third destroys. That was not the case at Nokia, where the strategic objective (ceaseless innovation) had transcended the specific industries of the company's operations (i.e., forestry, rubber, and cable)" (11). The company's commitment to innovation sustained its essence. Diversification changed only the superficial details.

Clearly, Nokia was established on two fundamental values: innovation and diversification. Who is at the helm of the corporation and what its primary product is has no impact on Nokia's continued success. The fundamental values of the organization charted a sustainable course, and personnel have followed that course to prosperity through the Russian Revolution, two world wars, and multiple global economic cycles.

What we have come to believe, then, is that except in the initial founding phases of an organization, the success of an organization is *never* about an individual. Success is about the institution itself. A "great" man or a "great" woman may initially champion the idea or the ideology on which an organization is established, but evidence to support the reality that one person operates singularly in sustaining an organization or movement is inadequate if not nonexistent (Badaracco, 2001; Webber, 1999). Even our Lord put together a group to promulgate His mission, and there has never been a greater institution than the Christian church. The church body (organism) of Christ is inspired and directed by a functional DNA—the Holy Spirit. But we digress.

Continuing the discussion, an organization's attempts to change are *never* more than temporary intruders—transplants— that are eventually rejected. A person who comes in with a fire in the belly and the vision to change the system is rejected as quickly as is an invading germ in a living organism. The antibodies attack and conquer the invader. The "learning organization" defined as an organization that learns is a myth. People learn. Organizations do not!

Recently, organizations have been involved in what can be loosely called the "systems-change" movement. But based on the premise that it is impossible for organizations to change on a genotypical level, we believe the systems-change movement is condemned to failure. With regard to change, organisms and organizations have only two options: They can continue as they are—unchanged or only phenotypically and temporarily changed—or they can die.

Any organization—a corporation, a city, a church, or a school, for example—may adapt to an imposed or inspired superficial change for as long as an influential individual or group of individuals is present. But when such change-agents move on, the system reverts to its original, fundamental traditions and practices. Only new institutions can sustain a change, because the very fact that they are new *is* the change. But, again, once established, even new institutions with pioneering philosophies and trail-blazing practices are likely to become fossilized.

We continue to wonder why more organizations are not established on the *concept* of change—that is, why change is not one of the fundamental values of more new enterprises. As described above, Nokia provides evidence in support of this idea. The founders of Nokia imbued their organization with the fundamental value of continuous change. That value—that DNA—supported rather than opposed radical changes in the product line as well as in the extensions of those lines throughout the world. Contrast the Nokia story with corporations such as organizations that identify closely with a given product line or ideology. Individual executives, managers, and other types of employees championed "phenotypical" changes that were sometimes even lauded as effecting "breakthrough" change—Lou Girstner at IBM and Lee Iacocca at Chrysler, for example—with the result being to maintain the organization's status quo that existed either before or after such changes were attempted. Detailing such changes in these organizations and others is beyond the scope of this chapter, but they provide examples that at least set the stage for the proposition that although organizations remain fixed, individual people can and do change.

Several learning theories, such as Vygotsky's sociocultural theory (Schunk, 2008) and Freire's (1998) educational theory, support the conclusion that individuals in small groups, often called teams, have what is perhaps the most potent power to improve their environments and to create new systems. Although such new systems often emerge from an existing organization, attempting to reform an established organization genotypically is wasted effort. Jesus, for example, did not change the organizations of His time. But His influence changed the people around Him. They, in turn, incorporated that change and created a new organization. Consideration of the dynamic nature of that organization is beyond the scope of this chapter.

Adventist higher education and change

The Seventh-day Adventist Church was built on a set of fundamental values, such as the beliefs in the seventh-day Sabbath, the second coming of Jesus, and the sanctuary as a metaphor for the end-time events. This church established its denominational foundation during the latter decades of the nineteenth century and the early decades of the twentieth century. Heated debates about the philosophy and practices of the church in some cases led to the divisiveness and disfellowship. Eventually, though, agreement was reached.

The Seventh-day Adventist Church is, after all, based on a particular theology that is laid out in a system of beliefs. If the church is to constitute a system of education, then it stands to reason that everything about the nature of that system, including the manner of teaching, would exemplify the church's basic theological tenets. All methods should embody redemption, reliance on the Word of God in both the written form and the created form, and preparation for the future that faith in that Word projects. In fact, the traditional educational literature of the Seventh-day Adventist Church does just that in publications by Ellen G. White, including but not limited to *Education*, *Fundamentals of Christian Education*, and *Counsels to Parents, Teachers, and Students*. And numerous classic Seventh-day Adventist authors on the subject have developed these concepts in harmony with the theological foundations of the church. Authors such as A. T. Jones ([undated], reprinted 1983); E. A. Sutherland (1915), L. A. Hansen (1968), R. S. Moore (1976), and Maurice Hodgen (1978) provided editorial views of the Seventh-day Adventist educational traditions, and they often decried the lack of fundamental adherence to what became known as the "The Blueprint" (Tucker, 2001, 311).

The early development of Seventh-day Adventist higher education was also fraught with intense controversy, including physical fights over issues that were believed to be of foundational importance (Valentine, 1992). The primary argument appeared to be about the basic purpose of institutions of higher education: Was their purpose to deliver a practical education in order to develop church workers? Or was their purpose to deliver a classical curriculum in order to prepare scholars who were also workers in the church organization? Ideologues were convinced that the purpose of Seventh-day Adventist higher education was to prepare missionaries, clergymen, and teachers to disseminate the teachings of the church, which was called "present truth." But scholars, who also agreed with the church's theology, were equally convinced that higher education needed to be a way to obtain a classical education. The scholars, represented by influential individuals such as W. W. Prescott, president at one time or another of the church's Battle Creek College, Union College, and Walla Walla College, prevailed, and the higher-educational system was established as a classical one. All efforts to change the classical system have failed, perhaps the most notable of which was the attempt made by E. A. Sutherland and his colleagues (discussed briefly below). The denomination's higher-education DNA had been set.

Let us state here that it *is not* our intent to dismiss the importance of foundational values. It *is* our intent to emphasize that foundational values must be entrusted to individuals in relatively loosely organized small groups or teams rather than to institutions. Individuals are more likely to interpret and apply values in ways that will meet the requirements of an ever-changing landscape—including that of the Seventh-day Adventist Church—while maintaining the fundamental values of the movement. When they act as institutional functions, organizational committees are more likely to base their decisions in terms of policies and procedures. When Ellen G. White wrote that "we have nothing to fear for the future, except as we forget the way the Lord has led us, and His teaching in our past history" (1915, 196), she was *not* discussing organizational policies and procedures. She *was* discussing faith-based values and experiences based on those values—the "blueprint," as it is often called. Yet even given her admonition, the system of higher education could not be changed from a classical format to a more experiential one. Is the future of Adventist higher education, then, just like its past, only longer lasting? Or will the future accommodate change that will bring Adventist education in line with the original, practical tenets of the church's founding individuals?

It appears that as an organization ages, it becomes more procedure driven than mission driven—that, in fact, all organizations naturally move from initial risk-taking to eventual process-maintenance. The Seventh-day Adventist Church seems to have followed that pattern. Consider the book *Education*. In 1903, Ellen G. White wrote what many educators consider to be one of the most authentic and practical instructional manuals written to date. The book presents a balance between scholarship and ideology, and even people who dismiss its inspired origin have agreed with its inherent value. We have consciously lived by the definition of "true education" as "the harmonious development of the physical, the mental, and the spiritual powers. It prepares the student for the joy of service in this world, and for the higher joy of wider service in the world to come"

(White, 1903, 11). A century later, *Education* was revised and condensed; in the definition of true education, the words "It prepares the student for the joy of service in this world, and for the higher joy of wider service in the world to come," were eliminated (White, 2000, 9). Although the abbreviated definition still has impact, its connection to a fundamental value of the church—that of its mission in terms of Christian service and eternal values—has been deleted. We would suggest that the revision is an example of forgetting "the way the Lord has led us in our past history" (White, 1915, 196).

The Seventh-day Adventist system of higher education could easily find itself in a situation that requires attempts to find meaning that has been largely "lost." As personal and organizational egos grow, so does myopia. What, for example, happened to the original mission? Has it been lost in our attempt to accommodate a changing world by changing Adventist theology? Adventists who live and worship in Europe have experienced firsthand the secularization of the church to a greater degree than have Adventists in North America, but the whole Western world appears to be floundering without a theological focus. Without a focus, it is easy to strive to be "great" without having defined what is "good." Denominationally, Adventists have adopted the unwieldy but universally recognizable hierarchical structure and have applied it to the denomination's higher-educational system—at times even at the expense of the mission of the church. Consequently, attempts to alter the established educational practices are as destined to fail as was the bold initiative of Madison College, described in the following paragraphs.

Early in the twentieth century, E. A. Sutherland and his colleagues attempted to introduce mission-oriented higher education to the Adventist educational system. In 1904, after years of difficult discussion about the role and function of Adventist higher education with the faculty and administration of Emmanuel Missionary College (EMC), in southwestern Michigan, Sutherland resigned as president of EMC, and with several colleagues journeyed south to establish Madison College, in central Tennessee (Gish and Christman, 1989; Dittes, 2006).

The inspiring story of the development of Madison is equaled only by the distressing story of its demise. Madison had been founded as a self-supporting Seventh-day Adventist higher-education institution, one that did not depend on the fiscal support of the denominational coffers. Madison's purpose was to deliver an education that was congruent with the church's mission—to develop workers who would disseminate the teachings of Jesus.

Madison was successful as an independent entity for six decades. In time, however, the initiators of this grand initiative retired and were replaced by people who claimed similar values but who were not skilled in the operation of such an institution and were, in fact, more connected with the traditional church institution. Within a relatively short time, the organization came to its end, with the assistance of both the parent church's institutional intervention and of external organizations who took over the assets and reordered Madison's purpose, bringing it into harmony with more traditional views—the strongest form of tradition creep. The Madison story came to an end institutionally, if not ideologically.

Several subsequent self-supporting Adventist institutions have had or are currently demonstrating similar histories, because their DNA is also alien to the DNA of the established system. To hope that Seventh-day Adventist higher education will adopt nontraditional approaches is equivalent to attempting an organ transplant without suppressing the immune system. In other words, although the initiatives seem successful for a period of time, they are not sustainable.

Conclusion and considerations

Why are there so many different religious denominations? And why are there variations in philosophy and practice within the denominations? The purpose of such diversity is not to promote Christianity, for all Christian sects promote the basic tenets of Christianity. Rather, organized religious orders and churches seem to depend more on the number of members and the values that divide—those elements that make them unique—than on a common truth.

The church is comprised of the corporate body of individuals. The church is not the formal organization. The organization has selfless, virtuous members. It also has selfish, unethical members. Mostly, though, it has members who are selfless at times and selfish at others, virtuous at times and unethical at others. In other words, the church is made up of human beings who are dedicated Christians, and, as individual humans with individual minds and hearts. They can effect change because they can depend on the positive force of their faith to guide them. When individuals organize as an institution, however, the potency of that influence becomes reduced, if not lost—and the result can be profane!

All this is not to say that religious organizations have no value. They do. Such organizations provide a structural base for cost-saving and organized approaches to achieve objectives inspired by the fundamental values that inspired the founding individuals. But given the genotype/phenotype metaphor as it applies to organizations, it is perhaps easy for organizational culture that has its roots in the now-distant past to forget its mission over time and to become more bureaucratically driven than mission driven. We wonder, can an organization's evolution from being mission driven to being procedure driven even be stemmed? All organizations seem to move from the initial risk-taking that prompted their establishment to the maintenance-behavior that marks their continuance. This process may be as natural as the human aging process.

Organizational practices are dictated by the DNA—the fundamental values—of the organization. Higher-education institutions are organizations, and they are subject to the same DNA-based restrictions as other organizations. With regard to Seventh-day Adventist higher education, the practice of delivering a more classical education along with applied subjects is firmly fixed and, at least to date, appears to be unchangeable. We believe that Seventh-day Adventist higher education could have adapted once to a "blueprint" form of delivery—but that format either would have had to be represented in the DNA from the beginning or the organizational framework would had to have been established as a fundamental value.

Perhaps it is time to recognize the value of the individual in the theory and practice of higher education. From their inception, higher education initiatives, which became institutions over time, were all directed at individual learners—people who wished to gain knowledge, skills, and understanding. Individuals—not organizations—drive the world. People are what matter. Only inspired human influence can improve the world. This is true in all types of organizations. It is true in government systems. It is true in corporate systems. It is true in family systems. And it is true in church systems—even higher education systems operated by church organizations. One by one or in small groups, we can make needed changes.

Bibliography

Argyris, C., and D. Schön. *Organizational Learning: A Theory of Action Perspective.* Reading, MA: Addison Wesley, 1978.

_____. *Organizational Learning II: Theory, Method and Practice.* Reading, MA: Addison Wesley, 1996.

Badaracco, J. L., Jr. "We Don't Need Another Hero." *Harvard Business Review* 78, no. 8 (2001): 120–128.

Carnegie Commission on Higher Education. *Quality and Equality: New Levels of Federal Responsibility for Higher Education* (1968).

Dittes, A. *Profiles of Madison College Pioneers: Their Role in the Rise of Loma Linda and the Southern Union.* Portland, TN: Dittes Publications, 2006.

Dixon, N. *The Organizational Learning Cycle: How We Can Learn Collectively.* London: McGraw-Hill, 1994.

Gish, I. and H. Christman. *Madison, God's Beautiful Farm: The E. A. Sutherland Story.* Nampa, ID: The Upward Way, 1989.

Freire, P. *Teachers as Cultural Workers—Letters to Those Who Dare Teach.* Translated by D. Macedo, D. Koike, and A. Oliveira. Boulder, CO: Westview Press, 1998.

Hansen, L. A. *From So Small a Dream.* Harrisville, NH: MMI Press, 1968.

Jones, A. T. *The Place of the Bible in Education: An Appeal to Christians.* Undated. Reprinted by Palmwoods, Queensland, Australia: Destiny Press, 1983.

Kerr, C. "Three Thousand Futures: The Next Twenty Years for Higher Education." *Carnegie Council on Policy Studies in Higher Education.* San Francisco: Jossey-Bass, 1980.

Leslie, M. "Experimental Drug Halts Chronic Organ Rejection." 'Scope. *Stanford Medicine* 16, no. 3 (Spring 1999): http://stanmed.stanford.edu/1999spring/.

Moore, R. S. *Adventist Education at the Crossroads*. Mountain View, CA: Pacific Press®, 1976.

Pedler, M., J. Burgoyne, and T. Boydell. *The Learning Company: A Strategy for Sustainable Development*. London: McGraw-Hill, 1991.

Schein, E. H. *Organizational Culture and Leadership*. 2nd ed. San Francisco: Jossey-Bass, 1992.

Senge, P. M. *The Fifth Discipline: The Art and Practice of the Learning Organization*. New York: Doubleday Books, 1994.

Schunk, D. H. *Learning Theories: An Educational Perspective*. 5th ed. Upper Saddle River, NJ: Merrill/Prentice Hall, 2008.

Steinbock, D. *The Nokia Revolution: The Story of an Extraordinary Company That Transformed an Industry*. New York: American Management Association, 2001.

Sutherland, E. A. *Studies in Christian Education*. Brushtown, NY: 1915. Reprinted by Teach Services, Inc., 2005.

Tucker, J. A. "Pedagogical Application of the Seventh-day Adventist Philosophy of Education." *Journal of Research on Christian Education* 10, Special Edition (2001): 309–325.

Valentine, G. M. *The Shaping of Adventism: The Case of W. W. Prescott*. Berrien Springs, MI: Andrews University Press, 1992.

Webber, A. M. "Learning for a Change." *Fast Company,* no. 24 (May 1999): 178–188

White, Ellen G. *Education*. Mountain View, CA: Pacific Press®, 1903.

_____. *Life Sketches*. Mountain View, CA: Pacific Press®, 1915.

_____. *True Education: An Adaptation of "Education."* Boise, ID: Pacific Press®, 2000.

GERALD D. LORD

Chapter 13

Faith-Based Higher Education: Reflections by an Accreditor

When I was first invited to make a contribution to this collection on faith-based higher education, as admirable as the idea for the collection might be, my initial reaction was that I would not be able to do it for at least three reasons. It was not that I did not want to write this chapter. In fact, I was intrigued by the opportunity to reflect on the subject matter at hand. My reservation was that as a staff member of the Commission on Colleges of the Southern Association of Colleges and Schools, I am bound by a strict confidentiality agreement. In short, I cannot reveal anything outside of the Commission's official disclosure policy about specific institutions. That is the way it should be in order to maintain the integrity of the peer review process of accreditation.

Moreover, as a staff member of the Commission, I must (and do) maintain objectivity in interpreting accreditation standards and in dealing with all the institutions to which I am assigned. So comments here should not be interpreted in any way as revealing any personal biases that might potentially influence any kind of accreditation decision regarding any of our member institutions.

Third, I knew that I could not, in this venture, speak for the Commission in any way. On the other hand, after nineteen years on the Commission staff, I have learned that anything a Commission staff member says is taken by some as having been spoken on behalf of the Commission, no matter what kind of disclaimer is given or what the circumstances might be. Nonetheless, I want to make that disclaimer very clear at this point. Nothing I say herein should be taken as speaking for the Commission on Colleges in any way or as reflecting its official position in any matter whatsoever. In fact, I cannot and would not presume to speak for the Commission. This piece reflects my own personal opinions, impressions, and judgments, none of which should be construed as influencing in any way my dealings with the institutions to which I am assigned as the staff liaison or, again, as speaking for the Commission.

Then I thought that, after having taken into account these restrictions and disclaimers, I might perhaps do an op-ed style of essay that might or might not be based on hard, quantitative research data, but which surely would emerge from a lot of accreditation visits to a wide range of higher education institutions over a substantial number of years. When the editors of this collection agreed to this approach, I proceeded to engage the issue. It has been a useful exercise for me personally.

One more prefatory comment: In this chapter, I am intentionally not referring to or including seminaries. They are special institutions in their own right in terms of professional clergy preparation. While much of what I say below might apply to them, I realize their uniqueness and have not intended to be referring to them when I have generalized. I do include undergraduate and graduate institutions, but at least some of what I have said probably does not pertain to seminaries as such.

The context

The history of American higher education, English and European too, for that matter, is primarily the history of ecclesiastical concern for educating clergy. Our oldest higher education institutions were founded for that purpose. Education for other professions, law, medicine, and teaching soon followed. The earliest higher education thus was private and church-related and faith-based. I need not expand further on this history here; the literature in this regard is replete. Suffice it to say that we now have a rich array of different kinds of higher education institutions, public and private and proprietary, large and small, technical and professional, liberal arts and vocational, research and teaching, all of which present, in this country, an enviable system of higher education which provides a singular range of choices for those seeking to better themselves. Faith-based or church-related institutions, as they have emerged from our earliest times, still comprise a strong part of this fascinating potpourri.

It is difficult to generalize about this genre of institution. Each institution is unique and distinctive in its own right with its own attributes and identifying characteristics. Most purport, in one way or another, to offer small classes, individual student attention, a caring community, a religious ethos in its own tradition to varied extents, an emphasis in some way on character-building, a certain worldview more or less well-defined, perhaps a certain approach to the teaching and learning enterprise and even to the academic disciplines, and a distinguished faculty of excellent, caring teachers. Most value good teaching over faculty research, and true caring about individual student welfare is usually a hallmark. Notwithstanding claims to the contrary, I would have to say that academic quality does vary as does, frankly, faculty quality. Some institutions offer very fine, rigorous, up-to-date degree programs; sadly, others raise questions in this regard. Most, but certainly not all, are accredited, usually regionally accredited.

Many are experiencing extreme financial difficulties, some even to the point of questioning survivability, and were doing so even before this latest recession severely taxed all higher education institutions. Most are heavily tuition-dependent, and a dip in student enrollment can be disastrous for them. So student recruiting becomes paramount, sometimes even to the point of sacrificing admissions standards. Scholarship budgets and tuition discounting get out of hand in the attempt to compete with the more attractive tuitions of public institutions. Institutional resources get spread ever more thinly, signs of that being faculty salary reductions and layoffs, unreasonable faculty teaching loads, reductions in library acquisitions, compounded deferred physical plant maintenance, annual operating deficits, reductions in total net assets and total unrestricted net assets, excessive use of lines of credit, and dangerously high indebtedness. Financial support from affiliated denominations varies, but is usually relatively low, thus placing a high priority on fund-raising for institutional administrators.

In the face of troubling financial realities, some institutions in this category have expanded their programs to try to attract more students. Some have gotten very entrepreneurial, sometimes out-stripping their means to support adequately the program expansion. Online courses and degree programs are commonplace, sometimes initiated without adequate faculty training and time for course development. Off-campus sites have proliferated along with use of adjunct faculty, leading to questions of quality and comparability. Adult degree completion programs, usually on an accelerated delivery schedule, have also multiplied, on the one hand performing a service, on the other, again, raising questions about quality and comparability and adequate support. Likewise, the initiation of joint degree programs and other kinds of academic relationships with unaccredited and/or institutions abroad might help the bottom line and give students a broadening experience, but does the accredited institution provide appropriate quality control mechanisms? Expansion of the institutional mission to begin offering advanced professional degree programs not offered before raises questions of institutional ability to support them. These and other issues might cause some to begin to wonder about the distinctiveness of the mission of this genre of institution and how well it can accomplish that mission while appearing to try to be all things to all people.

Happily, some private institutions of this genre are strong enough and stable enough financially to have weathered the recession in reasonably good shape, but even they are facing challenges in this regard. Usually a solid endowment, sound financial planning, and consistently strong fund-raising performance are to be thanked for their relative strength. In this economy, the financially strong are managing through hardships and remaining strong, while the financially weak are getting weaker. That in and of itself raises accreditation questions.

For what it is worth, I do not understand the terms *church-related* and *faith-based* to be necessarily synonymous. Neither are they mutually exclusive. It might, in fact, not be a useful distinction, but I personally do distinguish one from the other. I understand a church-related institution to be affiliated in some formal way with a specific denomination or religious tradition. These institutions vary in terms of the amount of denominational influence they reflect in their campus ethos and programs and in terms of the amount of support, financial and otherwise, they receive from the denomination. Their campus atmosphere might be liberal or conservative. They might espouse broadly conceived worldviews or narrowly focused, sectarian, fairly rigid approaches to life and learning. They might be entirely open to all points of view in the traditional sense of a broad liberal arts education, or they might have mission statements that define their posture as being much more restrictive or narrow, or at least less tolerant of other views. Religious practices might be more or less dominant in the campus ethos. Most of them, in my experience, fall somewhere in between the extremes I have outlined here.

An institution might or might not be church-related and still consider itself to be faith-based. The term *faith-based* is a commonly used self-identification at institutions that try to appeal to a broader constituency than a single denomination. They would typically be considered, at least in my experience, to be more conservative, evangelical, even fundamentalist Christian in worldview and in the posture in which they seek to shape their students. They would typically call themselves nondenominational evangelical Christian. Campus-wide worship experiences would be common, even mandatory, and would reflect this tradition. A religious emphasis would usually be a very important element in the campus ethos, which would also attempt to embody biblical predominance and faithfulness and genuine piety, sensitivity, and caring. This context and approach would be evident in the institution's mission statement, in its catalog and recruiting materials, and in its campus life in general.

While there are major research universities that are church-related, few of them would consider themselves to be faith-based, if my descriptors above are at all accurate. Church-related institutions run the gamut from two-year colleges to doctoral-level institutions. Many, if not most, of the faith-based institutions are baccalaureate or master's level institutions, some offering a professional doctorate or two. They tend to be smaller in terms of enrollment and more geographically focused in terms of student origins and service area. Their student bodies might be less diverse in most respects, certainly so in terms of religious tradition.

Possibilities

It is the case that church-related and faith-based institutions of higher education can literally be life-changing and life-transforming for their students. Many of them offer opportunities to students which they would never otherwise have. They can open up whole new worlds for many of their students who never knew these worlds existed. Many of them serve students who are first-generation college students and thus open up new vistas for them. To provide a sensitive, caring, supportive environment for learning in which students are known to faculty and staff as individual persons, not just as one of a sea of faces in a vast lecture hall, is a calling to be treasured. The strong liberal arts foundation that many of these institutions offer undergirds character formation, enriches lives, and forms the backdrop for a lifetime of learning and growing.

There are all kinds of theological and philosophical ways of talking about the advantages of this genre of institution: to love God with one's mind, to reunite knowledge and vital piety as John Wesley put it, to ground persons in a faith commitment, to prepare persons for lives of service to God and neighbor, to teach how to live in responsible community, to build Christian character (if the institution is in fact Christian in orientation), to shape civil discourse, to imbue civic responsibility and responsible citizenship, to ground professional and social skills in a particular worldview, to foster a broad understanding of the world around us and how we got here, to name just a few. Indeed, the literature is rife with these kinds of assertions, much of it more than mere recruiting rhetoric, so I need not add to it here. The possibilities are almost limitless for those who think creatively about the prospect.

These kinds of institutions can provide a wonderful alternative for many students who can most benefit from them. They add gloriously to the warp and woof of that colorful tapestry we call higher education in this country, which would not be the same without them. That is why they must be supported and not allowed to wither and die. That is why we must raise capable leaders to guide them through the challenges they face. That is why they deserve the best governing boards we can muster. In many ways, the future of our very culture is at stake.

Potential pitfalls

These kinds of institutions do in fact face potential pitfalls that could jeopardize their credibility, their identity, and possibly their very existence. They should continually ask themselves the question, "What does it mean to be church-related or faith-based in this increasingly secularized, pluralistic society in which three college roommates could be of the Christian, Hindu, and Muslim faiths?" If the answer to this question is too broadly conceived, they risk losing their identity and singular contribution and sacrificing their unique mission on the altar of trying to please others. If their answer to this question is too narrowly and rigidly conceived, they risk devolving into sectarianism, into a too-narrow worldview, and losing their rightful place in the world of ideas in which they can articulate with some measure of credibility their mission, call, and commitment as they see them. At both ends of this spectrum is the real danger of pride, intolerance, arrogance, even Manichaeism, in which they have the absolute gnosis, the absolute truth, and the rest of the world is absolutely wrong.

Closely attendant to this point is the time-honored, revered principle of academic freedom. In its best sense, academic freedom is the freedom to pursue truth wherever the quest leads, unfettered by doctrinal bonds that might be threatened by the search. Intellectual curiosity is a vital ingredient of a true scholarly community, including students as well as faculty, and must not be stifled if the most basic goals and principles of higher education are to be preserved. Unabashed, unleashed exploration is the key to successful teaching and learning and to developing the critical thinking skills so necessary for a successful, full, and rich life.

Academic freedom should not be construed as allowing faculty members the right to say anything they wish about any nonacademic matter or even to disagree with the administration over administrative issues. It is to say that faculty members' rights to explore, present, research, write, publish, and discuss all sides of issues, controversial or not, that fall rightly within their academic disciplines, are to be respected and maintained at all costs. That is true unless the mission statement of the institution includes an inviolate doctrinal stance, and faculty members know exactly what those terms are before agreeing to accept an appointment to the institution's faculty. Under these terms, faculty members may be required to sign a statement of faith, but only if they know about it before signing a contract to teach at that institution.

In a related area, institutions of this genre are also vulnerable to overzealous governing boards which sometimes, either collectively or individually, go beyond their policy-making authority and responsibility and intrude into the administrative affairs of the institution, rightly the prerogative and province of the administrators employed to implement the policies of the board. For example, accreditation standards clearly stipulate that the curriculum lies within the purview of the faculty. For governing boards to have approval authority over textbook selection and bookstore stock, or to abridge the faculty's right to free speech within the bounds of the institution's own policy on academic freedom, or to mandate the hiring or firing of certain faculty members or other persons would likewise be out of bounds. Furthermore, the governing board must be able to demonstrate that it is free from undue external influence, in this case particularly that of religious bodies, and is expected to protect the institution from such undue external influence.

I have already alluded to other kinds of potential pitfalls above, financial stress, for example. Ways to avoid or minimize this potential problem include invoking appropriate financial and budgetary discipline, that is, practicing good stewardship, and practicing responsible financial management and planning. Fund-raising and long-term development and endowment growth are crucial to the future well-being of the institution. Sound academic planning is also required so as to avoid watering down the academic quality of programs. There are, of course, other issues that might bear mentioning here, but my point is that competent leadership in all of these areas will determine institutional success or failure in the long term. Caring oversight and attention to that issue might just be the most important fiduciary responsibility of governing boards.

Paradigm

I have had but one exposure to Seventh-day Adventist higher education. I do not wish to sound patronizing, but that one experience was impressive to me. I was privileged to be assigned to work with Southern Adventist University during its reaffirmation of accreditation process some number of years ago. Throughout the years in which I worked with that institution, a deep-seated concern for academic quality and integrity was evident in all of my dealings with it. Institutional personnel took the reaffirmation process seriously and were conscientious in their participation in accreditation and all of its required reporting.

I recall quite well my visits to the campus, both my staff advisory visit and the peer review reaffirmation committee visit. I sensed and felt on campus a deep, sincere spirituality and piety, not in a cloying, overly sentimental sort of way, not with a lot of hoopla as on some campuses, but with a quiet devotion and commitment to a commonly held faith and set of values and religious traditions. All of this appeared to be in a context of intellectual curiosity and a profound respect for the teaching and learning enterprise.

The people on that campus, the faculty, staff, and students, seemed to know who and whose they were and to be quite comfortable with that identity. I did not get a sense of narrow sectarianism or unconsidered rejection of other points of view. On the contrary, they seemed to be open to a range of possibilities, all the while being able to engage these possibilities from the strength of their own convictions. In short, the institution appeared to me to have a wholesome academic atmosphere and to be a wholesome community in spirit and demeanor. Moreover, the food in the campus dining facility was extraordinarily good. So creative were the menu and food preparation, I never missed meat at all!

In many ways, it seemed to me that this campus, this institution, lived out a wonderful embodiment of what a good church-related or faith-based higher institution is called to be and to do. No institution is perfect. Every institution can improve, as accreditation standards expect. This institution appeared to me to be exemplary of what this genre of institution can and should be in surprising aspects, in ways I did not expect. If developing students as whole persons and forming their character and moral virtues without stifling freedom of inquiry is a laudable goal, then, without putting too fine a point on it, surely this institution is worthy of emulation in this regard.

Postscript

In this article, I have tried to point out the importance of church-related and faith-based higher education institutions in the rich mix of higher education opportunities in this country and, increasingly, abroad, as our institutions expand internationally. Certainly, Seventh-day Adventist institutions make a vital contribution to this range of educational possibilities.

The church has always been a service organization and has always taken seriously its responsibility to help develop human potential and enrich human experience, to ease suffering and to lighten the darkness and burdens of ignorance. This salvific potential has never been more crucial to our social, cultural, religious, economic, and political well-being in this world, to say nothing of our hope for the next.

This time of increased diversity in so many venues is hardly the time for an established voice of reason and religious tradition to withdraw from the conversation. If we are to regain any semblance of civility in the polis, of responsible citizenship in the commonweal, of mutual respect and reciprocal concern for the neighbor, of reconciliation, of shalom, then surely we need the shaping influence of the love of God and love of neighbor in higher education, complete with all the implications of what that might mean. And, in many respects, scientific and technological advances enhance our potential of meeting this challenge if we think creatively together about the most prudent approaches to their employment. This is only one of many unique contributions church-related/faith-based institutions can make to this enterprise which, after all, has never been more important, more imperative, than it is now.

TED W. BENEDICT

Chapter 14

Truth and Tenure

There are several common obsessions which we encounter when we read or listen to communication among Seventh-day Adventists. Examples include our choice of foods, our worry about the mechanics of salvation, and those whisper-behind-the hand questions and answers about creation versus evolution. These, and a few others, dominate our communication stream, but underlying them all is the theme of the importance of truth and, though not quite the same thing, of Truth. A motivation that drives the truth theme is the urgent need to be somehow different from others. If we could be just like others and still be correct, our denomination would probably disappear. *Different* is not our usual word for this distinction; we prefer to think of ourselves as *peculiar,* and several of our precious doctrines serve this purpose for us.

The task of preserving this uniqueness falls often to our clergy, and even more to our teachers. So, the teaching profession is, for us, essential to our community identity, health, and survival. This is a weighty responsibility for anyone to carry. However, it is odd that we have not enthusiastically learned to trust either our preachers or our faculty members to do this for us. Teaching is often regarded as a fall-back job, something like selling insurance or real estate. There is, in some of our corners, a strong anti-intellectual attitude, just as we find it within the more general American public. We must learn to deal with it.

In addition to the church attitude toward persons who teach, the view of the teacher that is held by American citizens generally is also a bit negative. He is very often displayed as uncombed, absent, forgetful, elsewhere, "triviating" his way from practical crisis toward unimportant catastrophe. The caricature suggests that we need to be there to help him find his glasses (all the while they are perched on the top of his head), his other shoe, his car, and his present wife. However, we really know that these are unfair fictions.

We've learned that great enterprises began in his garage, grand ideas spring out of his poetry and music and formulas, tumors shrink before his chemistry, and governments change at his urging, all to serve us more fairly. We need his visioning and his hard-headed innovativeness. Our leaders pass with us through his classrooms and labs. The worlds of geography, geology, and geometry yield to his insistent curiosity. Our many-cultured society feeds on his ideas about the values we must recover and preserve. So, we treasure his services to society, though we reluctantly reward him richly enough to put beans, okra, and rice on his family table.

Our American community recognizes that his existence is essential to the stability and health of our society, and that a free market for ideas and information is required to sustain our politics, religion, and commerce. We may not always agree with, or even understand, the professor with his stub of chalk, but we must not deny that we all need him.

A fine teacher, even on the Seventh-day Adventist campus, regards himself as a member of an intellectual group whose margins extend far beyond his own school. The scholarly and technical literature he feels obligated, or even called, to explore is a universal, not just a church resource. He thinks of himself as a scholar, distinguishing between his missions of training and educating. He lives within a professional world that has its code of ethics and whose members can be encouraged and trusted to monitor it, and he has chosen to adopt a particular style of living. He exists on the margin of what is already known, finding excitement and fulfillment in searching for the truth about the portion of a universe that is within his chosen discipline.

Given these orientations, he sometimes finds himself at odds with the church and campus administrators, who have their somewhat different concerns. They remind us that the school, as an institution, has among its missions the conservation of understandings that are presently known and believed, as well as the defense of the established order. The administrator prefers that new ideas will be, as a priority, reconciled with the past, and only reluctantly and quietly included in our view of our future.

Both the teacher and the church/school

administrator are reportable to the larger constituency and its subconstituencies, and their interests and fears are a constant backdrop against which the teacher must do his business. Though there are differences in goals among these groups, those goals are all driven by an underlying compulsion to serve truth, or even, Truth. This is, of course, worthy of our support and praise.

But there is a problem which we should not ignore. Our vocabulary about matters of truth is flawed because the term is ambiguous. Like other important abstractions, such as love and sin and beauty, we have worn it out by using it in so many and so very different ways. I love chocolate and my wife and my dog. Sleeping in can be a sin, and (remembering Solomon's song) my daughters are lovely beyond compare because their necks are like the pillars of the temple.

Perhaps, then, because academic freedom (our topic in this chapter) is so closely related to the idea of the truth that deserves our active protection, we should take a few lines to decide what we mean when we use the word here. I will begin by noting some misconceptions about the nature of truth, and comment on what truth is *not*.

Truth is not a thing. We cannot bottle it. It has no existence as an object. An apple or an artichoke cannot be true. The appropriate question here to ask is whether (a) they exist, and, if they do, (b) what name we should use when we want to refer to them. These are good questions, but they are not about the *truth* of an artichoke or an apple.

Truth is not quantifiable, or measurable. One instance of truth is not more or less true than another. Truth is a bit like pregnancy; an assertion cannot be a little bit true.

Truth is not a person (nor a Person). Please hold your fire! I realize that Jesus told us that He is the Way, the Truth, and the Life. These assertions are metaphors. There may be an implied truth here, but as it stands, His statement about the temperature of hell is not truth. We need to continue hearing while He keeps talking to us, leading us to our own discovery of His truth. I believe that He is eager to do just that, for those of us who have ears. The disciples often had to ask Him to do this for them, and He can do it for me too, if I am curious.

Truth is not an eternal abstraction that exists somewhere else, a model in heaven for the statements we make here on earth. That otherworldly concept is a Socratic-Platonic-Aristotelian idea that has had a strong influence on Paul's thinking, and also on Seventh-day Adventist thinking. We must be cautious when we talk that kind of language, lest we slip naively into a mystical religion, or buy into the theology of Aristotle by way of Saint Thomas Aquinas, accepting the notion that there are seven levels of hell and paradise.

So, then, what *is* truth?

It will help us if we first ask where it may be found. If we are looking for truth, where will we see it? What will it look like?

Truth is always *about* something; it doesn't exist by itself. The very short answer to this question is that truth is found in the assertions which we make in our human languages. Truth is an attribute of a statement, usually of the form of a claim that some thing has a particular characteristic, that something represented by *A* has the attribute of *B*-ness. Such a statement can be said to be a statement of fact (apples again), and may be either so or not, depending on whether the relationship of A and B-ness in the sentence or formula can be observed in the real world where A and B-ness exist. Thus, fact, a statement of fact, and truth are not the same. A fact is a thing, a statement of fact is an assertion about a thing, and truth is a verified statement about a thing. When we fail to distinguish among these concepts, we can unconsciously muddle our thinking.

We can observe this, as we have pointed out, in the parables of Jesus, who sometimes used a heretical assertion to demonstrate an implied truth. An example is His story about the rich man and Lazarus, describing a scene in (nonexistent) hell where the two kinds of residents, though both dead, can communicate with each other. The story is a fiction, it is not true, but its *implied* point is true. Some of us, having grown up in the days of "really-truelies," find this use of metaphor, simile, analogy, allegory, or parable disturbing, though as children we had no particular trouble with the stories of Uncle Arthur or Eric B. Hare. Similarly, Ellen White recommended Bunyan's book, *Pilgrim's Progress.*

Parenthetically, I suggest that Jewish literature, in any of its early languages, found these "as ifs" a very useful mode of explication. I think that there is a caution here for our translators and for us as translating readers.

With this established as a brief background, we can now look at the hazards that are inherent in teaching, especially on the college or university level. In a neutral sort of way, we can note the surprising plurality of perspectives that exist among us. This is surprising, precisely because each of us assumes that he, of course, is both normal and correct. As a tourist in Europe and as part of a Seventh-day Adventist group mostly from Lincoln, Nebraska, I was shocked to see the differences between that group and me. They regarded this Californian as a representative from quite another religion, and I couldn't understand some of their attitudes (for example, toward a meat diet, and about the status of women). Although we shared the same denominational membership, we had limited common ground when we discussed theological matters. Both of us were correct. Of course, we were each in our subcultural worldview.

If the teaching professional is seriously committed to a search for (new or forgotten) truth, he is going to be in trouble with someone. That is a part of his job description, and there is no escaping that possibility. He regards the search itself as an ethical, even a moral, imperative, a responsibility to his profession and to us. His conscience tells him this. He has been educated to believe it, and the search is respected and honored within his disciplinary community. Within his institutional community, though, on his home campus, he will be subjected to a variety of criticisms.

There is another concept here that must be asserted. The scholar-teacher is a professor. That implies that he is a person who professes something. His is a serious business. He does it to fulfill himself. More importantly, for our discussion here, he professes truth for the benefit of the communities to which he belongs. Our church, our society, and even our world, stand to gain from his work, and to lose profoundly if he does not do it and do it well. So, to protect these community values, the professor deserves some kind of job protection, not for his benefit, but for ours. This concept is most important, and it is crucial to our argument. So I repeat it: we must offer him some protection, not for his benefit, but for ours. The benefit to him is a by-product.

Now, we should identify some of those persons or groups from whom the professors need protection. Who might they be?

There are well-meaning persons who consider that their investment of money and time in schooling should guarantee reinforcement of existing truths, plus simple preparation for a desired employment. For them, new ideas are both suspect and wasteful.

There are those who suffer motion sickness whenever someone rocks their boat.

Others consider the content of instruction to be a commodity to be sold, bought, and preserved, and deviation from the package to be a violation of a contract.

Some feel that, whatever else a teacher may do, his primary purpose must be to develop and display loyalty to the organization. Anything critical of the institution which they feel is the only embodiment of all truth is, by definition, almost criminal disloyalty.

Some administrators have been taught to function in a *machismo* mode, where any kind of perceived misbehavior by a teacher (a hired hand) must be dealt with instantly and decisively. Time taken for review and consultative judgment is thought to be an evidence of weakness in leadership.

Generally, new ideas contemplate revision or abandonment of older ideas. This seems dangerous, even when the details of the danger are not clear. The proponents of exploration and amendment are also a danger, and we should remove the danger. A standard stratagem is to replace the person. So, to avoid evaluation of the message; we terminate the messenger.

Many times the innovator intrudes into an argument that is already in progress. He is then likely to look like an enemy to both sides, a straying soldier wandering around in no man's land between the trenches, and he becomes a target for both sides. This sometimes happens when the opponents are firmly established, the argument is ancient, and the contenders are afraid to shoot directly at each other.

These are some of the risks and their common origins. They, and others, are real, as our recollection of Seventh-day Adventist institutional history will immediately demonstrate. Being real, then, we need to ask a question.

What are the features of appropriate protection?

Again, I would suggest that some of our present practices do not offer good protection. One that would seem to flow from our Christian view of life would urge that we trust in the integrity, the good will, the natural paternalism, the innate fairness of our administrators and board members. My observations and experience clearly demonstrate that this is unwise because it is hasn't worked and so is unreliable. Administrators' judgments made under the stress of the immediate moment are far too deeply affected by matters not pertinent to the issues of particular cases. Quiet settlements, made for the best interests of the faculty member, usually operate to deny his legal rights. Further, judgments made by compulsive whimsy can easily create serious legal and financial liabilities for the school and the church. Procedural matters should be set out in advance, reviewed by legal counsel, and embodied in documented school policy. What, then?

A first requirement for a satisfactory solution will retain administration's rights to reduce expenses to fit an effective budget. This means that if the school does demonstrably not need his services, either for financial or for curricular reasons, the professor position may be terminated. If his behavior when doing his work violates professional ethics, demonstrates incompetence, or endangers the health, safety, or morals of his students, the professor may be fired. His administrators may rightly expect the professor's instruction to respect institutional beliefs, especially those that were specified and agreed to be important when he was initially employed.

The professor may be hired, initially, on a trial basis, a kind of "probation" that is limited to a specified time. During that probationary period, he is granted the same freedoms that are given a tenured faculty member, because those freedoms are essential to his professional activities. During this probationary period, his work is reviewed and his employment is renewed annually.

If the reviews are favorable and he is repeatedly rehired, at the end of the probationary period his employment is no longer subject to annual review. This new status is recognized as "tenure." It is important to note that the teacher who has "tenure" may, nevertheless, be terminated for the causes listed above. The most important change in his status is that before being tenured, he carries the burden of proof that he shouldn't be terminated, while after being given tenure, the institution bears the burden of proof that termination is appropriate.

In any case, the act of termination must, in order to be Christian, fair, and legal, follow a carefully specified procedure. We will call this protocol "academic due process." It will require that the professor be advised of the specific charges against him, that he be given time and access to records and advice that he may need in order to prepare his response, that the issues be investigated by a committee of his academic peers who are competent to make recommendations to the administration regarding a decision. The administration, properly, makes the final decision.

The ideas and ideals that I am recommending are not new or untried. They are a time-tested part of the traditional fabric of American higher education. They are documented in the literature of the American Association of University Professors (AAUP), dating from 1915 in a general way, and from 1940 in the form of its "Statement of Principles," both found in *Academic Freedom and Tenure,* edited by Louis Joughin. I strongly urge all educators to read and think about it. This understanding of uncomplicated fair play has become established in American higher education, and it is also consistent with labor laws, which are largely based on this practice. There is no requirement for membership in the AAUP for either individuals or institutions.

Some will object to this kind of procedure as an intrusion by outsiders into the affairs of the church and its schools, seeing it as something like a labor union pronouncement. They may view it as limiting executive authority. However, I have had extensive experience with faculty affairs following either an *ad hoc* or a negotiated, documented policy during my career, in both private and public school settings, and I assure you that the AAUP stand on the value, the necessity, and the ethics of true education are comfortably consistent with the mission of Seventh-day Adventism.

Further, there are objections that a systematic defense of freedom in intellectual matters weakens church authority. I contend that it does not do so; instead, such defense is essential to the growth of trust in the integrity of our most fundamental beliefs. This position can, I contend, be developed out of our Scripture and can be heard in the voice of Ellen White.

Her assertion that "truth can afford to be fair" implies, I believe, that the search for it can also be fair. And it can be Christian, professional, and legal, useful for teaching, reproof, correction, and for training in righteousness.

If this kind of truth protocol is a good thing, and I believe that I have demonstrated that it is, then it should be implemented at every one of our institutions of higher learning. That means, I think, that we will put our negotiated and documented policies regarding our respect for truth, for academic freedom, and for academic due process into our institutional bylaws and faculty handbooks. Such documents will clarify our mission and our goals, and establish the boundaries within which our teachers can live out their professional obligations to their colleagues and students, and inform our boards of trustees, for the ultimate benefit of us all.

Section 4

The Future of Seventh-day Adventist Higher Education

VINITA SAUDER, LORETTA B. JOHNS, AND JIMMY KAJAI

Chapter 15

Awareness and Perceptions Among Adventist College-Bound Youth Regarding Adventist Higher Education

The Seventh-day Adventist denomination operates fifteen accredited colleges and universities in the North American Division (fourteen campuses and one distance education university) with a combined enrollment of 26,571 students (Archives and Statistics, 2008), but only a quarter of college-bound Seventh-day Adventist youth attend these institutions. Seventy-five percent of college-going Seventh-day Adventists attend public institutions or other private colleges and universities (General Conference Commission on Higher Education [GCCHE], 2005).

To find out why more Seventh-day Adventist youth aren't attending the church's colleges and universities, a nationwide study of Adventist students between high school graduation and their first year of college was conducted for the Association of Adventist Colleges and Universities (Sauder, 2008). A major finding of the study was that awareness of the Seventh-day Adventist colleges and universities in North America is almost nonexistent among Adventist students who attend public high schools instead of Adventist academies. Results from a telephone survey from this study demonstrate that Seventh-day Adventist colleges and universities are not reaching out to the majority of Adventist students who attend public high schools; three-quarters of these students report no recruiting contact from a Seventh-day Adventist college. Compounding this lack of awareness is the fact that more and more Seventh-day Adventist youth, up to 70 percent, are choosing to obtain their high school education in the public school system or with other private Christian high schools, instead of in Seventh-day Adventist academies (Gillespie et al., 2004), so they are less likely to know about the benefits of a Seventh-day Adventist education.

Background for the study: Numbers of Seventh-day Adventist youth decline, ethnic proportions are changing

Important data regarding Seventh-day Adventist demographics and college-bound Adventist populations were published in a 2008 report titled "Seventh-day Adventists in North America: A Demographic Profile," by Monte Sahlin and Paul Richardson from the Center for Creative Ministry; the study was commissioned by the North American Division Secretariat. The report indicates that there are 1.2 million Seventh-day Adventists in North America, with 177,581 children between zero and fourteen years of age, and 141,604 young people between the ages of fifteen and twenty-four.

In spite of what appears to be large numbers of children, only one Seventh-day Adventist family in five currently has school-age children in the household. Since the last demographic survey was conducted in 1990, the number of Adventist families with school-age children has declined by 25 percent (Sahlin and Richardson, 2008), resulting in a smaller pool of potential students in the Adventist community. The median age for an Adventist in North America is fifty-one, compared to a median age of thirty-six for citizens of the United States and thirty-five in Canada. Additionally, in the last two decades, the population of retired people among Seventh-day Adventists has doubled. Sahlin and Richardson call this the "graying of Adventism."

In the Sauder (2008) study, a larger proportion of minority students, 57.3 percent, participated in the nationwide survey than did Caucasians, at 41.9 percent. This is explained by the changing ethnic composition of the church, which should inform the formulation of future enrollment strategies for the Adventist colleges and universities. The ratio of Caucasians in the Seventh-day Adventist Church in North America has declined over the last twenty years to only half the membership. By 2030, Caucasians will not be the majority, but neither will any of the four largest ethnic segments; rather there will be a "majority minority" in that African Americans, Hispanics, Asians, and other ethnicities combined will be larger than the percentage of Caucasians (Sahlin and Richardson, 2008).

Most important to enrollment discussions is that 43 percent of Seventh-day Adventist households with children are Caucasian; 26 percent are African American, 22 percent are Hispanic, 5 percent are Asian, and 6 percent identify themselves as multi-ethnic or from another ethnic category. This indicates that there already exists a "majority minority" in terms of the Seventh-day Adventist population with upcoming college-age students in the household.

In *Seeking a Sanctuary: Seventh-day Adventism and the American Dream,* Malcolm Bull and Keith Lockhart (2007) report that the racial balance in Adventism is very different from that of other Protestant churches as well as from the United States as a whole. While other churches are fairly homogenous, Adventism is very racially mixed, providing a unique cultural mix. While Caucasians are significantly underrepresented in Adventism when compared to the national population, African Americans are represented at twice the national rate, making them the "most successful" of the minority groups in the church (Bull and Lockhart, 2007, 147). This may help to explain the high percentage of minority participants (and the 24 percent African American response) in the study's telephone survey.

Despite reports of the significant decline of young people in the Seventh-day Adventist Church, the good news is that Seventh-day Adventists in North America are a well educated people, according to Sahlin and Richardson (2008); the percentage of church members with a college degree is more than double that of the general population in the United States. The majority of Seventh-day Adventist Church members, 61 percent, have a college education; so if one takes the number of young people of college age estimated in the demographic report and multiply it by 61 percent, there are up to eighty-five thousand Seventh-day Adventist young people in the market for a Seventh-day Adventist higher education. For Adventist colleges and universities struggling with enrollment numbers who wish to attract more Seventh-day Adventists, this report provides a ray of hope. However, these numbers represent different demographics in terms of ethnicities than previously existed, and the majority of Seventh-day Adventist young people are not attending Seventh-day Adventist academies, which means the work of recruiting the church's youth is more challenging than ever before.

The church worries about Seventh-day Adventist enrollment in its colleges and universities

The topic of Seventh-day Adventist student enrollment in the church's colleges and universities has received much attention in the Adventist press over the last decade, as church officials worry about the possible enrollment loss of Seventh-day Adventists in each institution of higher education. While total enrollment at the North American Division colleges and universities has been steadily rising, the percentage of Seventh-day Adventist students enrolled has not kept

Seventh-day Adventist Enrollment in North American Division Colleges and Universities, 2008

Institution	Adventist Enrollment	Total Enrollment	% Adventist Enrollment
Andrews University	3,034	3,419	88.74%
Atlantic Union College	302	388	77.84 %
Canadian University College	300	352	85.23 %
Columbia Union College	407	994	40.95 %
Florida Hospital College of Health Sciences	388	3,693	10.51 %
Griggs University	1,258	1,258	100.00 %
Kettering College of Medical Arts	80	821	9.74 %
La Sierra University	1,300	1,899	68.46 %
Loma Linda University	1,901	4,115	46.20 %
Oakwood University	1,581	1,865	84.77 %
Pacific Union College	1,023	1,453	70.41 %
Southern Adventist University	2,427	2,777	87.40 %
Southwestern Adventist University	299*	823	36.33 %
Union College	873	914	95.51 %
Walla Walla University	1,318	1,800	73.22 %
TOTALS	*16,491*	*26,571*	*62.06 %*

Note: Adapted from "Annual Statistical Report," by Archives and Statistics, 2008, from http://www.adventistarchives.org. (*Southwestern Adventist University reports that this number does not accurately reflect their Seventh-day Adventist enrollment numbers because they are having database issues. If the authors were to generalize Southwestern's Adventist enrollment to 85.4 percent, which is an average of their reports in the nineties, the total percentage of Seventh-day Adventist enrollment in the NAD colleges and universities would be 63.59 percent.)

pace over the last twenty years. When aggregated, the North American Division colleges and universities have a base of 62.1 percent Seventh-day Adventist students (figures are from 2008), but the variance between the fifteen colleges and universities is large. Union College in Nebraska is at the high end with 95.5 percent of its enrollment self-reporting as Seventh-day Adventist; Walla Walla University in Washington is at 73.2 percent; Loma Linda University in California at 46.2 percent; and Kettering College of Medical Sciences in Ohio reports 9.7 percent.

Why such wide variances in Seventh-day Adventist enrollment? Each college and university has a different mission, different target markets from which they draw students, as well as a different philosophy regarding the desirability of a homogeneous or heterogeneous mix of the student body in terms of religious faith. In addition, some of the colleges and universities offer primarily graduate programs or have adult completion degrees that draw in non-Adventist students.

To assess the unity, integrity, and financial viability of the Seventh-day Adventist system of higher education, including an assessment of the enrollment of Seventh-day Adventists in church colleges and universities across the globe, church leaders initiated a General Conference Commission on Higher Education in 2000, and the research group conducted surveys, compared statistics, and issued reports in 2003, 2004, and 2005. The Commission expressed concerns about a possible drift toward secularization in the Seventh-day Adventist colleges and universities, based on the evidence provided by authors George Marsden (1994), James Burtchaell (1998), and Robert Benne (2001), who collectively demonstrate that when colleges founded by a denomination lose an enrolled majority base of young people of the founding faith, it is often difficult to resist the slide toward generalization and a loss of distinctiveness, including pressures to move away from required chapels and worships, and the lifestyle restrictions generally considered appropriate for Christian colleges and universities.

Robert Benne's (2001) *Quality With Soul: How Six Premier Colleges and Universities Keep Faith With Their Religious Traditions,* measures a college's "church relatedness" with a matrix using a continuum of factors, with "orthodox" colleges and universities having the majority of students from the sponsoring tradition, "critical mass" colleges and universities having between 30 to 75 percent of their students from the founding faith, "intentionally pluralist" colleges and universities having only a small minority of students from the faith, and "accidentally pluralist" colleges and universities no longer recording the number of students from the faith. Following this model, a college with small percentages of students from the faith may eventually lead to a weakened connection with the founding religious heritage.

According to the Final Report of the General Conference Commission on Higher Education (GCCHE, 2005), the Seventh-day Adventist Church views its colleges and universities as training grounds for future church and lay leaders; therefore, the enrollment of significant percentages of Seventh-day Adventists in its colleges and universities is very important for the succession of future church leaders. To encourage more Seventh-day Adventist youth to enroll and to increase the number of Seventh-day Adventist students in the church's colleges and universities, the GCCHE (2005) recommends that the church develop marketing and financial incentive strategies.

> The church needs to take a serious look at how best to finance higher education and how best to reverse the trend of large numbers of church youth choosing non-Adventist institutions for their higher education needs as opposed to our own institutions (GCCHE, 2005, 9).

Response to the concerns about secularization in the reports of the Commission was mixed. The chief academic officers of the colleges and universities in the North American Division maintained that the problem of too many non-Adventist students was of more concern in other countries, where enrollment of non-Adventists is often the majority (AAAA, 2004).

While the academicians had doubts about the concerns outlined by the Commission, the reports were read with great interest by the chief enrollment and marketing officers in the Adventist Enrollment Association who were beginning to collaborate together to recapture a target market that had quietly grown over the last fifty years—Seventh-day Adventists who attend public high schools and colleges rather than Seventh-day Adventist academies and colleges.

Although twelve of the fifteen colleges and universities are independently owned by one of the nine union conferences in the North American Division (and three of the colleges and universities are owned and operated by the General Conference), there has been a history of stiff competition and territorial wars for students between the colleges and universities, until the members of the enrollment association realized that it would be easier to work together to recapture that elusive market of Seventh-day Adventist youth than to work independently. The Commission's call to bring more Seventh-day Adventist youth into the Seventh-day Adventist colleges and universities dovetailed with a goal of the college marketers who saw the potential of losing future generations of Seventh-day Adventist students if concerted action and an effort to recapture awareness and relevancy with Seventh-day Adventist college-bound youth were not emphasized. To this end, the Sauder (2008) study was conducted, sponsored by AACU and designed with cooperative planning and participation by the Adventist Enrollment Association.

Academy youth a no-growth target market

With a few exceptions, Seventh-day Adventist colleges and universities have traditionally devoted a majority of their marketing and recruitment resources to the more than one hundred academy campuses in the North American Division. Seventh-day Adventist academy students represent a relatively easy recruitment opportunity, or "low hanging fruit," according to college enrollment managers. The academy students are already acclimated to a Seventh-day Adventist educational environment and value the benefits of the total environment of opportunity on a Seventh-day Adventist campus, academically, spiritually, and socially. College recruiters visit academy campuses multiple times a year, holding junior and senior interviews, speaking in classes, and sometimes conducting Weeks of Prayer. In each union, colleges and universities hold an annual College Days event for the academy students. In addition, the Adventist Enrollment Association, in a collaborative effort, sponsors an annual college fair circuit (begun in 1999) on all one hundred plus academy campuses in North America, providing the fifteen colleges and universities a venue to showcase the entirety of the accredited Seventh-day Adventist higher education opportunities at each academy.

However, in contrast to the aggregated total enrollment of the North American colleges and universities, which has steadily increased, the enrollment at Seventh-day Adventist academies has not followed the same trend. Over more than two decades, from 1986 to 2008, academy enrollments have declined 18.9 percent. Several academies have closed or merged.

While the colleges and universities have increased enrollment in aggregate, the increase has not happened equally across all campuses. A third of the colleges and universities have struggled with enrollment declines from their enrollment positions twenty years ago; two colleges have maintained approximately the same enrollments over the decades. Eight of the colleges have experienced growth over the last twenty years, with the largest growth experienced by Florida Hospital College of Health Sciences (mostly non-Adventist students), Southern Adventist University, Loma Linda University, and Union College.

With the nationwide academy enrollment declining dramatically, and with the majority of Seventh-day Adventist youth enrolled outside the denominational system of church schools, the job of the college and

Seventh-day Adventist Higher Education in North America

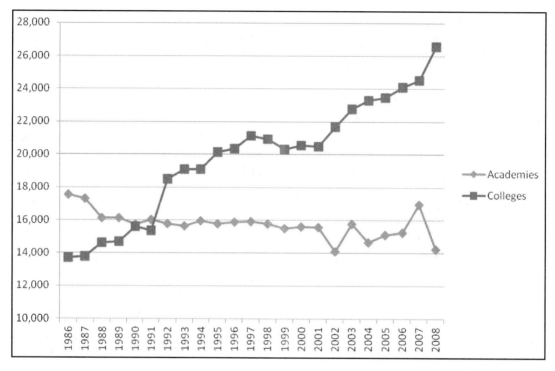

NAD academy and college enrollments, 1986–2008. From *Annual Statistical Report,* by Archives and Statistics, 1986–2008, retrieved April 27, 2010, http://www.adventistarchives.org; and *Annual Report,* by North American Division Office of Education, 1986–2008, Silver Spring, MD.

university enrollment office in attracting Seventh-day Adventist students becomes more difficult. The Adventist Enrollment Association has recognized that any future enrollment growth from Seventh-day Adventists is likely to come from the population of young people enrolled in the public school system. The enrollment group is now trying to enhance the recruiting efforts of the fifteen colleges and universities by providing increased emphasis, funding, and focus on prospective Seventh-day Adventist students who attend public high schools, other private high schools, and homeschools.

Where are the youth?

Now that membership in the North American Division has topped a million, it is difficult to find, target, and communicate with all of the Seventh-day Adventist college-age youth. The task of identifying who the school-age youth are and where they live is most difficult. Although each conference in North America is connected to a central Web-based data warehouse called E-Adventist, to which church clerks upload church membership records, this database is highly restricted. There is no central list of church attending youth maintained by the church, nor provided to the elementary schools, academies, or colleges for the purpose of recruiting the youth of the church. Each school is expected to figure out where the young people are by itself, through word of mouth, the goodwill of pastors and church clerks, or from parents and students seeking information. The only coordinated use of E-Adventist by the North American Division is the collection of all the membership addresses for nationwide monthly mailings of the church magazine, *Adventist World,* and for conference newsletters and union magazines.

Reaching the Seventh-day Adventist youth through Seventh-day Adventist Church publications or Web sites is also not an ideal option. Advertising is very expensive in church publications, and the one weekly church magazine, *Insight,* whose target audience is high school youth, is not delivered by subscription to the home but in batches three months in advance to the churches. Since *Insight*'s distribution is dependent on many variables at each church, it is not a guaranteed way of reaching every youth.

The Sauder/AACU Research Study

In order to do target marketing and strategic planning well, an approach based on research is optimal, so this study was designed to provide analysis of the Seventh-day Adventist college enrollment situation as well as recommend a marketing direction for marketing and enrollment managers. It was against this backdrop that the research study led by Sauder (2008) and the Adventist Enrollment Association developed. The study was commissioned by the Association of Adventist Colleges and Universities (AACU) and conducted to fill in the gaps in knowledge about Seventh-day Adventist college-bound youth. What do Seventh-day Adventist youth think about Seventh-day Adventist colleges and universities? Are there differences in perception and attitudes between the Seventh-day Adventists who attend the Seventh-day Adventist academies and the Seventh-day Adventists who attend public high schools, homeschools, or other private high schools?

The study was constructed to occur during a very specific time in the life of students—during the summer after high school graduation, but prior to attendance at college in the fall. The purpose of the study was to explore the views of Seventh-day Adventist youth on the factors (both motivators and barriers) that influence their college choices. The study grouped Seventh-day Adventist students according to the type of high school they attended; three groups were named and compared throughout the study:

1. Academy/Adventist College (students who graduated from a Seventh-day Adventist academy and were headed toward a Seventh-day Adventist college)
2. Non-Academy/Adventist College (students who graduated from a public school, private non-Adventist school, or homeschool, and were headed to a Seventh-day Adventist college)
3. Non-Academy/Other College (students who graduated from a public school, private non-Adventist school, or homeschool, and were headed toward a non-Adventist college)

The study's main research question was "Why are Seventh-day Adventists not attending Seventh-day Adventist colleges and universities in greater numbers?" Supporting research questions were:

1. What level of awareness of the North American Division colleges and universities is there among Seventh-day Adventist youth?
2. What college attributes are motivators and important influencers to the Seventh-day Adventist young person, and how are the Seventh-day Adventist colleges and universities perceived to perform on the attributes viewed as important?
3. What are the barriers to choosing a Seventh-day Adventist college?
4. What college marketing messages resonate with Seventh-day Adventist youth?
5. What are the most effective ways to communicate with Seventh-day Adventist young people regarding college choice?

A "mixed methods" approach was selected for the research methodology, applying both qualitative and quantitative techniques in a sequential two-phase design. The first phase of the research was an explorative study through focus groups conducted in Los Angeles and Nashville. Focus group participants were Seventh-day Adventist students and parents from the three groups in the study. A professional moderator guided the focus groups, while enrollment managers observed from behind two-way mirrors. The insights discovered from the focus groups then shaped the building of a survey instrument for use in a nationwide telephone survey, which comprised the second phase of the study. The in-depth phone interviews, lasting an average of eighteen minutes each, were conducted by a professional firm using computer-assisted telephone software connected to a database of purchased and provided names specific to this study. All of the students in the database were Seventh-day Adventist.

Findings and recommendations

From the dataset selected from the telephone interviews of 253 Seventh-day Adventist college-bound youth, 64.8 percent were non-academy students and 35.2 percent were academy students. Of the non-academy students, 82.3 percent attended public high school, 12.2 percent attended a non-Adventist private school, and 5.5 percent were homeschooled.

The differences among the three groups of students were compared using crosstabulations and Chi-square, showing frequencies, percentages, standard residuals, degrees of freedom, and p values. An absolute standard residual value of 2.0 or greater, combined with an alpha p value of less than .05, was used to indicate a statistically significant difference between the groups. Perceptual maps were also constructed to visually track the scores from the three groups using college choice criteria and college performance scales.

The findings indicate that where a student goes to college is clearly related to the type of high school attended. Students who attend an academy are more likely to attend a Seventh-day Adventist college. A surprising finding was that students who attend a private non-Adventist high school are also more likely to attend a Seventh-day Adventist college, while students who attend a public high school are more likely to attend a public college or a private, non-Adventist college or university.

Ethnicity plays a part

African American: The study discovered that Seventh-day Adventist African American students attend public high schools at a significantly higher rate (72.1 percent) than all other Seventh-day Adventist ethnicities. Seventh-day Adventist African Americans are also attending non-Adventist colleges and universities at a significantly higher rate than other ethnicities (74.1 percent).

Caucasian: Compared with other ethnicities, it was found that a significantly higher percentage of Caucasians attend Seventh-day Adventist colleges and universities after graduating from a Seventh-day Adventist academy.

Hispanic: The study found that the Hispanic students are also attending public high schools at high rates, which confirms the Ramirez-Johnson and Hernandez (2003) study, *Avance,* which found that the majority of Hispanic youth, up to 77 percent, are enrolled in public colleges and universities. However, the *Avance* study also uncovered a desire among Hispanics to attend Seventh-day Adventist colleges and universities, indicating that 61 percent of college-age Hispanic youth would select a Seventh-day Adventist college over a public school if given the choice. The

Avance authors suggest that colleges and universities should be more aggressive in their recruitment of Hispanic Seventh-day Adventist young people, and should aim their marketing at the churches where they are likely to reach Hispanic youth. "Where should the colleges and universities wanting to reach Hispanic Seventh-day Adventists go? There is only one answer—the local church—since Hispanic youth are not attending Seventh-day Adventist academies" (Ramirez-Johnson and Hernandez, 2003, 116).

From the findings of the Sauder (2008) and *Avance* studies, it appears that there is a definite recruiting market among the Hispanic, African American, and Asian youth for Seventh-day Adventist colleges and universities in North America. For the most part, Seventh-day Adventist minority students are not attending Seventh-day Adventist academies, and, for the most part, they are also not attending Seventh-day Adventist colleges and universities.

Factors influencing college choice: Cost

While no significant difference between groups was found with regard to household income, cost surfaced as a factor of concern in the Los Angeles focus group and was rated by a large percentage of the Non-Academy/Other College group as a key concern. Because of this concern, affordability and the availability of financial aid need to be prominent in communicating with this group. According to Lewison and Hawes (2007), marketing approaches should create value among prospective students and not focus on the negative aspects of price and cost. Obstacles should be seen through the lens of value (Hayes, 1993), much like the buyers of iPods or any other popular retail brands do not focus on the price but on the brand experience and the value they receive from the product. However, because a university operates within a service environment and not a retail environment, marketing strategies and roles may be different (Liu, 1998). A positive financial planning approach needs to be taken with families concerned with the cost of attendance, providing examples of other families in similar circumstances who were able to achieve their educational goals. Particularly in an uncertain economy, it is especially important to emphasize educational value and benefits, as well as offer a financial planning approach to affording a private college education.

Students headed toward Seventh-day Adventist colleges and universities in the survey reported receiving more financial aid than the students headed toward public colleges and universities, irrespective of household income. This is true in general for all private colleges and universities, since private schools offer more grants and scholarships due to their higher cost (Council of Independent Colleges, n.d.).

Factors influencing college choice: Parents

If a student's parent or parents attended a Seventh-day Adventist college, there is a significantly higher likelihood that the student will attend a Seventh-day Adventist college, even if they are not enrolled in a Seventh-day Adventist academy. The converse is also true, in that if a student's parent or parents did not attend a Seventh-day Adventist college, there is a significantly higher likelihood that the student will not attend a Seventh-day Adventist college. The influence of parents and family members, sometimes referred to as "significant persons," in relation to college choice is well documented in literature. Students who did not attend a Seventh-day Adventist academy, but who planned to enroll in a Seventh-day Adventist college, appear to be dependent on their link to family and friends in their choice to enroll at a Seventh-day Adventist college, and these students rank their parents as one of the most effective ways of reaching them. Parents of these students are very important influencers in the college decision.

In the long term, then, if more and more students attend public high schools and public colleges and universities, the parental role model effect may be less effective in encouraging enrollment in Seventh-day Adventist colleges and universities as this group of Seventh-day Adventist students become parents themselves.

Are students who don't attend Seventh-day Adventist schools really connected to the church?

Among Seventh-day Adventist administrators who work in the denomination's churches, conferences, or schools, there is typically anecdotal discussion about the probability of a lack of a good connection to the church among students who do not attend Seventh-day Adventist academies or colleges. It is often believed that these students are not well grounded to the church. The Sauder (2008) study demonstrated that this "myth" is untrue, in that there is no significant difference between groups with regard to church attendance or Sabbath observance. Committed Seventh-day Adventists are found equally in all groups.

Factors influencing college choice: Awareness levels

The focus group students in both Nashville and Los Angeles showed a marked lack of awareness about Seventh-day Adventist colleges and universities, particularly among the non-academy groups. In the Los Angeles group of non-academy students headed toward public colleges and universities, the moderator commented, "None of you selected a religious school. Were you considering one?" There was silence. "No," came the answer from around the room. The moderator began to read off the names of the Seventh-day Adventist colleges and universities. "Tell me if you've ever heard of them." After a few college names are read, one student asks, "Are these in, like, California?" "No, they are all over the country," the moderator replies. This finding of an almost complete lack of awareness was repeated in the telephone survey. Unaided, non-academy graduates could only name three of the fifteen colleges and universities.

Academy graduates recalled the names of Seventh-day Adventist colleges and universities at twice the rate of public school graduates.

Parent focus groups were also conducted in Nashville and Los Angeles and parents were similarly unaware that the Seventh-day Adventist Church supported fifteen colleges and universities. The parents reacted the strongest and seemed annoyed that the church or their pastor had not communicated this with them. Parents in Los Angeles wondered why all of the non-Adventist colleges and universities were soliciting their children, and why none of the Seventh-day Adventist colleges and universities had contacted the student or the parent.

It is noted that the non-academy group was most aware of Andrews, Loma Linda, Southern Adventist, and Oakwood. With the exception of Southern Adventist, the other three are all General Conference–sponsored universities, with world-church funding provided through special annual offering calls and mentions in church services around the world on specified weekends. This may explain why awareness levels among the non-academy group were higher for those three universities, a testament to systematic communication in the churches leading to higher awareness levels.

Interestingly, awareness about Seventh-day Adventist colleges and universities was also very low in the 2003 *Avance* study. "Assume that Hispanics are unaware that your institution exists" (2003, 116). "Not only are church institutions missing an entire population of potential students, but Hispanic Seventh-day Adventist youth are being denied the opportunity for the Christian higher education that can be so valuable both to their temporal and their spiritual well-being. Seventh-day Adventist higher education needs to make the Hispanic community an integral part of its constituency" (2003, 115).

The lack of awareness is the most significant finding of the Sauder (2008) study. It is obviously critical for the church and its colleges and universities to create higher awareness levels in the Seventh-day Adventist population. A foundational principle in marketing is to create awareness of a brand; without it, consumers will not know about the benefits of purchasing the product (Kotler, 1972).

College choice motivators

There are large differences between the academy and non-academy groups regarding which factors are important and which offer the main reasons for choosing a college. For the non-academy graduates headed to non-Adventist colleges and universities, top motivators are affordability, closeness to home, high-quality education, best program in their major, and classes taught by professors and not teaching assistants. For students who planned to attend Seventh-day Adventist colleges and universities, the top motivators are spiritual environment, students sharing same spiritual beliefs and values, and classes taught by professors and not teaching assistants.

As described in D. W. Chapman's (1981) conceptual model of college choice, which provided the theoretical framework for the research project, there is a confluence of factors, attributes, and events that come together to form a student's college choice, so there is never one factor that operates alone. A pattern of differences clearly emerged between students headed toward Seventh-day Adventist colleges and universities and students headed to other colleges and universities. Students headed toward Seventh-day Adventist institutions consistently placed importance on the spiritual environment and on friends and students sharing the same beliefs and values, a sort of social networking factor. These groups value what Seventh-day Adventist colleges and universities have to offer.

On the other hand, the students who did not attend Seventh-day Adventist academies and who were not headed toward Seventh-day Adventist colleges and universities valued factors that confirmed findings in 2002 by the Institute for Higher Education Policy. Students going to public institutions were more likely to choose location or price as main reasons over their peers at private colleges and universities (Cunningham, 2002).

During analysis of both the focus group findings and the telephone survey, it was surmised that the reason the non-academy group did not value the spiritual environment factor when provided the initial list of factors, is because of the complete disconnect with this group in terms of awareness, and the lack of conversation regarding the distinctiveness available on Seventh-day Adventist campuses. It is interesting to note, however, that when read a list of positioning statements toward the end of each focus group session, a finding which was repeated on the telephone interviews, this group of students found the statement, "Adventist colleges can offer you spiritual growth and spiritual opportunities that you simply can't find elsewhere," as making them more interested in attending a Seventh-day Adventist college. In fact, this group rated the statement at a higher aggregate percentage than the other two groups. It was by far the most motivating of the statements. Why did this group not value or mention the spiritual environment factor in earlier questions and then rate this statement highly toward the end of the survey? We believe the answer can be discovered from the focus group observations.

In the focus groups, a sort of transformation took place among the students headed toward non-Seventh-day Adventist colleges and universities. As the topics progressed and the moderator began mentioning a spiritual environment and associating with friends of like beliefs, it was interesting to see the concept dawn on them. It was obvious they had never thought about this before. The moderator, although of Lutheran background, almost found himself in an evangelistic position concerning the benefits and offerings of a Seventh-day Adventist college. As the students were slowly "educated" and "exposed" to the attributes commonly associated with Seventh-day Adventist campuses, they began to engage with the moderator in dialog about the value of a spiritual environment. The same sort of phenomenon happened in the parent groups. While fascinating to observe, it points out the lack of familiarity these students have with Adventist college environments, as well as the value of education, communication, and conversation about the values and distinctiveness that Seventh-day Adventist colleges and universities offer.

For those students who are looking for a faith-based academic environment, who desire a highly personalized education, and for a campus that affirms their Seventh-day Adventist beliefs and values, an Adventist college may be ideal.

"Professors who know you by name" is a highly prized attribute in the non-academy group, and was discussed in the focus groups by these students as well. They described classes at public universities that had two hundred to three hundred students in them; the small classes and personal interaction available at an Adventist campus was appealing to them. One non-academy student headed toward an Adventist college in a Los Angeles focus group said, "SDA schools will try extra hard to help you out, but in public school they don't give you that much attention."

In the Nashville focus groups, religion tended to be mentioned as a higher priority for college choice in all the groups. Students who had attended a public school felt it was more challenging than attending an academy, since teachers and peers could not understand why they could not play sports on a Friday night. One public high school student headed to a Seventh-day Adventist college said, "Being Adventist is not a normal thing; nothing beats being with other Adventist kids."

The marketing myth: Reputation for high quality education

It is often heard in conversations among Seventh-day Adventist college faculty that the reason the non-academy students do not choose Adventist colleges and universities is that they do not perceive the institutions to be of good enough academic quality. This study appears to have soundly repudiated that myth. All groups of prospective students (those who were not aware of any of the Seventh-day Adventist colleges and universities were not included in these results) rated the Adventist institutions high in terms of perceptions of academic excellence and reputation. In fact, the reputation for high-quality education attribute scored almost the same across the groups measured—as highly important, but also with good performance by the colleges and universities.

Professors are often heard to say, "We need to really market how great our academic excellence is because that will draw in more students." The study demonstrated that, while the attribute "reputation for high quality education" is a foundation, it is not a marketing differentiator among the groups. This came out clearly in the focus groups as well. Students are not choosing Seventh-day Adventist colleges and universities for their excellent academic programs (which they rank as important and they also perceive the colleges to have); instead they are choosing Seventh-day Adventist campuses over public universities because of the differentiators involved with spiritual growth opportunities, personal attention from caring faculty, and lifelong friendships with students holding similar beliefs and values. These are the differentiators that Seventh-day Adventist colleges and universities must market. The differentiators, however, only work properly as long as academic excellence is maintained as a foundation and strong academic programs exist that interest students. This study does not suggest that academic excellence can be abandoned or should not be mentioned; rather it must be the bedrock of each institution, and fostered and communicated as the strong base upon which the differentiation rests. It is possible to highlight excellent academics through an attribute all groups find important—the personal attention from faculty. Marketers and recruiters may be able to use faculty connectedness, a hallmark of teaching excellence, to emphasize the quality learning environment with engaged faculty and students at Seventh-day Adventist colleges and universities.

College-choice barriers

The largest barrier to attending a Seventh-day Adventist college is lack of awareness, followed by lack of knowledge of the benefits of attending a Seventh-day Adventist college, and the lack of recruitment contact among the non-academy group. One parent in a Los Angeles focus group said, "I noticed that other colleges were asking for Abby. I would like the SDA colleges to ask for the children that are in the church. None of these colleges contacted us or sent a letter. They should be saying, 'Why don't you join our college? Why don't you come over here? This is what we offer.' There was none of that."

Of the students surveyed by telephone, significant differences exist in the level at which the student groups are being recruited. A total of 71.0 percent of the Academy/Adventist College group were recruited by an Adventist college or university, in contrast to only 44.8 percent in the Non-Academy/Adventist College group and 22.6 percent in the Non-Academy/Other College group. Students are more likely to attend if they are actively recruited and have knowledge about certain colleges and universities. Unless the youth in the non-academy groups are approached by Seventh-day Adventist colleges and universities, additional enrollment from these groups cannot be expected.

Secondary barriers are cost, lack of scholarships, location too far away, lifestyle restrictions (mandatory worships, conservative dress code rules, diet restrictions), a strict or opinionated environment, no legitimate sports programs, and a desire to attend a big-name school.

The barriers regarding lifestyle restrictions and opinionated environments mirror the Maguire Associates study conducted in 2001 among seventy Christian colleges and universities who were members of the Council for Christian Colleges and Universities. Barriers to attendance in that study included concerns about "closed-mindedness" and strict rules. However, it is important to note that colleges and universities that provide a spiritual environment and are connected to particular denominations often require chapel attendance and other rules considered "strict" as a way of showing distinctiveness and fostering a different environment than is found on the campuses of public colleges and universities. Marsden (1994), Burtchaell (1998), and Benne (2001) demonstrate collectively that it is in the best interest of a denominational college to retain the distinctiveness of chapels, worships, and lifestyle requirements. Without them, the college becomes like any other college and loses its faith-based distinctiveness over time.

Marketing messages: What would make students more interested?

Ten positioning statements were tested in the focus groups and eight positioning statements were tested in the telephone surveys. Among all groups, both in the focus groups and in the telephone surveys, the top three messages that were most motivating and the most likely to increase interest were:

- Adventist colleges can offer you spiritual growth and spiritual opportunities that you simply can't find elsewhere.
- At Adventist colleges, you have easy access to professors who

- understand the value of providing personal attention to each student.
- At Adventist colleges, you can develop lifelong friendships and relationships with students who share similar beliefs and spiritual values.

It is interesting to note that the three top messages are also found in prior research regarding Seventh-day Adventist enrollment. D. W. Hunt's (1996) study identified top factors that families consider most important when sending students to Seventh-day Adventist boarding academies: a spiritual environment, concerned and caring teachers, and school climate. Philip Mainda (2001) addressed the factors influencing school choice among the Seventh-day Adventist population in Michigan and discovered that for grades K–12, there was a significant relationship between school choice and the parents' perceptions of spiritual values-based education. Minder (1985) conducted a study in the Lake Union Conference and found that attendance at a Seventh-day Adventist K–12 school substantially increased the probability of the student being baptized into the church and retaining membership, as well as a relationship between scholastic achievement and the development of high moral standards and positive spiritual lives. Could these school choice factors be timeless differentiators for Seventh-day Adventist families regardless of the school, whether elementary school, academy, or college?

Other studies confirm the significance of the spiritual environment for college choice. Gunnoe and Moore (2002) found that religious schooling fosters religious commitment by creating religious peer groups of friends for adolescents, which in turn reinforces the parental view of the importance of religion. Pascarella and Terenzini (1991) and Astin (1977, 1993) demonstrate a significant religious decline in religious attitudes, values, and behaviors during the college years with one exception: those students who attend denominationally affiliated colleges and universities. Enrollment in church-related colleges and universities tends to support and strengthen students' existing religious values and behaviors. By contrast, secular institutions tend to exert the strongest negative influence.

Lee (2001) identifies the college years as impressionable years when attitudes are susceptible to change, and Willimon (1997) reports an openness during this time of transition from youth to adulthood to explore and experience religion. It is clear that the college years are a time of questioning, searching, and movement, and a "time of transition from other control to self-control where decisions of faith and religion move from being imposed by parents to a faith that becomes inherent in the individual" (Henderson, 2003, 26). Pascarella and Terenzini (1991) indicate that there is evidence of a link between the religious values of the faculty and the tendency among students to change their religious commitments. Where faculty expressed greater commitment to religion, students felt supported in their values and commitment.

Henderson (2003) explored data from 16,000 students and 133 colleges and universities to study the change over time in religious commitment while at college. He reported an overall decline in church attendance, hours per week spent in prayer and meditation, and a self-rating of spirituality. There were twenty-one Seventh-day Adventist students in his sample, but no Seventh-day Adventist colleges and universities; the Adventist students were attending public or other private institutions. Among the Adventist students, 25 percent reported switching to the Catholic faith while in college.

The importance of the spiritual environment, personal attention, and close contact with caring, believing faculty, cannot be underestimated as a differentiating and motivating factor in college choice.

The local church is important for effective communication to students

The non-academy and academy groups have marked differences in their survey responses regarding the best methods of communication to reach Seventh-day Adventist students. The academy group values college fairs at the academies, academy counselors, and college recruiters. The non-academy groups cited church events, church pastors, college mailings and e-mails, and college fairs near their church. For high school students not attending academy, it is clear that the local church is the central hub of Adventism for these students. This is a critical finding with many practical implications. To reach the non-academy group, communication must go through the church as a central resource point. Colleges and universities need to consider the church pastors as vital partners in communicating with this target audience.

Because of the pastors' importance as a communication channel for non-academy youth, colleges and universities and the Department of Education in the North American Division should devote special effort at keeping pastors informed regarding the offerings and benefits at all fifteen of the colleges and universities. Churches should be supplied with ample materials for the college consortia brand, including posters with all the colleges and universities listed, bulletin inserts, literature, and a way to request that a college fair come to their church area. This should not be a job for the college consortium alone. The leadership of the North American Division, if it is indeed a goal to increase the enrollment of youth in Seventh-day Adventist schools, should mount a campaign of education for its ministers and make this important at ministerial conventions and church meetings. We are called to this task by the General Conference Commission on Higher Education: "The church looks to Seventh-day Adventist higher education for its next generation of leaders" (GCCHE, 2005, 3) and "The church needs to take a serious look at . . . how to best reverse the trend of large numbers of church youth choosing non-Adventist institutions for their higher education needs as opposed to our own institutions" (9).

The colleges and universities should focus time and attention to visiting churches in their unions regularly to connect with students and families, and bring materials to spread the word about the benefits of a Seventh-day Adventist college education. Many of the colleges and universities have begun excellent programs to connect with local churches in recent years, and are taking important steps to reach Seventh-day Adventist youth who do not attend academies. Some current programs that should get special mention include the following:

- Union College's enrollment office operates Matchbox Ministries, which sends out groups of students to the local churches.
- La Sierra University's enrollment office spearheads an intense local church ministry program, taking teams of students to churches in the metropolitan Los Angeles area.
- Southern Adventist University's enrollment office recently started a YES Ministry program, for Youth Encountering Salvation. Teams of students travel to churches to hold youth programs.
- Andrews University hosts an annual youth event for students attending public high schools and has a dedicated staff member on the enrollment team devoted to partnering with youth ministers in the conferences and churches of the Lake Union to reach out to the non-academy youth.

What actions can be taken?

A fundamental recommendation resulting from this study is that Seventh-day Adventist colleges and universities, in partnership with the North American Division Department of Education, need to create a comprehensive, integrated, and coordinated marketing plan to reach all Adventist youth, particularly those not attending the Seventh-day Adventist academies. As part of the plan, the colleges and universities should cooperate on a common branding strategy for the AACU college consortium. Gone should be the days when individual colleges and universities battle it out for name recognition and try to steal academy students from each other's territories. The current smattering of eclectic, individual strategies, with some colleges and universities heavily funded and others funded sparingly, is not serving the Seventh-day Adventist youth effectively. Awareness levels of the colleges and universities are simply unacceptable for a denomination that values higher education so highly and has spent so much funding to keep it viable.

Like other denominational college consortia that have already gone down this road (the Lutheran, Catholic, and Churches of Christ college associations), Seventh-day Adventists will be more effective and more successful at influencing non-academy students to enroll in Seventh-day Adventist colleges and universities if they will market themselves together and brand themselves together as a coordinated system of colleges and universities with an overarching set of educational benefits and strengths common to all.

This cooperative approach should extend to the conferences and churches across the country as well. While the Adventist Enrollment Association has made great strides in reducing the territorial battles among the unions and their colleges and universities, the old territorial barriers and attitudes still exist in many conferences, unions, and churches. There is a reluctance to assist in efforts that might promote colleges outside their union, for fear of hurting the institution located in their union and supported monetarily by the union. This sort of territorial mind-set should be put aside in the interest of young Adventist students, who need to know that a college that fits them well might be located outside their union territory. It should be the preference of every church leader to have a Seventh-day Adventist student enrolled at any of the Seventh-day Adventist colleges and universities, rather than have them enroll at a public university. A common, cooperative strategy will allow more to be accomplished together than individually. The philosophy of "a rising tide lifts all boats," to coin a popular, descriptive phrase, means that working together to create momentum and achieve a common goal will benefit all.

The biggest form of competition for all of the Seventh-day Adventist colleges and universities are the public institutions, so rather than worry about individual union territories, the colleges and universities should unite to increase awareness of the excellent alternatives available at church-sponsored institutions by using the knowledge of what motivates Adventist students in their college search. The core of a good brand strategy is knowing which attributes and factors of the brand have the most impact (Keller, 2002). A brand differentiates based on what makes it—in this case, a group of colleges and universities—unique (Burge and Gunther, 2003).

While the foremost finding of the study is the lack of awareness, the second most critical finding is the importance of the spiritual environment as a college characteristic that is differentiating and meaningful to Seventh-day Adventist young people, regardless of whether they attended an Adventist academy or a public high school. The opportunity to practice their faith and grow spiritually in a place where friends and faculty share their beliefs is an important college-choice factor that makes the majority of youth interviewed in this study more interested in a Seventh-day Adventist college. This is a differentiating factor shared by all fifteen Seventh-day Adventist colleges and universities in the Association of Adventist Colleges and Universities, and should be widely communicated.

First strategic steps taken by AEA and AACU

When the research project was first envisioned, the enrollment teams of the fifteen colleges in the Adventist Enrollment Association began to take the first few baby steps on the road to marketing collaboration and communicating systematically with Seventh-day Adventist youth who don't attend Seventh-day Adventist academies. AACU, as the sponsoring organization for the collaboration, helped launch the formal Joint Marketing Committee in 2003 and funded the first research project, which began in 2005.

By late 2005, the Joint Marketing Committee initiated the first joint direct mail campaigns, pilot tested approaches to joint community and church-based college fairs, and initiated joint calling campaigns to limited numbers of youth as the budget allowed. In addition, a common application was developed and made available on a joint Web site, www.adventistcolleges.org, which went live in 2007. Initial efforts began on joint publicity in all the unions, as well as joint advertising in church magazines, listing all the colleges under a common slogan.

Most important, the joint marketing materials have a consortium branding approach based on this research study, with all accredited North American Division colleges and universities listed together. The common themes on the materials include the top three messages found to generate the most interest among students from all three groups in the study (spiritual opportunities, friends in the faith, and personal connections with professors).

These efforts have led to a comprehensive marketing and enrollment strategy that has grown more sophisticated and successful, resulting in thousands of applications and hundreds of enrolled students each year as AACU seeks to reach all Adventist youth in North America, including those attending public schools.

While the early joint marketing efforts were organized by volunteers, AACU voted to fund a marketing director, the first full-time employee of the college consortium, in the summer of 2009. Initial funding for the position was contributed by the colleges and universities, the union conferences in the North American Division, and a benevolent educator passionate about the mission to reach out to young people and invite them to be educated in Adventist institutions. Rob Weaver, a former chair of the Joint Marketing Committee and a former vice president for enrollment at Union College, stepped into the role in October 2009, and has continued to build an innovative "Adventist Choice" strategy that reaches not only high school seniors, but also sophomores and juniors, as well as parents. Weaver publishes the monthly *Adventist College Strategy: Joint Marketing Report*, which tracks statistics and progress toward the annual enrollment goals. A second research project is now underway, which will further refine AACU's marketing strategy.

As N. Clifford Sorensen (2002) wrote in the *Journal of Adventist Education* regarding the North American Division colleges and universities collaborating together on various projects, "We can surely praise what occurred serendipitously . . . with respect to joint endeavors. However, today's environment requires a more comprehensive and coordinated approach" (49). With vision and foresight, Sorensen identified the need to commit the proper human and monetary resources to the collaborative process to make it work and to make it last, in order to benefit the youth of the church.

Given our long history of vigorous and competitive individuality, successful cooperation will require both a carefully crafted strategy and the identification of mutual benefits within partnership agreements. We must define outcomes and expectations and commit the necessary human and monetary resources to this process, which cannot be viewed as a short-term or one-time quick fix operation. In summary, many factors will impede or stall consortium efforts. Most if not all can be overcome by dedicated and unrelenting effort (Sorensen, 2002, 50).

It is time for the Seventh-day Adventist Church and the Seventh-day Adventist colleges and universities to work together as a system, in a systematic way, to communicate the advantages and benefits of a Seventh-day Adventist higher education to all church constituents. Each Adventist young person in North America should have the opportunity to consider all of the Seventh-day Adventist colleges and universities and be aware of the opportunities available. It is only in this way that the church will stabilize a vibrant future for Seventh-day Adventist higher education in

North America and continue to provide a healthy strategic base of Seventh-day Adventist young people for each institution. Well-educated leaders grounded in service to the Master are the future leaders of our church, and it is time to devote resources and attention to crafting solutions to the problems unearthed in this research study.

Bibliography

Adventist Association of Academic Administrators. *AAAA minutes*. Anacortes, WA: Author. November 2004.

Archives and Statistics. *Annual Statistical Report*. 1986–2008. Retrieved April 26, 2010, http://www.adventistarchives.org.

Astin, A. W. *Four Critical Years: Effects of College on Beliefs, Attitudes, and Knowledge*. San Francisco: Jossey-Bass, 1977.

———. *What Matters in College? Four Critical Years Revisited*. San Francisco: Jossey-Bass, 1993.

Benne, R. *Quality With Soul: How Six Premiere Colleges and Universities Keep Faith With Their Religious Traditions*. Grand Rapids, MI: William B. Eerdmans, 2001.

Bull, M., and K. Lockhart. *Seeking a Sanctuary: Seventh-day Adventism and the American Dream*. Bloomington, IN: Indiana University Press, 2007.

Burge, R., and S. A. Gunther. "The Way You Wear Your Hair: What Brand Really Means for Higher Education." *Admissions Marketing Report* 14, no. 1 (January 2003): 7–14.

Burtchaell, J. T. *The Dying of the Light: The Disengagement of Colleges and Universities From Their Christian Churches*. Grand Rapids, MI: William B. Eerdmans, 1998.

Chapman, D. W. "A Model of Student College Choice." *Journal of Higher Education* 52, no. 5 (1981): 490–505.

Council of Independent Colleges. *Making the Case*. (n.d.). Retrieved July 7, 2006, http://www.cic.edu/makingthecase/data/sources.asp#comparative_alumni.

General Conference Commission on Higher Education. *Global Report and Recommendations* (vol. 1). Silver Spring, MD: Author, September 2003.

———. *Final Report of the General Conference Commission on Higher Education*. Washington, DC: Author, October 2005.

Gillespie, V. B., M. J. Donahue, B. Gane, and E. Boyatt. *Valuegenesis: Ten Years Later: A Study of Two Generations*. Riverside, CA: Hancock Center, 2004.

Gunnoe, M. L., and K. A. Moore. "Predictors of Religiosity Among Youth Aged 17–22: A Longitudinal Study of the National Survey of Children." *Journal for the Scientific Study of Religion* 41, no. 4 (2002): 613–622.

Hayes, T. J. "Image and the University." *Journal of Marketing for Higher Education* 41 (1993): 423–425.

Henderson, S. J. "The Impact of Student Religion and College Affiliation on Student Religiosity." Unpublished doctoral dissertation, University of Arkansas, Fayetteville, 2003.

Hunt, D. W. "The Factors That Impact Marketing and Enrollment in Seventh-day Adventist Boarding Schools." Unpublished doctoral dissertation, University of Virginia, Charlottesville, 1996.

Keller, K. L. "Building Customer-Based Brand Equity." *Marketing Management* 10, no. 2 (July–August 2001): 15–19.

Kotler, P. "A Generic Concept of Marketing." *Journal of Marketing* 36 (April 1972): 46–54.

Lee, J. J. *Changing Worlds, Changing Selves: The Experience of the Religious Self Among Catholic Collegians*. Los Angeles, CA: University of California, Los Angeles, 2001. (ERIC Document Reproduction Service No. ED451825.)

Lewison, D. M., and J. M. Hawes. "Student Target Marketing Strategies for Universities." *Journal of College Admissions* 196 (Summer 2007): 14–19.

Liu, S. S. "Integrating Strategic Marketing On an Institutional Level." *Journal of Marketing for Higher Education* 8, no. 4 (1998): 17–28.

Maguire Associates. *Attitudinal Study of Prospects, Inquirers, Parents of Inquirers, Non-Matriculants, and Matriculants*, 2001. Retrieved March 4, 2006, http://www.ccu.org/projects/marketreearch/channel.reports/default.asp.

Mainda, P. O. "A Study on Selected Factors Influencing School Choice Among the Seventh-day Adventist Populations in Southwest Michigan." Unpublished doctoral dissertation, Andrews University, Berrien Springs, MI, 2001.

Marsden, G. M. *The Soul of the American University: From Protestant Establishment to Established Nonbelief*. New

York: Oxford University Press, 1994.

Minder, W. E. "A Study of the Relationship Between Church-Sponsored K–12b Education and Church Membership in the Seventh-day Adventist Church." Unpublished doctoral dissertation, Western Michigan University, Kalamazoo, MI, 1985.

North American Division Office of Education. *Annual Report*. 1986–2008. Silver Spring, MD: Author.

Pascarella, E. T., and P. T. Terenzini. *How College Affects Students: Findings and Insights From Twenty Years of Research*. San Francisco, CA: Jossey-Bass, 1991.

_____. *How College Affects Students: Vol. 2. A Third Decade of Research*. San Francisco: Jossey-Bass, 2005; Washington University.

Ramirez-Johnson, J., and E. I. Hernandez. *Avance: A Vision for a New Mañana*. Loma Linda, CA: Loma Linda University Press, 2003.

Sahlin, M., and P. Richardson, *Seventh-day Adventists in North America: A Demographic Profile.* Milton Freewater, OR: Center for Creative Ministry, 2008.

Sauder, V. "Marketing Seventh-day Adventist Higher Education: College-Choice Motivators and Barriers." Unpublished doctoral dissertation, Andrews University, Berrien Springs, MI, 2008.

Sorensen, N. C. "Forming Partnerships Within Adventist Higher Education." *Journal of Adventist Education* 65, no. 2 (2002): 48–50.

Willimon, W. H. "Religious Faith and the Development of Character on Campus." *Educational Record* 78 (1997): 73–79.

RICHARD OSBORN

Chapter 16

Broadening the Context of Challenges Facing Adventist Higher Education

Introduction

Throughout the nearly 140 years of Seventh-day Adventist higher education, Adventists have been good fire fighters, putting out the immediate fires that arise, but not dealing with the causes that created the fire. Another analogy might be dealing with health challenges when some preventive care might have precluded a more serious illness. In the case of higher education, the challenge is often dealt with in a reactive way rather than by being proactive in analyzing the broader context, both in advance and while in the middle of a challenge. Board members, university administrators, faculty, staff, church leaders, constituents, parents, and students sometimes think their situation is isolated and unique without realizing that the root causes of the challenge may have been predicted in advance and, oftentimes, shared by similar faith-based colleges, secular universities, K–12 schools, and even other church institutions such as the local congregation. This kind of myopic thinking sometimes sets up references to the "good old days" when such problems supposedly didn't exist, although they have more likely been forgotten in the nostalgia of thinking that everything used to be better.

This chapter encourages a focus on the broader context of challenges that will be faced by Seventh-day Adventist higher education and, in some cases, all higher education during the upcoming decades. Rarely is the challenge unique to the individual university. If that context is analyzed in a proactive manner, decision-making can become more effective because it will grow out of the collection and analysis of data and research.

Because information can quickly become dated, in this chapter, the broader trends will be focused upon from the first decade of the twenty-first century with illustrative data that can be used as a model for research in the second decade of the current century.

Trends of importance

1. Loyalty by church members to Adventist higher education and other church institutions cannot be assumed.

For much of its history as a denomination, the Seventh-day Adventist Church could count on the vast majority of its members supporting the church's institutions, including the local congregation, tithing and giving principles, Adventist hospitals, church publications and periodicals, health food products, K–12 schools, and its colleges and universities.

For example, my great-grandparents, in the early 1900s, moved from a homestead they built by hand near the great Columbia River in Washington in order for my grandfather to be able to attend a Seventh-day Adventist elementary school and academy just being started in Meadowglade, Washington. This emphasis on the importance of attending a Seventh-day Adventist K–12 school and, subsequently, Walla Walla College, was part of the church's culture and is the reason Adventists, given the size of the denomination, have such high educational accomplishments. While he attended Walla Walla College, his parents would sell an acre of land each year to help fund his education. Following graduation from college, he entered church employment in the church's printing establishments, leading several college presses and serving as a missionary to Argentina in a similar capacity before eventually finishing his career at the Pacific Press Publishing Association.

Such loyalty to the church and its institutions, including higher education, is rare today and will become less so in upcoming decades. While we might despair and think this is only a problem in Adventism, all denominations, institutions, and even the political structures of our society face similar challenges. It's become part of the culture that any institution will have to prove its worth to each new generation and cannot assume to have anyone's unquestioning loyalty. This change in culture will fundamentally change the way higher education markets itself to upcoming generations.

What are some specific examples of declining loyalty to the church?

Reduced tithe increases—During the first decade of the twenty-first century, tithe increases surpassed the Consumer

Price Index (CPI) by a small amount but should have been higher given an increased membership. However, at the beginning of the second decade, in the aftermath of a deteriorating general economy, many conferences experienced an actual decline in tithes and offerings. During much of this period, the percentage increase in per capita giving did not keep pace with the increase in the CPI. Most observers feel that younger generations do not have the same commitment to giving tithe and offerings as the World War II and baby boomer generation, so worries exist about the future strength of tithe as these population groups age and die. Some younger generation members are very generous in giving to specific projects, but loyal commitment to giving a "faithful" tithe and generous offerings to the local church is declining. Most churches report those giving offerings or tithe at less than 50 percent of their book membership. This is not a sign of vitality for congregational life. Most Adventist universities rely on generous subsidies from their sponsoring union conference which, in turn, relies on faithful giving by members to local conferences to supply these subsidies. If these trends continue, the ability for subsidies to remain at the same level is questionable when unions, conferences, and local churches are challenged to maintain their own budgets because of reduced giving. Given a greater proclivity for project giving by younger church members, universities may need to appeal to these members to make up for lost subsidies in future years. On a more fundamental level, reduced giving by members also indicates a lowered commitment and belief in the church's giving principles, which becomes part of a bigger problem for the overall morale of the church. Is it possible for a university to overcome these kinds of attitudes exhibited at the congregational level, or is the university a reflection of the broader challenges being experienced at other church levels? The answer to this question will say much about the future of Adventist universities.

Decreased church attendance—The percentage of those on the membership books who attend church is not a statistic kept by many conferences, but most feel this has been declining over the last few decades. The number of attendees is counted, including visitors and unbaptized children, so it's hard to determine accurate numbers. Roscoe Howard, former president of the Mid-America Union and former secretary of the North American Division, reports that one of the few studies ever done by a union, on this question, discovered that his union had an attendance rate of 48 percent of the membership number in 2005 and 51 percent in 2006. These percentages include visitors and children, which would lower the rate of actual members in attendance. Sabbath School attendance is even worse, with this important time for Bible study becoming a relic of the past in many churches. In some centers of Adventism, attendance remains strong for the worship service, but many small, rural churches, and even those in large secular cities, is discouragingly low with more gray hair evident than the joy and sound of vibrant children's Sabbath Schools. It's possible that the percentage of potential Adventist children attending K–university programs is similar to the percentage attending church on a regular basis.

Charles Sandefur, former president of ADRA and former president of Rocky Mountain and Hawaii Conferences and the Mid-America Union, makes the following observations:

> I do know, though, that after taking attendance counts conference wide in Hawaii and Rocky Mountain and union wide in Mid America my general rule of thumb has been that about 38–40 percent of on-the-books members attend on any given Sabbath and I bet it holds pretty true nationwide except in unusual situations where, for instance, all the inactives have been dropped from the books or there is exceptional vitality, thus improving the percentages.
>
> I've had a burden for accurate Sabbath morning attendance counts for a long time since it is the single best indicator of the health and vitality of a church and in fact probably "drives" other factors such as tithe paying and loyalty to Christian ed, etc. People who attend church are more likely to send their children to church school, pay tithe, etc., probably more than the other way around. Longitudinal attendance trends also track "real" growth and outs those churches who baptize a ton of people but don't have growing attendance which means there are lots of drop outs. It's pretty hard to find a church where attendance is growing but tithe, baptisms, active ministry is shrinking. Same for the opposite: few churches decline in attendance but have active outreach, tithe growth, strong children's programs, etc.[1]

Adventist higher education can only be strengthened to the extent that local congregational life and enrollment in K–12 Adventist schools can be revitalized. A way must be found for energizing church members, especially young adults, to become more joyful and committed to the mission and life of the Seventh-day Adventist Church, through regular participation in the church's activities, Sabbath School, worship services, evangelism, service, and financial contributions.

Later in this chapter, evidence will be

presented that the Seventh-day Adventist Church in North America is experiencing stagnancy in many indicators.

Broadening the context, the Seventh-day Adventist Church is not the only one to be experiencing these difficulties. One of the most provocative analyses comes from Reggie McNeal, a leadership trainer for the Southern Baptist Church. The power of his words should challenge all to think of the implications for the Seventh-day Adventist Church.[2]

> The current church culture in North America is on life support. It is living off the work, money, and energy of previous generations from a previous world order. This plug will be pulled either when the money runs out (80 percent of money given to congregations comes from people aged fifty-five and older) or when the remaining three-fourths of a generation who are institutional loyalists die off or both.
>
> Please don't hear what I am not saying. The death of the church culture as we know it will not be the death of the "church." The church Jesus founded is good; it is right. The church established by Jesus will survive until he returns. The imminent demise under discussion is the collapse of the unique culture in North America that has come to be called "church." This church culture has become confused with biblical Christianity, both inside the church and out. In reality, the church culture in North America is a vestige of the original movement, an institutional expression of religion that is in part a civil religion and part a club where religious people can hang out with other people whose politics, worldview, and lifestyle match theirs. As he hung on the cross Jesus probably never thought the impact of his sacrifice would be reduced to an invitation for people to join and to support an institution. . . .
>
> So far the North American church largely has responded with heavy infusions of denial, believing the culture will come to its senses and come back around to the church. This denial shows up in many ways. Many churches have withdrawn from the community. An alternate form of denial has been the attempt to fix the culture by flexing political and economic muscle. Still another form of denial shows up in the church's obsession with internal theological-methodological debates designed to determine who the true believers are while the world is headed to hell in a handbasket. . . .

Among many solutions, he suggests the following:

> A missionary culture will need to begin keeping score on things different from what we measure now. These may include how many ministry initiatives we are establishing in the streets, how many conversations we are having with pre-Christians, how many volunteers we are releasing into local and global mission projects aimed at community transformation, how many congregations are starting to reach different populations, how many congregations use our facilities, how many languages (ethnic and generational) we worship in, how many community groups use our facilities, how many church activities target people who aren't here yet, how many hours per week members spend in ministry where they work, go to school, and get mail.[3]

Adventist universities have gone through several generations of Americans including those described as the Lost Generation (born 1883–1900), the G.I. Generation (born 1901–1924), the Silent Generation (born 1925–1942), the Boom Generation (born 1943–1960), the Generation X (born 1961–1981), and now the Millennials (born 1982–now) with other possible designations for those being born today. The Millennials who represent the traditional age of those currently attending college have been described, by those who study each generation, as possessing seven traits—special, sheltered, confident, team-oriented, conventional, pressured, and achieving.[4]

The Millennials bring to the church the special challenge of being more spiritual than previous generations but not committed to institutional religion. However, some have been noticing a strong core of very conservative and traditional students among today's students who are becoming more assertive in their witness, creating an interesting blend in dealing with "baby boomer" professors who still carry a lot of baggage from the Vietnam War era and the theological debates of the 1960s and 1970s. In some ways, they are very traditional but, in other ways, they are more open to greater diversity of lifestyle practices, spiritual disciplines, and worship practices. In addition, a new generation of parents, often called "helicopter parents," have higher expectations of ongoing involvement in the lives of their children while in college, which creates new challenges and expectations. Before long, the Millennials will have their own children in K–12 and in Adventist universities. Within what broader context will those children function? How can Adventist universities proactively study their needs and motivations within the broader culture they will become part of as they enter adulthood?

One of the greatest challenges facing the church is the high dropout rate of young adults in congregational life. Yet, this is where the energy driving the church and its K-university system develops. Can Seventh-day Adventist universities be vibrant without a high level of involvement by young adults who often come from second and third generation families? For universities in North America to have a dynamic and growing future, a renewed vision for what the church is and can become in order to create renewed loyalty among members will be essential. In order for colleges to grow, increased attention must be focused on improved attendance rates at Sabbath School and church. Broadening the context to what is happening in a local congregation is crucial for the strength of Seventh-day Adventist higher education.

2. The changing demographics of the church, including the declining income levels of church members, will continue to create some of the biggest challenges for the continuing success of Seventh-day Adventist higher education in future years.

During the peak period of higher education enrollment, the church's demographics were largely Anglo, with many of childbearing age coming from a middle-class income level. The face of the church has dramatically changed in the last two decades and will continue to do so in upcoming decades. The impact on higher education will reverberate throughout the system as these changes take place, not only posing challenge, but new opportunities.

What are these demographic trends?

The graying of Adventism—In the first decade of the twenty-first century, the average age of church members increased. The median age for the Seventh-day Adventist community in North America, including the unbaptized children in church families, was fifty-eight. The median age for the general public was thirty-six in the United States and thirty-seven in Canada. Among native-born Anglo and African American members, the median age was even higher. As Paul Richardson of The Center for Creative Ministry wrote,

> These demographic realities affect many things. There are more than 1,000 local churches in the North American Division that have no children or teens at all. The pool of people in the age group who might attend Adventist schools is getting smaller and smaller. Fewer and fewer congregations have enough teens, young adults or even young couples to provide the critical mass necessary to conduct a youth group and other activities that have always been the lifebeat of Adventist churches.[5]

The graying of Adventism means that there will be fewer young people of university age compared to earlier decades with this trend continuing into the future.

Declining membership growth rates—While North American church membership is growing, barely enough new members are being added to compensate for those dying or leaving. One sample year would be July 1, 2005 to June 30, 2006, when 37,334 members were added for a 3.4 percent accession rate; however, more than 27,000 members were dropped due to death, apostasy, or missing, which translated into a net gain of only 9,829 out of a total membership of slightly more than one million.[6] Net membership growth rates, which averaged 3.23 percent in the 1970s, 2.42 percent in the '80s, 2.05 percent in the '90s, but only 1.86 percent in the first half of the twenty-first century, do not bode well for the future when coupled with an aging membership. Universities cannot count on dramatic membership increases, either through traditional or nontraditional evangelism or birth rates, to increase their enrollments.

Dramatic growth in Hispanic membership—The greatest growth in church membership in the twenty-first century has been among Hispanics, especially first generation immigrant families who find special appeal in the teachings of Adventism taught through traditional evangelism. With the Seventh-day Adventist Church divided into eight regional unions composed of several states within each union, the Pacific Union, located in the western part of the country, might serve as an example of where other parts of the country may be headed. In 2005, this union was composed of 58.4 percent Anglo, 20.2 percent Hispanic, 13 percent African American, and 8.4 percent Asian Pacific. In 2010, Hispanics, comprising some 20 percent of the membership, added 35 percent of the new members, while enjoying the highest overall retention rate among all ethnic groups. This may be typical for many regions in Adventism.

Is this growth only taking place in the church? The broader context finds that these growth figures among Hispanics are similar in the general population of the United States, where half of the population growth is coming from Hispanics, with a median age of twenty-six, compared to the general population's median age of thirty-six.[7] These growth rates project a time within three decades when there will be no majority population in the United States, with that level already reached in some states. By 2012 projections are that "majority" births (Anglos) will drop below 50 percent. Asian, black, and Hispanic children already make up 47 percent of children under the age of five. Anglo and Asian birthrates are already below replacement level, which then increases the impact of higher Hispanic birthrates and immigration.[8]

In upcoming years, Hispanics will represent the largest growth potential for Seventh-day Adventist universities, but along with that potential will come challenges. Because Hispanics attend college in the least numbers and persist to graduation at the most problematic rates for all ethnic groups, universities will be challenged to dramatically increase enrollment from this important ethnic group, especially taking into consideration the income levels of many Hispanic families. Another problem will be the large number of undocumented Hispanics who are members of Seventh-day Adventist churches in some states. They will be hard to find in order to recruit and, unless immigration laws change, undocumented graduates will find it challenging to get work or to be accepted into graduate school upon graduation. In addition, they are not eligible for any state or federal student financial assistance, meaning that universities will have to find institutional resources to help them attend. Because many potential Hispanic students come from first generation families, the lack of basic language skills will require universities to have strong learning centers to provide tutoring, which can also be utilized by all students on campus.

Two other challenges for increasing Hispanic enrollment represent some of the most valuable character traits of this ethnic group. Hispanics hate debt, and yet most students today have to borrow money in order to attend a university. These families will need to be convinced that there is "good" and "bad" debt. Another challenge for primarily residential campuses is the Hispanic love of family, meaning that it's challenging for them to leave home in order to live in a dormitory. Campuses will need to create a strong sense of community and family to help make Hispanic young people feel comfortable leaving home.

Economic status of members—The church has perceived itself, in earlier decades, as being largely composed of successful middle-class families, but more recent evidence shows otherwise, with a growing trend toward an increasing lower income or lower middle-class base. What is the evidence?

In a study, now more than ten years old, on the demographics of religious subcultures, the lower middle-class proportion of Seventh-day Adventists is illustrated when compared to thirty religious groups (including those with no religion and agnostics.) Incidentally, this report takes up one entire page in the country's leading consumer behavior college textbook.[9]

- The **median annual household income** of Seventh-day Adventist members was $22,700, placing the denomination twenty-first out of thirty. (The highest was the Jewish faith with $36,700 and the lowest was the Holiness tradition with $13,700.)
- The percentage of **home ownership** for Seventh-day Adventists

was 54.6 percent, placing Adventists at twenty-fifth out of thirty. The Brethren represented the highest level at 81.4 percent and Muslims the lowest at 43.3 percent.
- In the category of **college graduates,** Seventh-day Adventists were 17.9 percent, ranking twenty-first out of thirty, with the highest being Jews with 46.7 percent and the lowest, Jehovah's Witnesses at 4.7 percent.
- In terms of employment of those **working full time,** Seventh-day Adventists were ranked twenty-eighth out of thirty, with 46 percent working full time, and the highest were Hindus at 64.1 percent while the lowest were Christian Scientists at 40.1 percent.

Since these figures are more than ten years old, evidence presented earlier might predict that Seventh-day Adventist percentages and rankings may have declined even further.

Monte Sahlin, drawing information about Seventh-day Adventists from the U.S. Congregational Life survey, completed in April 2001, of members attending church on a specific Sabbath or Sunday, demonstrates that of those Seventh-day Adventists attending church on the Sabbath during the time that the study was conducted:

- 15 percent made less than $10,000 in annual household income, compared to 10 percent in the U.S. Census
- 21 percent made $10,000 to $24,999, compared to 19 percent
- 27 percent made $25,000–$49,999, compared to 29 percent
- 18 percent made $50,000–$74,999, compared to 20 percent
- 9 percent made $75,000–$99,999, compared to 10 percent
- 10 percent made $100,000 or more, compared to 12 percent[10]

The 2006 results of the Cooperative Institutional Research Program (CIRP), conducted by UCLA of freshmen students in American colleges, can help compare family incomes at four-year religious colleges to Pacific Union College (PUC), located in Napa Valley, California:

- 14.9 percent of PUC students came from households making less than $30,000, compared to all religious college families with 12.7 percent.
- 30.6 percent of PUC students came from households making less than $50,000, compared to all religious college families with 30.7 percent.

- 31.5 percent of PUC students came from households making $100,000 or more, compared to all religious college families with 29.1 percent. (PUC's high Asian student population may be one of the factors at this income level.)

Both groups clearly are divided, with a substantial number coming from low and high income families, illustrating the financial challenge for both segments.

These figures, which will probably worsen in upcoming decades, illustrate that many church members are either very poor or in the lower middle-class, with some in upper income groups. Taking into consideration the low income level of many members, family income levels may represent the greatest threat to the future of Seventh-day Adventist higher education in upcoming decades as the cost of higher education increases.

3. Adventist universities will not be able to depend on increasing their enrollment because of increased K–12 enrollment.

K–12 Seventh-day Adventist school enrollment has been on a steady decline over the last two decades. Here are some evidences of the broader context which do not bode well for the future.

- In 1994, with a membership of 822,150, primary schools had 51,927 students amounting to 63 students per 1,000 members. This ratio declined by 2005 to 43,284 students, or 42 students per 1,000 members.
- Secondary enrollment declined from 16,722 students, or 18 students per 1,000 members, to 16,313 students, or 16 students per 1,000 members.
- K–12 enrollment peaked in 1976 with 76,342 students, while the 2008–2009 enrollments reached a new low point with 54,074 students. This represents a 29 percent loss of enrollment, with only 4,000 more students than the church enrolled in 1956.
- A large number of K–12 schools closed in the last two decades. Between 1999–2008, 177 Seventh-day Adventist K–12 schools closed. This represents a 17 percent loss. Many of the schools closed were in small rural areas where church membership has decreased, as has the general population. Not only have Adventist schools been challenged in the broader context of rural communities, but public schools have experienced similar problems compared to a time when farming was a key part of the economy.

Projections from the North American Division Office of Education, which have been accurate in the past, show no expected increases, but actual declines in twelfth grade graduates from Seventh-day Adventist secondary schools into the foreseeable future.

Why are these enrollment figures important? The largest percentage of enrollment in most Adventist universities has come from Seventh-day Adventist high schools, known as academies, but this source is no longer the dependable source that it once was for stable enrollment growths. Actual declines should be expected.

Taking into consideration the broader context, are Adventist declines in enrollment expected for the entire nation? In an analysis done by the Western Interstate Commission for Higher Education in 2006, including all states, with projections through 2015, roughly 60 percent of the states show declining numbers of high school graduates, with another 16 percent showing no increase. Three out of four states show flat to declining numbers of high school graduates.[11]

4. Seventh-day Adventist higher education enrollment has the potential for overcoming demographic, financial, and K–12 enrollment challenges.

In contrast to declining K–12 enrollment patterns, Seventh-day Adventist higher education institutions in North America show increases. College/university enrollment increased in 1994 from 18,955, or 23 students per 1,000 members, to 23,492 students in 2005 for the same ratio per 1,000 members of 23 students. A similar pattern is expected to continue through the end of the decade. K–12 education has not kept pace with membership growth, while higher education enrollment has. However, much of this growth in higher education came at six institutions—three healthcare institutions—Florida Hospital College of Health Sciences (FHCHS), Kettering College of Medical Arts (KCMA), and Loma Linda University, with much of the growth at these three from nonchurch members; three colleges that became universities—La Sierra University and Southern Adventist University with significant graduate school growth, and Oakwood Adventist University with major undergraduate growth—and one international university with large growth in the Seventh-day Adventist Theological Seminary—Andrews University. Other Adventist colleges experienced significant declines during this period. Those with increased enrollments indicate that the healthcare field has high potential for growth, especially given the recent passage of a new healthcare system for the United States, which will add millions of new patients. Graduate level education, in areas such as business, also appear to represent a growth area.

Even though academy enrollments are expected to decrease, the pool of potential college students may actually become more positive. Monte Sahlin's 2004 study of the Columbia Union, extrapolated to North America, projects that the pool of Seventh-day Adventist eighteen through twenty-two years old will increase from 43,224 in 2007 to 53,711 in 2015.

These numbers indicate that many Adventist students either are not attending college or are going to colleges not affiliated with the denomination. In order to save money, some start in local community colleges to complete their general education requirements, but few of these students eventually transfer into Seventh-day Adventist colleges. Community colleges actually have very low rates of students completing a four-year degree anywhere. Others choose public universities because of lower cost and perceived excellence of product. Others attend non-Seventh-day Adventist Christian colleges, and some from wealthier families select prestigious private institutions. No reliable study has ever been done of the percentage of "faithful" Adventists, defined as those going to church on a regular basis and giving financial contributions to the church, but one hears estimates that anywhere from 50 percent to 70 percent of eligible Seventh-day Adventist students do not attend a Seventh-day Adventist university or college. All of these represent potential markets for Seventh-day Adventist universities in upcoming decades. This could mitigate some of the earlier negative information about K–12 enrollment.

Two of the healthcare oriented institutions, Florida Hospital College of Health Sciences and Kettering College of Medical Arts, which were founded to serve the needs of local communities, serve a large nonchurch member population, which raises the question about whether marketing to a more general Christian population might make up the difference for some of the demographic trends mentioned earlier. While Seventh-day Adventist universities already accept many nonchurch members, if this becomes more necessary for survival, issues will become more central about what is taught, what lifestyle rules are maintained, who is hired, where money is raised, and the composition of college and university boards.

Expanding the Adventist enrollment base will not be that easy. Many avowedly Christian students might come from public schools, where they have had to stand up for their religion, or from conservative Christian schools hoping to find an Adventist campus on fire for Jesus Christ. Instead, they find many Adventist students in a normal psychological developmental process trying to figure out if they even want to continue being Adventists, which can be very disillusioning to students from public schools. One of the roles of Adventist professors and staff is to help guide students through these normal stages of faith development.

On the other hand, some public school students might be enrolling just to get a good academic education and will be bothered by the more conservative rules of Seventh-day Adventist culture, or even the ability to understand the language and theology of Adventism. One example would be talk about "non-Adventists," which is unfamiliar and troubling language for those not of the Seventh-day Adventist faith.

In contrast, when students go to other Christian colleges, they know why they are there—to continue their strong Christian education in a setting with many different denominations sharing a few Christian teachings in common, but without a strong distinctive theological emphasis of a particular denomination.

Another issue will be how Adventist professors teach such subjects as creation and evolution or human sexuality with a more diverse student population. These kinds of issues will become part of the broader context of debates taking place in upcoming years over the identity and soul of Adventism, with conservative Adventists demanding a more traditional education than will be acceptable to new markets.

5. One of the greatest challenges to maintain and increase enrollment in Seventh-day Adventist universities in the future will be the ability of students to put together financial packages to enroll.

During the first decade of the twenty-first century, the average cost of tuition, room, and board at four-year private colleges, including several Adventist universities, rose to over $30,000 per year. While pressure is being exerted by the federal government to reduce annual increases, these costs will continue to increase. Some may assume that these increases, which have often been greater than the CPI, result from the greed of administrators and professors to get more pay. In reality, much of the increase goes beyond the CPI because of major increases in healthcare costs similar to other organizations and businesses, increased financial aid for students, and increased necessity for meeting the needs of students with learning challenges. Given the income levels of Adventist families mentioned earlier, the ability of Adventist students to attend a Seventh-day Adventist university will become increasingly challenging, especially for those from middle-class families who aren't eligible for any government financial assistance.

Many church leaders have argued that Adventists who do not have their children in church schools just haven't created the right priorities, forgetting that church workers, themselves, enjoy a generous education subsidy for their children. It's true that a handful of parents, who then become "stereotypical" parents, spend money on fancy vacations, boats, large houses, and new cars rather than sending their children to church-sponsored schools or universities. But many parents still truly sacrifice to have their children in Seventh-day Adventist schools.

One local conference treasurer tried to create a budget for two scenarios in order to discover the possibility of enrolling a child in a church elementary school with an annual tuition cost of $4,320. For a single parent making $40,000 per year and with one child and living on a very modest budget, the shortage between income and expenses came to $10,920 a year if they paid tithe and had their child in a Seventh-day Adventist elementary school. For a two-income family with two children making $75,000 a year, the shortfall came to $16,898 per year. Many Adventist families do not earn this kind of an income and are barely eking out a living that allows them to put food on the table and handle the basic necessities, in too many cases, using credit cards to handle their expenses. In the case of these two scenarios, these parents are faced with the unpleasant choice of paying tithe or having their children in church school.

Let's place these families into the context of an Adventist university. When putting together a financial package, a student would begin with the calculation of the family's expected contribution, but few American or Adventist families have saved anything for college. The student might earn $1,200 to $1,500 during the school year, and possibly another $1,500 in the summer, but this would barely cover the cost of books, which average well over $1,000 per year, and other basic needs such as transportation, clothing, and other lifestyle necessities. The federal government is increasing the amount of Pell grants, and a Perkins loan is also available for low-income families. Some states provide special grants for low-income families.

So where will families turn to make up the rest? Pressure is increasingly being placed on private universities to offer tuition discounts from the "sticker price," which then places pressure on the university's budget. In essence, students who can afford to pay tuition—although a majority of the tuition discounts are not need-based but centered on merit, such as high grades, leadership activities, athletics, and music—pay a higher tuition to subsidize the cost of these tuition discounts. Funding these tuition discounts has represented the largest change in the budgets of most private universities over the last two decades from a time when nothing was spent for financial aid to today when a significant portion of the budget goes for this need. In 2008, the average discount rate for freshmen in private universities amounted to 42 percent with many Adventist universities in the 30+ percent range, except for the healthcare related institutions, which don't fund any tuition discounts.[12] These rates have been steadily increasing every year over the past decade with no end in sight. In addition to higher tuition costs to fund these discounts, universities have relied on donations and endowment income for funding. Ironically, universities with the largest endowments have experienced the biggest challenges with their budgets, after a steep decline in their investments in 2009, compared to institutions with lower endowments, such as Seventh-day Adventist universities, who were well below the average endowment for similar institutions.

Even after considering all of these forms of financial assistance, students usually come up short in putting together a financial package, which then forces them to borrow money from the federal government or private lenders. This leaves the typical student saddled with debt, upon graduation, with averages around $20,000 but some well into the $100,000+ range.

The new federal law on student loans will limit their obligation to repay those loans to 10 percent of their income in the future, which will help. However, students now and in the future will increasingly be making a business decision about attending an Seventh-day Adventist university rather than attending to broaden their horizons by getting a general education within a Seventh-day Adventist context in addition to obtaining high quality career preparation. For some in high paying careers such as medicine, paying back the loans will be a lower challenge than for other professions. Students will ask themselves, "If I'm going to end up with this amount of debt, will I be able to get a job that will enable me to make payments for many years on that debt? Is it worth a chance?" Career opportunities in service fields such as teaching, social work, or ministerial work will be severely tested in the future unless employers can develop plans to help graduates with the repayment of debt.

6. Seventh-day Adventist universities are not immune to challenges being experienced by most small Christian and independent universities in North America.

In 2006, the Association of Physical Plant Administrators (APPA), the National Association of College and University Business Officers (NACUBO), and the Society for College and University Planning (SCUP) held a conference on "The Campus of the Future: A Meeting of the Minds," which included a presentation regarding Standard & Poor's analysis of the condition of American higher education.[13] They focused attention on industry concerns about what they called the weak state of higher education with an emphasis on the following issues:

- Rising costs of healthcare, insurance, and utilities
- Pensions
- Rising inflation and energy costs
- Cost thresholds (Can colleges afford to provide needed financial aid with incomes failing to grow?)
- Deferred maintenance (How will it be funded?)

They then emphasized the following concern:

> The weakest portion of the sector is tuition dependent, underendowed colleges capped by the ability to pay on the revenue side and rising costs on the other side.

Did these issues and concerns describe Seventh-day Adventist colleges during the first decade of the twenty-first century? The answer is a resounding "Yes."

What percentage of Seventh-day Adventist university income is derived from tuition? In most Seventh-day Adventist institutions of higher learning, the percentage of the budget derived from student tuition amounts to more than 80 percent. This means that a downturn in enrollments seriously jeopardizes the viability of many Seventh-day Adventist universities.

Do Seventh-day Adventist universities have any financial cushions or reserves? How about endowments?

A sample year reveals that in 2005 the total value of endowments reported by the Council for the Advancement of Education for all Seventh-day Adventist universities amounted to over $360 million compared to Harvard University, which had the most with $28.9 billion. However, Seventh-day Adventist universities get some of the most generous subsidies from their sponsoring church organizations compared to other faith-based universities. In 2005, total giving by the General Conference and unions in the North American Division to the fifteen universities in North America amounted to over $54 million. In a sense, this represents an ongoing endowment. How large an endowment would be needed to create $54 million on an annual basis? Using a 5 percent investment payout, this would be the equivalent of a $1.087 billion endowment. If we were to add the actual total endowment of $360 million to the $1.087 billion equivalent endowment for the church subsidy, the total endowment value for the church would amount to $1.4 billion. This would place the combined endowment value at thirty-third on the list of most valued university endowments. This represents a significant investment by the church in its universities.

While impressive when combined, the endowments are too low to help compensate for sudden financial challenges from a lower enrollment or emergency needs on individual campuses. Generally, a university should have $90,000 per student in an endowment for a healthy operation, but in 2006 Loma Linda University was the highest with $70,773 per student and Southern Adventist University held second place with $10,332 per student. The overall mean, including LLU's much higher amount, was $15,040 per student.

Ironically, high endowments became a serious challenge for American universities in 2009 when the stock market declined, resulting in many endowments being reduced in value by over 40 percent. Those institutions that relied upon high investment income from large endowments ended up having to make more serious adjustments than institutions that were highly tuition driven and not relying on endowment income to fund high percentages of their budget.

In spite of the lowered values of endowments, most would agree that Seventh-day Adventist universities need to grow alternate sources of revenue, including larger endowments, greater annual gift giving from donors, and income from successful businesses to be prepared for downturns in enrollment and possible reductions in church subsidies. These needs will become even greater in upcoming years to counteract the problematic trends cited earlier of being tuition dependent and under-endowed.

The church has gone through various phases in how its universities were constructed. Through the 1960s, the sponsoring union or General Conference would take on the responsibility for funding the construction of all buildings along with help from the university's operating funds. In more recent years, universities have been expected to raise most of the cost of new buildings through their own fund-raising efforts, which has been the focus to the detriment of building endowments. In addition, many donors have liked the satisfaction of seeing physical buildings constructed and, sometimes, named after them. The creation of new endowments will take on greater importance given the larger costs of running universities and the need for greater student tuition discounts, faculty salaries, and deferred maintenance of many old buildings

One of the largest endowments "given" to our institutions are the lower salaries paid to Adventist university professors and administrators compared to those that they could earn on other campuses. The salary differential represents their "living endowment" to the church.[14] If dollars were needed in an endowment to cover this savings paid at 5 percent this would be the result:

Lower earnings of:	Represents an endowment of:
$20,000	$400,000
$30,000	$600,000
$40,000	$800,000
$50,000	$1,000,000

Not only are these professors, administrators, and staff employees providing a major donation to the church through their lowered salaries, they are among the most important human resource assets as the church moves into the future.

Solutions can be found

Too many Adventist universities exist

from year to year, just barely balancing budgets dependent almost completely on the next enrollment cycle in an incredibly difficult balancing act. Since most are tuition driven with more than 80 percent of the budget coming from tuition and some help from church subsidies, financial security depends on the next enrollment cycle. Little is left to buy the essential equipment and resource materials to stay current in the academic fields being offered. Is just staying open sufficient, or can the vision of the leaders who, with great faith, established Seventh-day Adventist universities, be recaptured? Can ways be found to become stronger without losing the mission? Think what it must have been like to operate a college during World War I or II, or during the Great Depression. Yet solutions were found in these even more challenging times.

Our son, Trevan, finished his seminary training a few years ago and is now a pastor in Richmond, Virginia. After going through a difficult field school of evangelism experience in Hunter's Point, the most crime-ridden area of San Francisco, he made the following provocative observations:

> The Adventist evangelistic series attempts to answer the question, "How will the world end?" I believe this has been the definitive question of Christianity throughout the existence of the Adventist church.

However, I believe a new question has begun to emerge and people are beginning to ask, "How can true life begin?"

The question that needs to be asked is, "How can true life begin for Adventist universities?"

By broadening the context through analyzing trends within Adventism and in the broader higher education world, the answers will become easier to find.

References

[1] E-mail from Charles Sandefur to Richard Osborn, February 4, 2007.

[2] Reggie McNeal, *The Present Future: Six Tough Questions for the Church* (San Francisco: Jossey-Bass, 2003), 2, 3.

[3] Ibid., 67.

[4] Neil Howe and William Strauss, *Millennials Go to College* (AACRAO, 2003).

[5] Center for Creative Ministry, *InnovationNewsletter*, November 1, 2006.

[6] Sandra A. Blackmer, "NAD Year-end Meetings 2006," *Adventist Review*, 28.

[7] "America by the Numbers," *Time*, October 30, 2006, 45.

[8] Sam Roberts, "Births to Minorities Approach a Majority," *New York Times*, March 12, 2010.

[9] From Michael R. Solomon, *Consumer Behavior: Buying, Having, and Being*, 5th ed. (Upper Saddle River, NJ: Prentice Hall, 2002), 430, as taken from Kenneth L. Woodward, "The Rites of Americans," *Newsweek*, November 29, 1993, 80.

[10] Monte Sahlin, *Adventist Congregations Today: New Evidence for Equipping Healthy Churches* (Lincoln: Center for Creative Ministry, 2003), 42.

[11] Jerry Scoby, Jon McGee, and Nathan Dickmeyer, "Small Colleges: When Roll Is Taken in 2015, Which Institutions Will be Present?" The Campus of the Future Conference, Honolulu, Hawaii, July 9, 2006 as reported in

The Chronicle of Higher Education, November 25, 2005.

[12] Jack Stripling, "Slashing Prices," *Inside Higher Ed*, March 31, 2010.

[13] Mary Peloquin-Dodd and Josh Stern, "Campus of the Future. Credit Quality & Bond Ratings: What Does the Future Hold?" Honolulu, Hawaii, July 11, 2006.

[14] Richard Osborn, "Everyone's a Philanthropist," *Adventist Review,* September 1998, 31.

CHARLES SCRIVEN

Chapter 17

Responsible Partisans: Ethics and Intellectual Accountability in Adventist Higher Education

Tony Campolo, the Philadelphia preacher and professor familiar on many Adventist campuses, often flies home tired from his speaking appointments. When his seatmate wants to know his name and what he does, the answer depends on whether Campolo feels like talking or not.

"When I want to talk," he says, "I say I'm a sociologist. And the person next to me says, 'Oh, that's interesting.' But if I really want to shut someone up I say I'm a Baptist evangelist. That generally does it."

Once, on a red-eye special, he told the man sitting beside him that he was a Baptist evangelist. But the man didn't retreat. "Well, do you know what I believe?" he said. "I believe that going to heaven is like going to Philadelphia."

Campolo was taken aback—Philadelphia?

The man explained that just as there are "many ways to get to Philadelphia," so there are many ways to get to heaven. You don't have to be a Baptist or even a Christian—"we all end up in the same place; how you get there doesn't matter."

Campolo was too tired to argue. He maneuvered himself out of the conversation as fast as he could and went to sleep. But several hours later, when the plane began its descent into Philadelphia, he woke up to gusting winds, heavy rains, and fog as thick as wool. The ride was rough and scary. Everyone was tense.

So Campolo, feeling pugnacious, turned to his seatmate and said, "I'm certainly glad the pilot doesn't agree with your theology."

"What do you mean?"

"Down in the control tower," Campolo replied, "someone is talking to the pilot: 'You're on beam,' the controller's saying, 'You're on beam,' and the message is: don't deviate from this."

Campolo went on: "It's foggy outside, and I'm glad the pilot's not spouting off about how he can get to Philadelphia any way he pleases. I'm glad he's saying to himself, 'The controller knows the best path to the runway, and I'm going to stay with it.' "

As for how to live the best life you can—how to get to "heaven," how to walk the road to fulfillment—Campolo's seatmate was very much like the modern educational establishment. From the viewpoint of conventional understanding, school is no place to take a strong position about morality and religion. On these matters the rule in school is, Don't be partisan and don't ruffle any feathers.

When Adventist education was developing in the second half of the nineteenth century, our pioneers were flat-out partisan feather-rufflers. In her first extended essay on education, Ellen White declared that the young can be trained "for the service of sin or for the service of righteousness." She said, too, that we should give them "that education which is consistent with our faith."[1] Percy T. Magan, describing the 1891 (and first-ever) Adventist education convention, said that what the reform participants envisioned was seen mostly in terms of making the Bible central to the curriculum.[2]

All the while the conventional secular orthodoxy, especially as regards higher education, was headed in another direction. The oldest colleges in the United States were sponsored by churches, but many were just then breaking their religious ties. Educational leaders were challenging, or even ridiculing, education that tries to instill in students a specific spiritual heritage with its own distinctive way of thinking and living.

At his inauguration in 1869, Charles Eliot, the Harvard president who cut the last links between the university and its original Christian patrons, mocked the teaching that tries to instill some *particular* set of beliefs about what is good and true. That may be "logical and appropriate in a convent, or a seminary for priests," he said, but it is "intolerable" in universities.[3]

Eliot perhaps gleaned his comparison from Cardinal Newman, who in *The Idea of the University* had declared more than a decade earlier that the university is neither a convent nor a seminary.[4] In any case, the misgivings about religious training in higher education were taking an ever-stronger hold. In 1904, DeWitt Hyde, who studied at Harvard while Eliot was there and soon afterward became the president of Bowdoin College, called the "narrowness" he associated with church colleges "utterly incompatible" with responsible higher education. "A church university," he declaimed, "is a contradiction in terms."⁵

To these educational leaders, in other words, teaching a general awareness was fine; teaching a specific religious heritage was suspect. Today, this sentiment still predominates. Partisan education, especially in matters religious and moral, is seen widely to be, at best, narrow, and, at worst, bigoted and victimizing. Responsible teaching does not inculcate a particular point of view or set of virtues; it rather imparts knowledge and skills sufficient, as Mortimer Kadesh writes, to enable the self to criticize its "social milieu" and to "form its being and determine" its wants.⁶ Even a teacher at a Southern Baptist college echoes the conventional understanding: "It's not my job as a professor to tell [students] what to think," the teacher told *The Chronicle of Higher Education* recently, "it's my job to *make* them think."⁷

I will show here why the historic Adventist understanding is closer to the mark than secular modern orthodoxy. My claim, made with a view to secularization *inside* as well as outside the church, is that teaching and learning in the Christian setting, including the Christian college, should be, as Ellen G. White insisted, "consistent with our faith." It should display (in its own way) the church's true identity; it should be, indeed, a deliberate strategy for building and bracing the circle of disciples. Bland neutrality is a mistake, and it is a dangerous mistake.

Let me begin by explaining a figure of speech I learned from my teacher and friend, Professor James William McClendon Jr., now Distinguished Scholar in Residence at Fuller Theological Seminary in Pasadena. In *Ethics*, the first volume of his *Systematic Theology*, he remarks that we humans exist "as in a tournament of narratives."⁸ What does he mean by the arresting phrase "tournament of narratives"?

His point, first of all, is that whatever idea or possibility confronts us, any day or any hour of the day, the way we respond—the way we think and feel and act—depends on the stories we're attached to. The stories, or narratives, we know and identify with shape our whole lives, our whole ethos or ethics. Narratives, in others words, are bedrock—bedrock for both personal and communal frame of mind—for insight, for attitude, for conduct.

The second point of the phrase concerns conflict. The narratives men and women identify with are many—across the total human landscape, beyond counting. And frequently, like contenders in a tournament, these narratives clash with one another, one story feeding this loyalty or outlook and another that. The result is variety in human culture, often welcome and often winsome. But more than anyone would like, the conflict of narratives feeds strife as well, including violent strife. We are sadly aware, we who inhabit the world of Sarajevo and Rwanda and (for that matter) the United States, that differences of faith, politics, morality, and custom occasion not only charm but also bloodshed.

These are the conditions we live in, and under these conditions, bland neutrality, I repeat, is a mistake. If uncharitable narrowness is also mistaken, that does not gainsay the point. Conflict is a fact, and bland neutrality leaves conflict, even violent conflict, unchallenged. Conflict is a fact, and bland neutrality puts blinders over people's eyes. Bland neutrality, in short, threatens society by feeding indifference—and then compounds the threat by feeding self-deception.

It is in this light that I want to advance my claim, namely, that *Christian education, including Christian higher education, should be partisan*. It should not be blindly or arrogantly partisan, but, without embarrassment and without apology, it should both build and brace the circle of disciples.

As we have seen, among the secular-minded, and to a surprising degree among the religious, antipathy to the partisan is widespread. The background to this antipathy is the Enlightenment. Kant declared that movement's ideal of the autonomous individual when he called his readers to thrust off dependence on others for direction. " 'Have courage to use your own reason!'—that," he said, "is the motto of the Enlightenment."[9] And with the ensuing shift to the self-governing, or self-defining, individual the meaning of respect for others veered toward noninterference, or even neutrality, with respect to differences of outlook and conviction. The partisan was now bad manners. Conflict was to be domesticated.

The motive was admirable. The Enlightenment grew into full flower on blood-soaked soil. The Thirty Years' War, religion-stoked and staggering in its brutality and senselessness, ended (more or less) in 1648, endowing Europe with a need and a lively desire for peace, or at least respite. Bloodletting had failed to resolve the doctrinal discord from which it sprang. As Stephen Toulmin writes, circumstances called for a means of determining truth that "was independent of, and neutral between, particular religious loyalties."[10]

But truth, despite these hopes, could not be determined in total independence of particular religious loyalties. Consider the idea that the individual is self-governing and self-defining, with no need to depend upon others for direction. This idea subverts—indeed, it was *meant* to subvert—accountability to authority, whether religious, familial, or communal. Autonomy was needed, so the thinking went, in order to fend off acquiescence to inherited prejudice and folly. But we each speak a human language, and every human language gives particular peoples, each with the particular narratives they have lived and told, the ability to communicate. What is more, every language bears the freight of stories past and so gives every user an inherited frame of mind. Thus no neutral vantage point exists from which the self may practice its alleged autonomy. In a world of many languages and histories, there can be no neutral point of view, no single pathway of knowledge available to everyone. How and what we think at all times reflects a storied past.

The point, despite conventional modern thinking, is not *whether* to be partisan but *how*. Even so, the narrative that shapes the dominant version of higher education continues to be that of the Enlightenment. The debate over "political correctness" sweeping the campus and the wider culture betrays, it is true, growing uneasiness about standard, educational assumptions. Still, the curriculum usually comes across as a kind of intellectual bazaar, catering, at least ostensibly, to autonomous selves in the process of forming their being and determining their wants without "direction" (as Kant put it) from others. Students are still said to be learning how to think, not what to think. It is still "narrow" and "sectarian" to inculcate a particular point of view, especially if the point of view involves religious or moral commitment. Except in defense of diversity itself, it is still bad manners, and bad education, to be partisan.

The deception in all this, or self-deception, is palpable. But antipathy to the partisan jeopardizes education in other ways as well. For one thing, it trivializes differences. When disagreements over faith, politics, morality and custom flame up in violent strife, as they often do, it is disingenuous to speak, in the customary, bleached-out phraseology, of mere "competing value systems," as though students were consumers meant to pick and choose like shoppers in a marketplace. To be or feign to be impartial is to push the truth away, to keep it at a distance. It is a kind of indifference, and it communicates indifference.

Far from being innocuous, the indifference damages humanity. For when in matters of faith and morals education must be too open to contain conviction, it can no longer fight off the tendency to spiritual coma that seems in any case to bedevil contemporary culture. Differences trivialized by neutrality feed the trivialization of morality itself—and examples abound: this is an age when expert witnesses can make ethical judgments seem repressive even at an incest trial; it is an age when "standards" at media command posts consist in whatever the market will bear; it is an age when lawmakers wring their hands over teen violence and still cast votes for murder weapons. The situation recalls what Yeats, in "The Second Coming," declared of an age without conviction: "Mere anarchy is loosed upon the world, / The blood-dimmed tide is loosed . . ."

Suspicion of commitment in the classroom does not, of course, produce students with no biases at all; it rather favors their "assimilation," as Patricia Beattie Jung writes, to the "prevailing cultural ethos."[11] The fiction of neutrality tends to baptize the status quo, with its implicit morality or immorality, and to nullify the stark alternatives. Antipathy to the partisan turns out, then, not just to trivialize differences, but also to protect whatever now predominates. Despite the homage paid to criticism, antipathy to the partisan is fundamentally conservative.

What this entire criticism of liberal education displays is the emerging awareness that the modern era, heralded by Descartes and the Enlightenment, is now passing. We are entering what some now call a "postmodern" era, with its key realization that outlooks are bequeathed to individuals, not discovered or created by them. How we see and live depends on the background—family, community, history—we each absorb growing up with our particular language and culture. Systems of thought and practice characteristic of particular communities may involve differences too deep to be adjudicated or even understood through simple conversation.

But does all this add up to irrationalism, add up to the tribalization, as one might say, of knowledge? This question is central to the issue of ethics and education. If we are left with mere subjectivity, if everything comes down to mere personal choice, how is anyone accountable? How does ethics, with its assumption that some attitudes and actions are right and some wrong, even have a place?

Nietzsche, who in the nineteenth century anticipated the shift to the postmodern, believed that the ideas we consider true are fixed and binding merely from long usage and endorsement within a particular group. One may employ strategies to promote or subvert a point of view, but it is impossible to adjudicate among contending points of view. So-called truths are only fictions to assist the "will to power," conventions whose conventionality has been forgotten.

But even if we accept the absence of a neutral viewpoint, it's still possible—and important—to make a vigorous argument for accountability, and thus for the importance of defending right against wrong. Sheer consent to rival truth claims, after all, is not just the embrace of charming or fertile disagreement; sheer consent is surrender to injustice and bloodshed, for these are what differences of faith, politics, morality, and custom all too often bring about. Writers such as Alisdair MacIntyre, James McClendon, and Nancey Murphy, who will figure prominently in what follows, argue that even though we see the world through our inherited frameworks, no framework must be a prison house. It is possible and important that conversation, both within and across the lines of human difference, should yield new increments of understanding and agreement. The shift to the postmodern does not, in other words, compel anarchy and resignation with respect to human knowledge.

In light of all this, let me now suggest the outlines of a postmodern conception of intellectual *accountability* for colleges of explicit Christian *commitment*. How can higher education under the church's auspices contend responsibly—with no retreat of mind or heart—in the human tournament of narratives? How can it nourish postadolescent minds with its own distinctive vision? How can it be partisan and still hold itself responsible to justify its partisan convictions?

To begin, let me say unmistakably that the partisanship in question is countercultural. From the biblical narrative, this is obvious enough: solidarity with God and God's Messiah means dissent from the wider world. Nevertheless, the lure of respectability within the surrounding, dominant culture has always tantalized the Christian community. As McClendon writes,

> The church's story will not interpret the world to the world's satisfaction. Hence there is a *temptation* (no weaker word will do) for the church to deny her "counter, original, spare, strange" starting point in Abraham and Jesus and to give instead a self-account or theology that will seem true to the world on the world's own present terms.[12]

What is true for the church is true for its colleges. Here, too, the endurance of distinctively Christian vision must be a matter of deliberate design. In its decisions about personnel, curriculum, and student life, the Christian college must renounce congenial neutrality, what is in any case artifice and self-deception, and embrace without apology its own heritage and discipline. In the tournament of narratives, anything less is a recipe for defeat. Anything less marks capitulation to "the unstoried blandness (and the mortal terrors) of late-twentieth-century liberal individualism."[13]

In the college setting, learning takes place under the leadership of teachers. So if the countercultural, the embrace of distinctive vision, is crucial for responsible Christian partisanship, a corresponding view of the teaching function is also crucial. In the guidance and inspiration of students, intellectual accountability allows, and indeed requires, commitment to a particular point of view.

Being responsibly countercultural means acknowledging the self-deception and emptiness in the platitude about teaching students how to think, not what to think. The platitude fits neatly with the

Enlightenment antagonism toward authority and obsession with personal autonomy. It reflects as well the earlier Socratic form of moral education, which trained students for criticism of convention without offering a positive account of the good in human life. The overall impact of a purely negative approach was to leave students without reasons for preferring one way of life to another, and thus without reasons to fend off the blandishments of purely private satisfaction.

In his play, *Clouds,* the Greek writer Aristophanes made this point with his imagination. A father named Strepsiades has a son who is a spendthrift and idler, with hardly any conscience at all. The father, desperate for change, brings his son to the school of Socrates in Athens.

Socrates arranges for the son to hear a debate between one teacher who is a stern guardian of traditional values, and another who is a smirking, self-indulgent enemy of these values. In the end it becomes clear that Socrates himself, though courageous and serene compared to both debaters, has more in common with the smirking critic of traditional values. It turns out that he has nothing positive to teach about how to live. He is like the tradition-hating debater in that his whole mode of teaching is to raise questions about traditional morality and to shoot it down. He ridicules inherited wisdom and those who try to instill it into the minds and lives of students. And it's all the worse because he offers virtually nothing to substitute for what he ridicules. He says nothing about what a person *should* aim for in life, nothing about the standards and convictions that *should* prevail.

Aristophanes is Socrates' critic; he thinks the situation is disastrous. So in his play, the fancy education at the fancy school in Athens leaves the son as selfish as ever. In the end he just doesn't care about anything but himself, anything but his own personal satisfaction. The wider world, and the people in it, don't meet any of his needs and don't even matter.[14]

In order to make advances in awareness and comprehension, the inquirer must first have been taught what to think, must first have been initiated into some actual way of life or type of practice. Knowing how to think presupposes some partisan account of the subject matter, some positive immersion into a tradition. Being partisan may, it is true, slump into narrow indoctrination. But it doesn't have to, and responsible partisanship is in any case fundamental: nothing positive can happen without it. The road to enlightenment requires advocacy as well as criticism.

Responsible partisanship engages the whole person. Yet another respect in which the learning environment at Christian institutions must swim against the current is in the attention paid to the total way of life—not just technical, calculating intellect but also feelings, imagination, habits, and virtues. The mere removal of ignorance—what the distinguished education writer Jacques Barzun reveres as the "prime object" of education[15]—calls for such attention, anyway, since study itself is a discipline involving virtues. Just paying attention and seeing clearly—traits important for scholarship as well as moral growth—require emotional involvement. As Martha Nussbaum argues, interpreting Aristotle, a person may know something as a fact—a connection as father or mother, say, to a child; or the benefit of unearned privilege relative to others in one's society—yet fail to take in the fact "in a full-blooded way," fail to confront or acknowledge what it means and what response it calls for. When a person lacks "the heart's confrontation" with what lies open to view, the deficit narrows vision and foils insight. Perception, to be complete, must involve "emotional and imaginative, as well as intellectual, components."[16]

But as with the bare noticing of facts, so with the emotion and imagination that deepen our perception: they, too, reflect personal experience over time. Emotion and imagination disclose stories heard and lived. They reveal communal ways of life. They make manifest the past and present habits, duties, and affiliations that constitute the evolving self. All this signals the need for attention to the whole person. Education must concern itself with character, with the total way of life. This matters, indeed, for the mere removal of ignorance; for positive enlightenment, it matters all the more.

That is why Parker Palmer, in *To Know As We Are Known,* his work on the spirituality of education, declares his opposition to "objectivism" in education. In this still-dominant (if perhaps fading) classroom pattern, students learn the "facts" from an emotional distance, like bystanders. Mostly, the heart has no role; in accordance with the "objective" ideal, what is investigated remains at arm's length, an object and nothing more. Yet this detachment, this denial of the connection and interdependence of the student and the subject matter, "leaves the inner self unexamined." And without attention to the inner self, Palmer declares further, humans tend to scorn the common good and veer toward arrogant manipulation of the world outside themselves.[17]

If mere technical expertise—the mere removal of ignorance—were truly the prime object of education, then few could be said to have received better training than the scientists who produced the first atom bomb. Before the initial explosion, their technical expertise smoothed the way toward the perfecting of their awesome creation. On the day after the first mushroom stained the sky, when the scientists stopped to agonize over what they had done, one said that "the glitter of nuclear weapons," had seemed "irresistible." The participants were overcome, he said, by "technical arrogance" that arose from their knowledge of what they could do with their minds.[18] They no doubt understood, at some level, that weapons with the capacity to lift a million tons of rock into the sky would bring unspeakable danger and death to humanity. But without confronting this fact "in a full-blooded way," through feeling and imagination as well as calculating intellect, they failed to see what it meant or what response it called for.

The story illuminates the point: education that plays down feeling and imagination, and pays no heed to training the entire self, including those habits, duties, and affiliations that give shape to feeling and imagination, is both indigent and undependable.

A third aspect of responsible partisanship is this: *it must acknowledge conflict, it must confront conflict, it must initiate students into conflict.*[19]

The same spirit and goal must infuse the responsible partisanship of Christian colleges today. If all education, to be complete, must engage the whole person, Christian education must do so in a manner appropriate to its own struggle in the tournament of narratives. It must acknowledge, and deal constructively and honestly, with the challenges posed by other points of view. Masking over differences feeds apathy by pushing truth away, whereas the point is to nourish passion and involvement.

In the second volume of his *Systematic Theology,* McClendon says that Jesus enrolled His followers "as students in his school, his open air, learn-by-doing, movable, life-changing dialogue." The purpose was "training" for world-changing witness; the method was "costly apprenticeship." Then he alludes to blind Bartimaeus, said by Mark to have received his sight from Jesus and immediately followed Him on His dangerous mission to Jerusalem. On the view suggested by the story, declares McClendon, "enlistment and scholarship are integral parts of one whole." Bartimaeus, occupied with Jesus' mission and immersed in its conflict, was "the paradigmatic Christian scholar."[20]

Alisdair MacIntyre, who himself suggests the need for "rival universities," says one task of responsible partisanship is "to enter into controversy with other rival standpoints." This must be done in order to challenge the rival standpoint, but also in order to test one's own account against "the strongest possible objections."[21] The pairing of enlistment and scholarship by no means entails, in other words, a flight from challenges or a refusal to give reasons and make adjustments. Within limits required by the maintenance of basic identity, the Christian college or university, like a responsible partisan journal or newspaper, must tolerate—must, indeed, seek out—lively confrontation with other points of view. This can happen, not just in the classroom or library, but through the selection of students or even faculty. Postmodern awareness puts the difficulty of the knowledge enterprise in bold relief, but accountability is still vital. Convictions must still be justified. To be responsible, partisan higher education must provide, or better, *be,* a context for accountability.

In certain academic disciplines and certain aspects of collegiate bureaucracy, the Christian institution may find itself in virtual consensus with models dominant in the surrounding culture. Consider the natural sciences. Here the Christian setting may evoke a distinctive framework for instruction—it may, for example, lead teachers to discourage the use of scientific knowledge for violent purposes—but the course content will no doubt reflect what broadly respected authorities have had to say. At the points, however, of profound difference—in the human sciences and the humanities; in the administration of student life—the only responsible conduct in the face of challenge is honest conversation. And this means readiness "to amplify, explain, defend, and, if necessary, either modify or abandon."[22]

In her book on *Theology in the Age of Scientific Reasoning,* Nancey Murphy argues that the right method for defending Christian convictions is exactly analogous to the scientific method. She writes from a postmodern point of view and relies on the distinguished philosopher of science Imre Lakatos. Christian communities, she says, are "experiments" in a "research program." The program has to do with the claims of the gospel. As in productive science, the convictions central to the research program must be held tenaciously. Secondary convictions may be held less tenaciously, but all—the central as well as the secondary—must be willingly subjected to testing. The testing is in the living out of Christian life, and in the meeting of objections to the beliefs and practices associated with that life. The objections are met either by displaying, through words or deeds, their deficiency, or by attempting to make adequate adjustments. Over the long run, evidence accrues that counts for or against the secondary or even the central convictions. The intent and hope, always, is for "new and more consistent models of the Christian theory."[23]

A paragraph gives short shrift to the nuance and complexity of Murphy's argument. She means to embrace the postmodern awareness of the limits and uncertainty of human knowledge while arguing for standards of evidential reasoning that defeat "total relativism" and reclaim accountability. Justifications cannot be absolute, even in the natural sciences. In the domain of moral and spiritual conviction, as in the human sciences, the difficulties are even greater. But when challenges are sufficiently understood to cause dismay—a common enough experience—they must be dealt with through honest, open conversation. The attempted justifications, as McClendon writes in his own discussion of these matters, may seem acceptable and effective only in the eyes of the person or community being challenged.[24] But the effort of justification, and the intent of framing new and more consistent models of the Christian theory, must be embraced. Otherwise, the partisanship so necessary for growth in knowledge becomes a barrier to growth and ceases to be responsible.

For colleges and universities of explicit Christian commitment, then, intellectual accountability requires a countercultural frame of mind, a willing dissent, that is, from the wider world and a deliberate advocacy of the church's distinctive belief and practice. In the exercise of such accountability, teachers should first of all be protagonists. Second, they should, in their teaching, engage the whole person, intellect and character alike. Third, they should acknowledge and participate in conflict; they should meet challenges with attempted justifications.

In these ways colleges that honor and reflect the church's narrative can address the "critical years" of postadolescence when, as Sharon Parks writes, the emerging self is especially open to "life-transforming vision."[25] In these ways such colleges, following their particular purpose of education, can embody and refine the practices of teaching and learning and thus create standards for these activities that assist congregations and eventually the wider world.

The genesis of modernity was, substantially, a hope for peace. But the attempt to realize the hope proved self-deceptive and, all too often, oppressive, not just in its hostility to differentiation but also in its drift toward compelled uniformity. My argument for partisan education is an acknowledgment, as Toulmin puts it, "of the unavoidable complexities of concrete human experience."[26] But as a call for responsible partisanship, it is also an evocation of a humane approach to discord: honest partisanship, involving mind and heart alike, fused with honest conversation and shorn of the need to injure or coerce. Here higher education can be a beacon—and especially Christian higher education, whose narrative, in decidedly *un*modern fashion, calls its partisans to peaceable and prayerful regard for those with whom it differs, including its mortal enemies.

The point of the Christian narrative is not resignation, it is transformation. In a sometimes winsome but often violent tournament of narratives, colleges embracing such an approach to discord and such a hope of transformation may and must stand tall.

References

[1] Ellen G. White, *Testimonies for the Church* (Mountain View, CA: Pacific Press®, 1903), 3:131, 159.

[2] The description appears in Emmett Vande Vere, ed., *Windows* (Nashville: Southern Publishing Association, 1975), 172, 173.

[3] James Tunstead Burtchaell, "The Alienation of Christian Higher Education in America: Diagnosis and Prognosis," in Stanley Hauerwas and John Westerhoof, eds., *Schooling Christians* (Grand Rapids: Eerdmans, 1992), 133.

[4] Quoted in Jaroslav Pelikan, *The Idea of the University: A Reexamination* (New Haven: Yale University Press, 1992), 39.

[5] Ibid., 132.

[6] Mortimer Kadesh, *Toward an Ethic of Higher Education* (Stanford, CA: Stanford University Press, 1991), 73, 79.

[7] Quoted by Courtney Leatherman in "Southern Baptist College Enters Carefully Into Women's Studies," *The Chronicle of Higher Education,* July 14, 1993, A13.

[8] James William McClendon Jr., *Systematic Theology: Ethics* (Nashville: Abingdon Press, 1986), 143.

[9] Quoted in James C. Livingston, *Modern Christian Thought* (New York: Macmillan, 1971), 1.

[10] Stephen Toulmin, *Cosmopolis: The Hidden Agenda of Modernity* (New York: The Free Press, 1990), 70.

[11] Patricia Beattie Jung, "A Call for Reform Schools," in Hauerwas and Westerhoof, eds., 117.

[12] McClendon, *Systematic Theology: Ethics,* 17.

[13] Ibid., 71, 62.

[14] See Martha Nussbaum, "Aristophanes and Socrates on Learning Practical Wisdom," in Jeffrey Henderson, ed., *Yale Classical Studies,* 26 (Cambridge: Cambridge University Press, 1980), 43–97.

[15] Jacques Barzun, *Begin Here* (Chicago: University of Chicago Press, 1991), 54.

[16] Martha Nussbaum, *Love's Knowledge* (New York: Oxford University Press, 1990), 79–81.

[17] Parker Palmer, *To Know As We Are Known* (San Francisco: HarperSanFrancisco, 1993), 33–39.

[18] Parker Palmer tells this story to introduce his argument. Ibid., 1, 2.

[19] McClendon, *Systematic Theology: Ethics,* 45, 44.

[20] James William McClendon Jr., *Systematic Theology: Doctrines* (Nashville: Abingdon, 1994), 32.

[21] Alisdair MacIntyre, *Three Rival Versions of Moral Enquiry* (Notre Dame: University of Notre Dame Press, 1990), 231.

[22] Ibid., 201.

[23] Nancey Murphy, *Theology in the Age of Scientific Reasoning* (Ithaca, NY: Cornell University Press, 1990), 196.

[24] James William McClendon Jr., and James M. Smith, *Understanding Religious Convictions* (Notre Dame: University of Notre Dame Press, 1975), 182.

[25] Sharon Parks, *The Critical Years* (San Francisco: Harper and Row, 1986), 17.

[26] Toulmin, *Cosmopolis,* 201.

STEVE PAWLUK AND GORDON BIETZ

Chapter 18

Where Might We Go From Here?

In the final chapter of his or her dissertation, the doctoral candidate generally identifies additional studies that could profitably be pursued, but that he or she was not able to include in the present dissertation research. So it is with this book. Even as it was being sent to the press, we thought of additional chapters that would have been useful and other voices that would have been interesting to include. But dissertations and books have to stop somewhere. And so we end our project here. Not with "The One Right Idea," but having attempted to present some important considerations, ideas, questions, and possibilities.

It is our hope that the reader's mind will be stimulated to, not only reflect on the issues herein presented, but to study and write and contribute in a productive manner to the conversation as well. A definition of insanity that is attributed to Albert Einstein is "doing the same thing over and over again and expecting different results." Change is difficult for conservative institutions, and all Seventh-day Adventist institutions of higher education are conservative when compared to the range of educational institutions of higher education in North America today, but it is clear that there needs to be change in Seventh-day Adventist education if it is to fulfill the mission of one of the key founders of Seventh-day Adventist education.

Our ideas of education take too narrow and too low a range. There is need of a broader scope, a higher aim. True education means more than the pursual of a certain course of study. It means more than a preparation for the life that now is. It has to do with the whole being, and with the whole period of existence possible to man. It is the harmonious development of the physical, the mental, and the spiritual powers. It prepares the student for the joy of service in this world and for the higher joy of wider service in the world to come (Ellen G. White, *Education,* 13).

We can't, and shouldn't, expect to offer programs and course content today that were designed to be relevant and to address the world of one hundred years ago when Ellen White wrote those words, but we recognize that her vision of the fundamental mission of education is as viable today as it was then. Information, understandings, issues, and society's questions and challenges have changed dramatically and have become exponentially more complex over the past century. But human nature still presents the same basic needs and aspirations. God's eternal principles continue to undergird the fundamental structure of our physical, social, and moral universe, but the applications of those principles must be renewed and applied in innovative ways in order to respond in a meaningful way to the questions and to address the needs of the twenty-first century.

We pray that the written "conversation" that this book offers will, in at least a modest way, encourage a renewed commitment to providing access to a high quality Christian Seventh-day Adventist education, which prepares God's kids, our students, for productive, joy-filled lives and effective service in today's world while helping them to look forward to the world to come.

Appendix: Author Information

Niels-Erik Andreasen, a native of Denmark, has been the president of Andrews University since 1994. He received a doctorate degree in religious studies from Vanderbilt University in 1971. From 1970 to 1990, he taught Old Testament in the United States and Australia, and served as dean of the School of Religion at Loma Linda University. In 1990, Andreasen was named president of Walla Walla University, a position he held until becoming the fifth president of Andrews University. He has authored publications on Old Testament scripture, theology, and Christian education, and has written three books: *The Old Testament Sabbath, Rest and Redemption,* and *The Christian Use of Time*. Andreasen is married to Demetra Lougani of Athens, Greece. They have a married son and two grandchildren.

Ted W. Benedict was born in 1919 to Adventist parents, educated in Adventist elementary schools, attended Pacific Union College's College Preparatory School, and earned a BA degree with two majors (speech and history) at the college in 1942.

After service from 1942 to 1945 (England, 67th General Hospital), he married Ruth Hardt of Loma Linda, and completed MA and PhD degrees at the University of Southern California.

He joined the Pacific Union College faculty in l947, and chaired the Department of Speech there until 1963. He taught at San Jose State University from 1964 until 1984. There he chaired the Department of Communication Studies and served as dean of Academic Planning. Growing out of his experiences with faculty tenure at PUC, he became a special assistant to three successive presidents at State, advising them about management of faculty problems related to tenure, discipline, and procedural matters, during the difficult days of student and faculty unrest and protests.

His home church was in Palo Alto, where he was ordained an elder. He served as chair of the Mountain View Academy Board, and on various boards of the Adventist Media Center and at La Sierra University. He retired from San Jose as an emeritus professor, and was awarded an honorary emeritus professorship at PUC in 2008.

He and Ruth built a home at the Sea Ranch in 1984, living there until moving to Monterey in 1998, where they are members of the Monterey Peninsula Seventh-day Adventist Church.

Appendix: Author Information

Since 1997, **Gordon Bietz** has served as president of Southern Adventist University—a graduate and undergraduate coeducational accredited university located in Collegedale, Tennessee. Before becoming university president, Bietz was president of the Georgia-Cumberland Conference of Seventh-day Adventists.

Bietz held several pastoral positions prior to serving as conference president. He was chaplain at Rio Linda Academy in California for six years, pastor at the Stockton Seventh-day Adventist Church in California for five years, and pastor of the Collegedale Seventh-day Adventist Church in Tennessee for thirteen years.

Dr. Bietz has authored several publications, including *Witness,* a book about Christian witnessing; *Parables of Fenton Forest,* a children's book of parables; and *Power for Mind and Soul,* a collection of devotional thoughts. In addition, he has written for professional journals and authored a weekly column in the "Faith and Family" section of the *Chattanooga Times Free Press.*

President Bietz graduated from La Sierra University in California in 1966 with a bachelor's degree in theology before receiving a master of divinity degree from Andrews University in Michigan in 1968. In 1976, Bietz received a doctor of ministry degree from Andrews University.

Bietz received a Merrill Fellowship from Harvard University in 1991 and attended classes at Harvard Divinity School, Harvard Law School, and the J. F. Kennedy School of Government.

His wife, Cynthia, is a receptionist at Southern Adventist University. Their twin daughters, Gina Gang and Julie Kroll, are physical therapists in Loma Linda, California, and Nashville, Tennessee, respectively. They also have six grandchildren.

Seventh-day Adventist Higher Education in North America

E. Grady Bogue is currently professor of Higher Education Administration and Policy Studies at the University of Tennessee (1991 to present). He served for eleven years as chancellor of Louisiana State University (LSU) in Shreveport (1980–1991), served for one year as interim chancellor of Louisiana State University in Baton Rouge, and was named chancellor emeritus of LSU Shreveport by the LSU Board of Trustees in 1991. He received a BS degree in mathematics (1957), a MS degree (1965), and EdD (1968) from the University of Memphis. Dr. Bogue earned the first doctoral degree granted by the University of Memphis and was named a distinguished alumnus of the university in 1986.

He has served as the chief academic officer for the Tennessee Higher Education Commission (1974–1980) and on the administrative staff at the University of Memphis for ten years (1964–1974), his last position as assistant vice president for Academic Affairs. He was an instructor of physics with the U.S. Navy from 1961–1964, and served as a communications electronics officer with the U.S. Air Force from 1958–1961.

Dr. Bogue has written nine books. His most recent book was released in August 2007 and is titled *Leadership Legacy Moments* (ACE/Praeger Publishers). Four other recently published books are *Quality and Accountability in Higher Education* (Praeger/Greenwood Publishers, 2003), *Exploring the Heritage of American Higher Education* (ACE/Oyrx Press, 2000), *Leadership by Design* (Jossey-Bass Publishers, 1994), *and The Evidence for Quality* (Jossey Bass Publishers, 1992.) He has published over sixty articles in such journals as the *Harvard Business Review, Leader to Leader, Journal of Higher Education, Educational Record, Phi Delta Kappan, Planning for Higher Education,* and *Trusteeship.* Over the past two decades, six of his speeches have been carried in *Vital Speeches of the Day*. He writes a bimonthly column, "On Leadership," for the *Knoxville Business Journal.*

He has been a consultant on planning and evaluation, assessment and accreditation, and leadership and governance to a wide range of colleges and universities, state level agencies, and corporations. He was an American Council Fellow in academic administration in 1974–1975. During his ACE fellowship year and the following five years with the Tennessee Higher Education Commission (1974–1980), Dr. Bogue directed the Performance Funding Project, which designed and implemented the first state level performance incentive policy in American higher education, a policy now in its twenty-fifth year.

He was a visiting scholar with the Educational Testing Service in 1988–1989 and a consulting scholar with Lipscomb University from 2001 to 2005. He has participated in exchange travel and lectures in China, France, Germany, and republics in the former Soviet Union, and has delivered papers at international meetings in France and Hungary.

Appendix: Author Information

V. Bailey Gillespie received his BA degree in theology and biblical languages from Loma Linda University, an MA in philosophical theological, and MDiv degree from the Seventh-day Adventist Theological Seminary at Andrews University, and his PhD degree from Claremont Graduate University with a focus on faith development and psychology of religion.

Dr. Gillespie's published works include *Religious Conversion and Personal Identity: How and Why People Change; The Dynamics of Religious Conversion; The Experience of Faith, Keeping the Faith: A Guidebook for Spiritual Parenting; The Textures of Grace in the Church;* and *Wise for Salvation—How to Study Your Bible.*

He is the chief investigator and publications editor of the massive research project on young people in Seventh-day Adventist schools entitled, *Valuegenesis: A Study of Faith, Values, and Commitment.* This research has been repeated every ten years—1990, 2000, and again in 2010. His published works associated with this research include *Faith in the Balance,* with Roger L. Dudley; *Ten Years Later: A Study of Two Generations;* and *Hey! Love Them and They Will Come.* He served as editor for the Project Affirmation resources *Perspectives on Values* and *Teaching Values,* and developed the North American Division teaching resource, *Potentials: Faith, Values, and Commitment in the Classroom.*

As director of the John Hancock Center for Youth and Family Ministry, he helped organize the Sabbath School study program *GraceLink*. He is a popular speaker and presenter for youth, young adults, and family ministry in the United States and abroad. He is married to Judith W. Gillespie, president of Gillespie Reporting and Document Management, Inc., in Riverside, California. Their son, Timothy Gillespie, is young adult pastor at the Loma Linda University Seventh-day Adventist Church and their daughter, Shannon Quishenberry Sievers, teaches English as second language at Redlands High School.

Seventh-day Adventist Higher Education in North America

Douglas Herrmann's career in education began on a spring day in Maryland during his senior year at Takoma Academy when he served as principal-for-a-day. Unaware of the omen in this appointment and undeterred by the "support" of his friends, he continued to prepare to be a teacher. His experience as a student missionary in Zaire provided more teaching experience. He began the financially compensated period of his educational career at Fortuna Junior Academy. After completing his master's in religious education at Loma Linda University, he taught religion at Loma Linda Academy (LLA). After seven years in the classroom, he fulfilled the sign he lived out years earlier during his senior year of high school—he became the high school principal at LLA and lasted 16 years and 364 days longer than in his first administrative term. He left Loma Linda Academy to serve as an associate superintendent of schools for the Southeastern California Conference and later as an associate professor at La Sierra University's School of Education. He returned to Loma Linda Academy in 2011 as the chief administrative officer. He is married to Merry and has three children—Brandon and his wife, Kristi; Stacy and her husband, Scott; and Dustin and his wife, Laura.

Appendix: Author Information

Loretta B. Johns is assistant dean for program development and evaluation for the School of Medicine at Loma Linda University in Loma Linda, California. She was formerly the chair of the Leadership and Educational Administration Department in the School of Education at Andrews University in Michigan.

Loretta earned a master's degree in educational psychology at Michigan State University and a doctorate at the University of Maryland. Her interdisciplinary doctorate combines learning research and methodology in business education and organizational behavior. Her research interests include the effectiveness of learning through assessment of student learning outcomes. She has copublished a chapter on issues in education, and co-authored articles in the *Journal of Research on Christian Education* and the *Journal of Adventist Education*. She has also published in *Perceptual and Motor Skills*.

She began her teaching career as a business education teacher at Battle Creek Academy in Michigan. Since then, she has taught at Columbia Union College, Andrews University, and Newbold College. In her role at Loma Linda, she focuses on program evaluation and assessment of student learning for medical students enrolled in the School of Medicine.

Her most rewarding time, however, is as wife to her husband, Warren H. Johns, and as mother to their daughter, Lorie G. Johns.

Seventh-day Adventist Higher Education in North America

Jimmy Kijai is a professor of research and statistical methodology for the School of Education at Andrews University in Berrien Springs, Michigan. He is a founding member and sits on the board of the Andrews International Center for Educational Research. He also serves on the editorial board of the *Journal of Research on Christian Education.* Malaysian by birth, Jimmy currently teaches graduate level courses in research and statistical methods in the School of Education at Andrews University. He holds a bachelor's degree in physics from Spicer College in India, and a master's and PhD in educational research from the University of South Carolina. He is a former high school science and math teacher. He has taught in Thailand, Kenya, Tanzania, Costa Rica, Jamaica and Trinidad. He is married to Lucia and has three grown sons. Jimmy is a member of the American Educational Research Association and the National Council on Measurement in Education. His research interests center around school effects. He is currently the principal investigator for a research on college experiences of Adventist students in Adventist and non-Adventist colleges and universities in North America.

Appendix: Author Information

Gerald D. Lord is associate general secretary of the General Board of Higher Education and Ministry of the United Methodist Church. As the CEO of the Division of Higher Education, he relates to the 120 U.S. schools, colleges, and universities affiliated with the United Methodist and to the almost eight hundred institutions in the Methodist tradition worldwide. He also oversees support programs for United Methodist collegiate ministries on over five hundred U.S. campuses and is responsible for administration of the Black College Fund, which assists the eleven United Methodist historically black colleges and universities. He serves as the executive secretary of the United Methodist Senate, the very first accrediting body in this country, which, along with regional accrediting agencies, ensures quality of educational institutions related to the United Methodist Church.

At the time of the writing of his chapter, Lord was vice president of the Commission on Colleges, the unit of the Southern Association of Colleges and Schools responsible for the accreditation of approximately eight hundred postsecondary degree granting institutions in the eleven-state southern region. At the commission, his responsibilities included assisting in coordinating the development and implementation of programs, policies, and procedures to aid institutions in meeting accreditation standards and improving educational programs; serving as staff liaison for over one hundred member institutions; and coordinating on-site institutional visits during the accreditation process.

Before joining the Commission on Colleges, he held faculty and administrative appointments in Emory University's Candler School of Theology and a faculty appointment in the University of Tennessee's Department of Political Science/Bureau of Public Administration with three years service in the U.S. Army in between.

A native of Mississippi, Lord lives in Atlanta, Georgia, where he is active in church and community affairs. He is married to Joan McCarty Lord, vice president of the Southern Regional Education Board. They enjoy two daughters, their spouses, and a very cute and smart grandson.

Seventh-day Adventist Higher Education in North America

Richard Osborn, associate director, Accrediting Commission for Senior Colleges and Universities, Western Association of Schools & Colleges (WASC), worked at all levels of education for the Seventh-day Adventist Church for thirty-nine years including service as an elementary school and academy teacher and principal in Maryland, Potomac Conference superintendent of schools, and Columbia Union and North American Division vice president for Education. For the eight years prior to joining WASC in 2009, he served as president of Pacific Union College, a highly ranked Adventist undergraduate college located in the Napa Valley, California. In his role at WASC, he oversees regional accreditation for a portfolio of around forty senior colleges/universities ranging from large University of California and California State University campuses to several faith-based and independent universities to small specialized colleges.

Osborn served as the founding president of the Association of Adventist Colleges and Universities, a consortium of the fifteen Adventist colleges/universities located in North America. He has also held leadership positions in major organizations including chair of the Association of Independent California Colleges & Universities, president of the Council for American Private Education, co-chair of Denominational Executives in Church-Related Higher Education, and a member of the Secretariat of the National Association of Independent Colleges & Universities. He graduated with degrees in history including a BA from Columbia Union College in Maryland (now Washington Adventist University), and a MA and PhD from the University of Maryland specializing in colonial Virginia history. He is married to Norma Keough, a pastor at the Pacific Union College Seventh-day Adventist Church.

Appendix: Author Information

Steve Pawluk serves as the provost of La Sierra University in Riverside, California. Prior to this, he was professor of administration and leadership and chair of the Department of Administration and Leadership of the School of Education at La Sierra. Pawluk's perspectives on Seventh-day Adventist higher education were sharpened, not only by his work at LSU, but also by his prior employment as the senior vice president for Academic Administration at Southern Adventist University in Collegedale, Tennessee, and as professor of education and the dean of the School of Education and Psychology at Walla Walla College (now University) in Washington. He also has experience as the superintendent of schools and youth director for the Montana Conference of Seventh-day Adventists, a district pastor who also spoke on a daily radio program on the local country and western station, a high school teacher, a reserve police officer, a welder, a licensed contractor, a city council member, and a door-to-door cutlery salesman.

Pawluk holds a doctorate of education from Montana State University, a master of arts in religion from Loma Linda University, and a bachelor's degree in theology from Loma Linda University, La Sierra. In 2004, he was awarded a leadership fellowship by the Milton Murray Foundation for Philanthropy that allowed him to complete a summer institute at the Graduate School of Education at Harvard University.

Pawluk's wife teaches at Loma Linda Academy and both of his children attended Seventh-day Adventist schools until their graduation from Walla Walla University.

Vinita Sauder is the vice president for Strategic Initiatives at Southern Adventist University. She previously served as vice president for Marketing and Enrollment Services there for thirteen years, during which time enrollment increased by more than one thousand students. She holds a PhD from Andrews University in educational administration and leadership, an MBA from the University of Tennessee in Chattanooga, and a bachelor of arts degree in communication from Southern Missionary College.

Vinita was a founding member and chair of the Joint Marketing Committee for the Association of Adventist Colleges and Universities from its beginning in 2003 to 2007, and is a past president of the Adventist Enrollment Association. She currently serves as a member of a research team conducting a comparative study regarding the outcomes, college experiences, and congregational involvement of Adventist graduates of Adventist and non-Adventist colleges and universities. She is passionate about advancing both the mission of Adventist higher education and the collaborative work among the North American Division colleges and universities.

Before serving as vice president, she was an assistant professor of marketing in the School of Business and Management at Southern, associate vice president for Academic Administration, and director of Institutional Research and Effectiveness. She also worked in marketing communications for Kettering Medical Center and Kettering College of Medical Arts in Ohio.

Vinita serves on the executive board of the Samaritan Center, a local social service agency, and is a member of the American Marketing Association. She enjoys travel adventures with her husband, Greg, and her two grown boys, Dustin and Nick.

Appendix: Author Information

President of Kettering College of Medical Arts, near Dayton, Ohio, **Charles Scriven** has worked as an editor, college teacher, pastor, healthcare trustee, and college president. Before coming to Kettering College, he served for eight years as president of Washington Adventist University (formerly Columbia Union College) in Takoma Park, Maryland, a suburb of Washington, D.C.

Dr. Scriven studied philosophy, theology, and social ethics at the Graduate Theological Union in Berkeley, California. His professors at the University of California included Robert Bellah, the author of *Habits of the Heart,* and James McClendon Jr., a leader in the renewed emphasis on stories and storytelling as a key to self-understanding. He has published many articles and several books, including *The Demons Have Had It: A Theological ABC, The Transformation of Culture: Christian Social Ethics After H. Richard Niebuhr,* and *How to Believe When You Hurt.* His most recent book, published in 2009 by Pacific Press®, is *The Promise of Peace: Dare to LIVE the Advent Hope.* His articles have appeared in *Spectrum,* the *Adventist Review, Ministry,* and numerous other Adventist publications, and also in *Christianity Today* and *Sojourners.*

Dr. Scriven has three children and six grandchildren. His older son, Jonathan, teaches at an international high school in southern France. His daughter, Christina, is a nurse in Chattanooga, Tennessee. His younger son, Jeremy, works as a compensation analyst at Adventist Health Care in Rockville, Maryland. He is married to Rebekah Wang, an internist and currently medical director for Clinical Quality at the Kettering Medical Center, near Dayton, Ohio.

Seventh-day Adventist Higher Education in North America

Ella Louise Smith Simmons holds a doctor of education degree from the University of Louisville (Kentucky) with concentrations in administration and the sociology and politics of education, and holds a honoris causa doctor of pedagogy degree from Andrews University (Michigan). She serves as a general vice president of the General Conference of Seventh-day Adventists in Silver Spring, Maryland, and has the distinction of being the first woman to hold that position. Here she provides professional and spiritual advisement to the Education Department, Women's Ministries Department, and, in an associate capacity, the Sabbath School and Personal Ministries Department. She provides leadership to several worldwide agencies, organizations, and university boards. She has served as provost at La Sierra University in Riverside, California; vice president for Academic Affairs at Oakwood College (now University) in Huntsville, Alabama; associate dean at the University of Louisville School of Education where she was also a tenured member of the graduate faculty in the Foundations of Education Department; and chairperson of the Department of Education at Kentucky State University. Her fondness for institutional evaluation involved her in accreditation work throughout the world for twenty-five years. Her grant-funded research and development endeavors focusing on education for underrepresented groups have yielded an array of successful programs, refereed publications, and church periodical articles over the years, and she has continued this interest as guest and program host on church and public television. She is married to Nord Simmons, a retired teacher and business owner. They have two sons, Darryl and Christopher; a daughter-in-law, Stephanie (married to Christopher); one granddaughter, Jannette; two grandsons, Evan and Connor; and a great-grandson, Jordan.

Appendix: Author Information

David Thomas was born on the African continent to British missionary parents. The first nineteen years of his life were spent living in Zambia, Kenya, Tanzania, and old Rhodesia. After high school at Helderberg College near Cape Town, he emigrated to the United States to go to college, where he attended Atlantic Union College, graduating with a degree in theology in 1975. During college, he met, and later married, Loralee Minty of South Lancaster, Massachusetts. After several years at the Andrews University Seminary, David returned to New England where he pastored for seventeen years, working in Massachusetts and Connecticut in both multi- and single-church districts. During this time he began working on a doctor of ministry degree, which he finished in 1999. In 1995, David moved his family across the country to College Place, Washington, to pastor a large, multistaff church. While in this pastorate, he was called to become the dean of the School of Theology at Walla Walla University, a position he currently occupies. David has published a number of articles on pastoral life and function, an article on teaching philosophy in Seventh-day Adventist schools, and he is currently working on a book on the subject of marriage, and another one on pastoral ministry. He hopes someday to publish a book on Christian apologetics. David is the father of two grown sons, Matthew and Jonathan, and he has a host of interests ranging from systematic theology to old cars to sailing to driving big trucks.

James A. Tucker, PhD, currently holds the McKee Chair of Excellence in Learning at the University of Tennessee at Chattanooga. Prior to this position, he was professor of educational psychology and director of graduate programs in leadership at Andrews University. Formerly, Dr. Tucker served as director of the Bureau of Special Education, Pennsylvania Department of Education; director of federal programs for the Department of Special Education, Texas Education Agency; and as a high school and elementary school teacher. Dr. Tucker is a leading authority on the subject of integrated educational program-development for at-risk students, including students with disabilities. He has served as a consultant to hundreds of school systems, both public and private, in more than forty-five states and provinces in North America, as well as in Brazil, Canada, England, Japan, Lithuania, Norway, and the West Indies. Dr. Tucker has published widely in the areas of special education, educational psychology, ethics, leadership, natural history, and the spiritual application of natural-history subjects.

Appendix: Author Information

Priscilla M. Tucker, PhD, currently is a professor in and coordinator of graduate studies in the Outdoor Leadership Program in the School of Education and Psychology at Southern Adventist University. She also serves as executive director of the Institute of Outdoor Ministry, an organization dedicated to teaching values through science and environmental education, and as director of communications for the Foundation of Leadership and Learning.

Formerly, Dr. Tucker served as president of Educational Directions, Inc., an Austin, Texas-based consulting firm; as executive editor of *Birding,* the bimonthly journal of the American Birding Association; and as managing editor of the *Journal of Research on Christian Education,* at Andrews University. Dr. Tucker also taught school at the junior-high school level and served as an instructor in the Department of Teaching and Learning at Andrews University.

Don Williams is senior vice president for Academic Administration at Florida Hospital College of Health Sciences. Don has worked in a wide variety of settings. He has been a church pastor, conference worker, academy teacher, college and postgraduate faculty member, and a college administrator. He and his wife, Merrie Lyn, have also had the opportunity to live and work in New Guinea as student missionaries, and eight years in Singapore. Don received his undergraduate degree in psychology and a master of divinity degree from Andrews University. He earned his PhD in professional counseling from Purdue University. He and his wife life in Apopka, Florida, and are the parents of two grown children and four grandchildren.

Appendix: Author Information

Dr. Randal Wisbey serves as president of La Sierra University. His career in Adventist higher education spans twenty-five years. Before coming to La Sierra, he served as president of Columbia Union College in Takoma Park, Maryland, and Canadian University College in Lacombe, Alberta.

He has also served as associate professor of youth ministry at the Seventh-day Adventist Theological Seminary at Andrews University in Berrien Springs, Michigan. His academic interests focus on generational studies, contemporary youth culture, and personal and corporate spiritual formation.

He received his doctor of ministry degree in 1990 from Wesley Theological Seminary in Washington, D.C., while serving as chaplain and assistant professor of Christian ministry at Columbia Union College. His dissertation considered the transformative role service plays in the lives of young adults. He also earned a master of divinity degree from the Seventh-day Adventist Theological Seminary in 1984 and a bachelor of arts degree in theology from Walla Walla College in 1980. A year as a student missionary in Jerusalem, Israel, teaching Palestinian high school students proved transforming to his personal life during college.

He is married to Deanna Clay Wisbey. Their son, Alexander, will begin his senior year at LSU this fall. As a family, they have enjoyed traveling throughout Europe, Israel and Egypt, Australia and New Zealand, and Central and South America. Their recent passion is adventure hiking, having completed the Mont Blanc Circuit and the Inca Trail trek to Machu Picchu.